County of Brant Public Library
Literary Angel Program

Donated
by
Reader's
Anonymous
book club

D1521738

COLLECTED POEMS OF ALDEN NOWLAN

Alden Nowlan, Study (detail), 2009, by Stephen Scott

ALDEN NoWLAN

collected
poems

Edited by BRIAN BARTLETT

icehouse poetry
an imprint of Goose Lane Editions

Edited by Brian Bartlett.
Cover and page design by Julie Scriver.
Frontispiece: *Alden Nowlan, Study* (detail), 2009, by Stephen Scott.
Used by permission of the artist. stephenscott.ca
Printed in Canada.
10 9 8 7 6 5 4 3 2 1

Library and Archives Canada Cataloguing in Publication

Nowlan, Alden, 1933-1983
[Poems. Selections]
Collected poems of Alden Nowlan / Alden Nowlan ; edited by
Brian Bartlett.

Issued in print and electronic formats.
ISBN 978-0-86492-960-0 (hardcover).--ISBN 978-0-86492-948-8 (EPUB).--
ISBN 978-0-86492-949-5 (MOBI)

I. Bartlett, Brian, 1953-, editor II. Title.

PS8527.O798A6 2017 C811'.54 C2017-902803-0
C2017-902804-9

We acknowledge the generous support of the Government of Canada, the Canada
Council for the Arts, and the Government of New Brunswick.

Goose Lane Editions
500 Beaverbrook Court, Suite 330
Fredericton, New Brunswick
CANADA E3B 5X4
www.gooselane.com

CONTENTS

Introduction

TO SHARE A THING SO HUMAN

Czeslaw Milosz once wrote of another great twentieth-century Polish poet, Wislawa Szymborska: "Poetry that speaks to the enduring and irreversible coordinates of human fate—love, striving, fear of pain, hope, the fleeting nature of things, and death—leads us to believe that the poet is one of us, and shares in that fate."[1] The same could be said about one of Canada's most distinctive and beloved poets, Alden Nowlan. He once wrote of a desire to leave behind "one poem, one story / that will tell what it was like / to be alive" ("Another Poem"). Many times he did just that, with candour and subtlety, emotion and humour, sympathy and truth-telling. Only now is the true range of Nowlan's poetic achievement finally available between two covers. *Collected Poems* offers in one volume all his poems previously published in three early chapbooks, eight full-length collections, "new and selected" compilations, and the script of a long poem for voices.

Nowlan takes us from nightmarish precincts of fear and loneliness to the embraces of friendship and family. He reveals our shared humanity as well as our perplexing, sometimes entertaining, differences. His poems colourfully reflect his childhood in Hants County, Nova Scotia, and his adult years in New Brunswick (Hartland, Saint John, Fredericton), but the autobiographical elements intersect with fantasies and a historical consciousness nourished by broad reading and deep curiosity.

Who was the man who wrote the poems? We are fortunate to have two substantial, quite different biographies of the poet (Patrick Toner's *If I Could Turn and Meet Myself: The Life of Alden Nowlan* and Gregory M. Cook's *One Heart, One Way: Alden Nowlan: A Writer's Life*), several prose memoirs by Nowlan, and many autobiographical passages in his poetry and fiction. In some senses the life is well documented, yet both biographies reveal that Nowlan highlighted aspects of his childhood and shaped a quasi-mythical version of his own beginnings. Over many years, for instance, he told even those closest to him that his mother had died,

---

1   Milosz, 1.

when in fact she would eventually outlive him. After leaving his native place, he had little to do with his only sister, Harriet, while he went on to call a cherished cousin "my sister." After his departure for New Brunswick, Nowlan also gave facetious names to places in Hants County, such as the Slough of Despond, the Road to Ruin, and Desolation Creek. (For years I thought "Lockhartville" was also a Nowlan coining, until I saw a highway sign for the community with that name in Kings County, Nova Scotia.) As an adult he recalled having survived "an almost incredibly loveless environment during my childhood"[2] and claimed, "I would have been happier on a desert island because then there would have been no one around to torment me."[3] Yet alongside depictions of repression, harshness, and cruelty within the family and the community, his writings dramatize acts of warmth and care given by many, including his grandmothers and his difficult, at times frightening, father. "Looking back as objectively as I can, I see my own childhood as a pilgrimage through hell," he wrote. "And yet I was seldom desperately unhappy and there can't have been many days when I didn't laugh."[4]

The title of one Nowlan collection, *The Mysterious Naked Man*, suggests the complexities of the person we see in his writings and in biographical accounts: no matter how self-revealing a person seems, much mystery enwraps the nakedness. We should keep in mind Nowlan's alertness to the shiftings and transformations of selfhood, the ways in which we think and act as different people on different days. In the final year of his life he cited André Gide's admonition "Do not understand me too quickly." At the same time he memorably said, "as time passes, we constantly are developing into different people, almost like a caterpillar developing into a butterfly, except that the butterfly then perhaps changes into a bird and the bird changes into something else. But at the same time, all the previous selves are inside us."[5] As his biographer Toner writes: "Nowlan maintained to the end that he was a collection of semi-detached and often contradictory selves, some isolated in time and space, others existing side by side to spring into being... in the presence of certain other personalities, all with their own multiple selves."[6] Early on, Nowlan wrote poems under the pseudonym Max Philip Ireland, and later he published a few satirical

---

2   Cook, *One Heart*, 55.
3   Pedersen, 262.
4   Nowlan, "Growing," 15.
5   Pedersen, 267, 293.
6   Toner, 13.

parodies as Bhikku Bannister, as well as writing a novel called *Various Persons Named Kevin O'Brien*. In a letter he once wrote humorously: "I must found a Society for the Popularization of Multiple Names as a Means of Recognizing the fact that Every Personality is Split."[7]

Nowlan's poems "Deuces Wild," "He Takes His Leave," and "What Happened When He Went to the Store for Bread" are among his finest meditations on chance and fate. He was very aware of how the courses of our lives are changed by seemingly very minor events, by something happening or not happening at a particular place and time. In a letter written in 1980, he commented: "As I look back, it seems to me that whatever I've become has been largely as a result of a series of accidents. I might just as easily have become a bum or a bank robber. We're all tied to the wagon of Fate."[8] His poetry not only laments the tragedies brought on by chance and circumstance but also marvels at gifts of unearned good luck. To concentrate on the whims of chance, however, is misleading if it downplays the significance of choice and will, which Nowlan clearly demonstrated at age nineteen, when he fictionalized a high-school education and a year's work for a local newspaper to make his escape from Nova Scotia and become a journalist in Hartland, New Brunswick, steering his life in a new direction.

ooooo

The place Nowlan left was Hants County, where he had been born in what he often described as the worst year of the Depression, and where he spent much of his childhood and adolescence in a house without central heating, electricity, telephone, or plumbing. In the first substantial interview he gave in his life as a poet, in 1963, he said:

> We were poor and isolated and I was alone a lot — like Huckleberry Finn, you know, not the Huck Finn that got his picture on sentimental calendars but the Huck Finn in Mark Twain's book, a beautiful, horrible book — and I was steeped in the Bible, saturated in a kind of Calvinist Baptist, almost Jewish theology, and when I was ten or so I thought of myself as a kind of apprentice prophet. I was going to be like Isaiah when I grew up, I guess. I even thought I had

---

7 Cook, *One Heart*, 55.
8 *Ibid.*, 299.

visions.... And I started to write them down because Isaiah
and Jeremiah and all those old fellows wrote their visions
down. The Words that the Lord spoke Unto His Servant,
Alden.[9]

This is a version of his youth that Nowlan would restate and rephrase
over the years, as in the most revealing of his memoirs, "Growing Up in
Katpesa Creek."

At Nowlan's birth in 1933 his father, Freeman Lawrence Nowlan, was
twice the age of his mother, fourteen-year-old Grace Reese. Years later
Nowlan would comment, "Child brides weren't terribly rare in rural Nova
Scotia in those days."[10] Hard-drinking, hard-working Freeman worked in
the local mill yet never landed a full-time job. "The Hard Times broke my
father," Alden later recalled. "They broke his spirit forever."[11] Over the next
six or seven years Grace's attentions to her children became increasingly
erratic, and Alden and Harriet were then cared for much of the time by
one of their aunts and by their grandmothers: Emma Nowlan (who in old
age step-danced, played autoharp, and exuberantly sang old hymns and
Irish ballads) and Nora Reese, who talked proudly of her deceased father,
saying that he "could scratch a living where a goat would starve." Nora's
descriptions of her father had an impact on her grandson: Alden later
recalled that before he was ten, "I knew that I was descended from classic
heroes."[12] Both Nowlan biographies include details of how his family
encouraged reading and storytelling, even though he never went beyond
grade four in school. Grandmother Nowlan took small amounts from
Freeman's paycheques to buy books for Alden; Grandmother Reese read
to him from *Pilgrim's Progress* and Petrarch's poetry. Freeman held books
in his lap and appeared to read to Alden but was mostly telling stories off
the cuff; before she left the family, Grace read him exciting ballads. Up
against the walls in Alden's bedroom, books were piled, helping keep out
drafts of cold air in the winter.[13]

After dropping out of school, Nowlan read for long hours at home,
often under the illumination of kerosene lamps. He would eventually
find jobs as a pulp-cutter, night watchman, and worker for the provincial

---

9   Cook, "Alden," 33.
10 Toner, 25.
11 Cook, *One Heart*, 25-26.
12 *Ibid.*, 39.
13 *Ibid.*, 33; Toner, 48.

Department of Highways. During 1946 and '47, he suffered from anemia, weak lungs, chronic fatigue, and perhaps malnutrition. The symptoms of poor health, along with his moodiness and extreme introversion, alerted Children's Aid, and he spent several months in a Dartmouth psychiatric hospital (the same facility in which Elizabeth Bishop's mother had lived her final eighteen years, dying there a year after Nowlan's birth). That experience was one source of his later poetry and fiction dealing with borderlands between sanity and insanity (see especially his moving, terribly authentic poem "Living in a Mad House"). After Nowlan's return to Stanley, a new library was opened in nearby Windsor, with a collection mostly composed of books donated by Hants and Kings County residents, including works by Dickens, Thackeray, Darwin, Dostoevsky, and Jack London; the adolescent Nowlan seemed to read them all, feeling a special affinity for London. He later recalled that the library was "separated from the village by eighteen miles according to the geographers but at least a thousand miles away if distances were measured by their effects upon our lives. The memory of those books, waiting to be read, pressing hard against the body, is as sensuous as the memory of a sleepy young girl's head against a young boy's shoulder, his lips in her hair."[14] That library continued to feed Nowlan's great hunger for books of many kinds, books that likely made him one of the most-educated teens in Hants County, despite his status as an early dropout.

ooooo

In March 1952, at the age of nineteen, Nowlan made the first major move of his life. Hartland, a town sixty miles upriver from Fredericton, would become his home base for the next eleven years. His good-humoured landlord and landlady, Charlie and Bertha Shaw, became like surrogate parents for him. He honed his plentiful, keen journalistic skills, gaining the admiration and trust of his employers and co-workers at the *Hartland Observer*. He overcame some of his deep shyness and joined groups such as the Knights of Pythias, Hartland Lodge No. 46, the Fish and Game Protective Association, the Potato Festival Committee, and the Hartland Board of Trade, while also maintaining a reputation for being a loner. For a brief time he managed a country and western band, George Shaw and the Green Valley Ranch Boys. He befriended a local named Richard

---

14 Nowlan, "Something," 8.

Hatfield, who would later serve as the premier of New Brunswick for many years and have his poet friend write speeches for him.

Years later Nowlan would recall that he started writing at the age of eleven but was twenty-five before he "started taking the writing—the work—seriously."[15] His first published poem appeared in the United States while he was still in Stanley, then in Hartland he more vigorously tracked down the addresses of literary journals (mostly American ones), mailed them his work, and had dozens of poems published—yet he still hadn't met another poet. That all changed with his correspondence and subsequent meeting with Fred Cogswell, a poet, University of New Brunswick professor, and editor of the *Fiddlehead*. Cogswell offered Nowlan his first friendship with a fellow poet, lent him books of Canadian poetry, and in 1958 published his first chapbook, *The Rose and the Puritan*. It was also in Hartland that Nowlan met Claudine Meehan (née Orser), a linotype operator at the *Observer*, and her young son, Johnnie. The second of his three early chapbooks, *A Darkness in the Earth*, would be dedicated discreetly "To C.M.," but in the future Nowlan would dedicate nearly all of his books at least in part "To [or 'For'] Claudine and Johnnie," often "with love." His love for Claudine and the strength of their marriage would give him great joy and help carry him through difficult times for the rest of his life.

After his first three chapbooks, Nowlan then published major collections with two Ontario presses: *Under the Ice* (1961) and *The Things Which Are* (1962). Though even a few favourable reviews included condescending phrases like "isolated chip-on-the-shoulder Maritime culture," "a certain backwoods ingredient," and "Dogpatch verse,"[16] overall the collections were highly praised, and Nowlan was recognized as both a bright star of Maritime poetry and a poet deserving national attention. Canadian poets whose example had helped move his poetry into greater structural and tonal freedom, such as Raymond Souster and Irving Layton, now read him with excitement. In the final interview of his life, Nowlan would say, "I've borrowed from everybody, I suppose. D.H. Lawrence, Thomas Hardy, William Carlos Williams, Sherwood Anderson, Robert Frost, Wordsworth, Chekhov, Robinson Jeffers, Whitman—and most of all, the King James Version of the Bible,"[17] but as his reading of his

---

15 Cook, "Alden," 32.
16 Toner, 110.
17 Cook, *One Heart*, 90.

contemporaries broadened, Souster, Layton, and other Canadians, such as Al Purdy and John Newlove, also inspired him.

The Hartland years were followed by the Saint John years (1963-68), when Nowlan worked as provincial editor and night news editor of the *Telegraph-Journal*, enjoyed what he considered the Dickensian vividness of the old port city, and felt relief from Hartland's gregarious atmosphere ("I've avoided meetings of all kinds the way I avoid poison ivy ever since I got out of Hartland, where I had more than enough meetings to last a lifetime"[18]). Saint John is also where Nowlan's thyroid gland developed a malignant tumour, and cancer soon spread to lymph nodes on his neck. Early in 1966 he spent six weeks in a hospital, undergoing three surgeries; in the fall, after cancer was again detected in his body, he returned to the hospital for radiation treatments. The brush with death deeply affected him and his poetry, in ways effectively discussed over thirty years later in physician-poet Shane Neilson's *Alden Nowlan & Illness*. Nowlan was very grateful for the *Telegraph-Journal*'s support, financial and moral, but the harsh reminder of mortality he'd received — and the energy-sapping labours of being a newspaper man — made him long for a lifestyle that would let him dedicate more time to what he liked to call "verse." The great value of his poetry was recognized in 1967 when his collection *Bread, Wine and Salt* (his first from the publisher that would be key in his later life, Clarke, Irwin) won the Governor General's Award.

The change Nowlan's style had undergone between his first books and *Bread, Wine and Salt* helps us identify his Saint John years as the most crucial in the broadening of his poetry's scope. By the time of *The Things Which Are*, his final collection published before he left Hartland, he had moved from the structural formalism dominating his earlier books to free verse. Much later he would say, "I think the writer I learned the most from technically was William Carlos Williams."[19] It would be a mistake to exaggerate the transition; there are free-verse poems ("Weakness," "Cattle among the Alders," "Child of Tabu") in the first chapbook, and Nowlan would continue to write poems in set rhyming patterns. But in the early 1960s the balance clearly tipped in favour of unique, improvised structures.

After Nowlan turned thirty, his poetry underwent another change. Though the more emotional poems in his first five books could hardly be described as detached, now a greater willingness to share details of his own

---

18   *Ibid.*, 84.
19   Pedersen, 282.

complicated self—and to put himself in the shoes of others—added new kinds of intensity to his poems. Again, we can exaggerate the difference: the three chapbooks include poems in which an "I" is central ("A Poem to My Mother," "When Like the Tears of Clowns"); and "Flossie at School" is an early Nowlan poem that confesses a shameful neglect at age ten in not standing up for a bullied classmate. Yet Nowlan's later shift toward more extensive, close-up explorations of his own sufferings and the sufferings of others can be seen by contrasting certain 1950s poems with others he wrote during the '60s. In "Marian at the Pentecostal Meeting" from Nowlan's third chapbook, for instance, satire overrides the "pity" it speaks of, whereas "Daughter of Zion" from *Bread, Wine and Salt* conveys through its wildly varied line lengths and unpredictable, excited rhythms the thrill of religious ecstasy. Likewise, in *Under the Ice* the poem "Georgie and Fenwick" might make the readers chuckle at two repressed bachelor brothers who face female flirtation and teasing "like rabbits frozen / with fear of the gun," but in a *Bread, Wine and Salt* poem, "The Wickedness of Peter Shannon," Nowlan steps inside the sensibility and shame of a teenager overwhelmed by sexual desire. Nowlan would always write poems of cool observation, including satirical poems, but the empathy in his writing intensified over time.

The desired change in lifestyle from full-time journalism arrived the next year when the University of New Brunswick appointed Nowlan as writer-in-residence, a position he would hold—with nerve-wracking periods of uncertainty about whether the funding would run out—until his death. Nowlan would live in Fredericton on the edge of the university campus longer than he lived anywhere else except Hants County. Both the Toner and Cook biographies, along with his poetry and his journalism, provide detailed accounts of his Fredericton years, including his friendships with people from many walks of life (law, medicine, music, teaching, theatre, politics, the military); his extensive written correspondence; his travels to England, Ireland, and Cuba; his rare contacts with people from his Nova Scotian youth; his ongoing struggles with what he variously called "Nancy Whiskey," "Colonel Booze," and "our brother Al Cohol";[20] and his pride in writing not just poetry but also newspaper columns, magazine articles, short stories, plays, and a local history.

After he died of complications from emphysema at the age of fifty in June of 1983, Nowlan's work continued to be honoured. In the fall after his

---

20 Toner, 255-56.

death, Fiddlehead Poetry Books gathered together his three chapbooks and first two full-length collections into the handsome volume *Early Poems*. A year later, Irwin Publishing released his second collection of short stories, *Will Ye Let the Mummers In?* In 1985, *An Exchange of Gifts: Poems New & Selected*, edited by Nowlan's friend and literary executor Robert Gibbs, appeared from Irwin. In 1988, Goose Lane Editions surprised many readers with *The Wanton Troopers*, a novel Nowlan had written in 1961 and shelved after two publishers turned it down;[21] that novel, a fictionalized version of Nowlan's childhood, mesmerizing in the clarity of its imagery and the depth of its characterization, is arguably the most powerful of all his prose works.

In 1970, while still alive, Nowlan found American readers after a small press in New York State published *Playing the Jesus Game: Selected Poems*. The book's insightful introduction by Robert Bly borrowed a metaphor from D.H. Lawrence to describe Nowlan as an "umbrella ripper," a poet who makes holes in "the protective layer that man builds up between himself and the chaos of the sky."[22] A decade after Nowlan's death, the Nineties Press in Minnesota published the selection *What Happened When He Went to the Store for Bread*, edited by Thomas R. Smith and including another appreciation by Bly. A new Canadian selected of Nowlan, edited by Patrick Lane and Lorna Crozier, was released in 1996 by the House of Anansi Press in Ontario. Then, in the first years of the twenty-first century, more signs of continuing interest in Nowlan arose with the publication of the two biographies and the choice of a selected Nowlan as the first in a new "World Series" of poetry collections from Bloodaxe Books in Northumberland, England.

ooooo

Alden Nowlan has often been associated with poetry that is, to quote from the back of *I'm a Stranger Here Myself*, "simple, direct, and very beautiful." That description is apt for many of his poems, especially later ones that seem unabashedly personal and unguarded; yet even riveting, emotionally "direct" poems like the masterpiece "He Sits Down on the Floor of a School for the Retarded" are far from "simple." Nowlan is sometimes a

---

21 A note in both editions of *The Wanton Troopers* gives the year of composition as 1960, but the Toner and Cook biographies cite 1961. Also, although several sources refer to the novel being rejected by one publisher, both Ryerson Press and McClelland and Stewart turned it down.

22 Bly, 5.

richly ironic poet, and irony works by indirection, as do tonal spaces where humour and seriousness overlap. Moreover, while he undoubtedly favours a vocabulary more Anglo-Saxon than Latinate and often writes sentences that gain much of their impact from their brevity, at other times he builds long, leisurely sentences. In "A Poem for Elizabeth Nancy," "Homebrew," and "Summer" (which I recall novelist David Adams Richards reading aloud to me with wonder and excitement, over the telephone, in the early 1970s), Nowlan writes image-rich single-sentence poems. The beginning of "Party at Bannon Brook" reads like a demonstration of two stylistic choices set side by side, the sinuous and expansive next to the compact and sharply focused:

> At the dead end of a road twisting snakelike
> as that out of Eden, in a hunting camp, the hoarse creek
>   crawling
> through the closed door like the wet ghost of some drowned
>   Adam,
> coughing water on the floor, I sprawl on a straw-filled bunk
> and drink rum with strangers:

> > The chef in his tall white hat
> > and apron embroidered
> > with ribald slogans,
> > spears steaks with slivers
> > of white pine, roaring.

Passages in Nowlan's poetry where such alternate syntactical strategies are put side by side are plentiful. From his final collection, the conclusion of the poem "The Weekend God" exemplifies an order the opposite of that beginning "Party at Bannon Brook." After stating the need for "a name for the Weekend God / of the working-class," the poem works through nine more lines discussing that need, then finishes with this stanza:

> Yes, there ought to be a name for the Weekend God.
> There ought to be shrines raised to him
> in places like Sudbury, in cities where at dusk
> the sun dissolves in acid, creating a sky
> of purple, scarlet and brass,
> like the garments of the Whore of Babylon,

like a blind man's last remembered
thunderous moment of sight.

A lesser poet than Nowlan might have ended the poem with the repetition of "there ought to be a name for the Weekend God," matching the poem's beginning with its ending, coming full circle and saying no more. Instead, Nowlan opens up the poem to a broad Canadian context (note that the specific place reference isn't to a Maritime location but to Sudbury, Ontario), the imagery of a factory-discoloured sky, two similes, and the poem's most densely textured sentence.

An over-emphasis on Nowlan's conversational modes of writing also undermines his poetic skills in handling lines, line-breaks, and pacing. The illusion of speech is so strong at times that it's easy to forget how much some of Nowlan's poetry is page-based, especially in free verse. In a 1975 interview, Nowlan discussed with much self-awareness his choices for crafting a poem so that its typographical character helps guide its moment-by-moment unfolding:

> [My poetry] attempts to find a typographical substitute for
> the purely visual and oral things that play such an important
> part in a conversation — facial expressions, gestures of the
> hands, intonations of the voice.... Some of the divisions are
> intended to make the reader slow down — to read certain
> words in units of five instead of ten, for instance. And
> sometimes the break adds an additional level of meaning
> in that the reader is led to believe that I'm saying one thing
> and then an instant later he finds that I'm saying something
> else which doesn't supersede the first thing, but amplifies
> it, or modifies it.... There's a deliberate instant of ambiguity,
> you see, which reflects the ambiguity of life.[23]

Nowlan's deft use of the page can be appreciated by comparing a prose watering-down of his "The Day's First Miracle" to the actual poem. This sort of poem might be compared to an Impressionist painting. The imagist ideal of uncluttered, direct presentation gives way to the impressions made by nearby phenomena on an observer. In prose, Nowlan's lines would go like this:

---

23 Metcalf, 52.

If the relationship between my window and the sun
differed, if I did not sleep by day and there were no need
for both blinds and drapes, or if either were another colour,
if the wind blew from any other direction, were weaker or
stronger, if this April were not unseasonably cold, if the
window were open more than a fraction—above all, if I
were not free this morning I would not have seen a vision of
the absurdly beautiful love-making of two golden dolphins.

As prose, the words make up a dense single-sentence paragraph that seems
to have little to do with Nowlan's own prose, especially with the economy
of phrasing he learned from his experiences as a news reporter and editor
and practised during his many years as a popular columnist. The original
poem, while identical in wording, syntax, and punctuation to the prose,
is a very different thing, and Nowlan's handling of the words *on the page*
makes it so:

If the relationship between
        my window and the sun
        differed,
                if I did not sleep
by day and there were no need
        for both
                blinds and drapes,
                                or if either
were another colour,
                if the wind blew
from any other
                direction,
were weaker or stronger,
if this April were not
        unseasonably
                cold, if the window were open
more than a fraction—
                above all
if I were not free
        this morning
        I would not have seen
                                a vision

of the absurdly beautiful
love-making
of two golden dolphins.

From having seen him read several times and having heard recordings of his readings, I have no memory of Nowlan ever reading this poem aloud. Perhaps he figured that its character is too integrated into its visual nature for it to work well orally. (While Nowlan became a beloved public reader of his own poetry, he said in a 1975 interview: "I don't write poems for an audience. An audience is a crowd. I write poems for one person at a time.... I'd rather talk with one person than speechify to a thousand."[24] On the other hand, Nowlan's readings of poems with a strong communal component, such as "Ypres: 1916," were unforgettable and remain so on recordings.)

∞∞∞∞∞

Some poems by Nowlan might be compared in musical terms to atmospheres or tone poems. These are concentrated pieces that give great importance to setting, and make mood and sensuous evocation dominate over character, narrative, or argument. "July 15," filled with images of heat, wind, trees, and grass, insists "Nothing is happening. / I do not strive for meaning." When the poem switches into wondering, "How long have I lain here? / Well, it is still summer. But is it the same / summer I came?" it opens into the possibility of a surreally speeded-up passing of time. "I must remember / not to ask myself questions," the poem says, but the difficulty of *not* asking questions — of letting mood be everything — is part of the poem's mood. "One Night in Christmas Week," "Cornflowers," "Hilltop at Night," and "The First Stirring of the Beasts" are other poems that create strong sensations of inhabiting the present, doing justice to the sensations and often ambiguous feelings of being alive in one time and place, whether in summer or winter, darkness or sunlight, restlessness or calm.

One element of Nowlan's poetry that has been questioned by some readers is its willingness at times to state rather than suggest, to generalize about human nature and risk the appearance of dispensing wisdom. Yet the range of his modes and voices seems to me enriched, especially from his collections published in 1969 and 1971, by a handful of poems that use epigrammatical or parable-like conciseness. A fine example is "The Bhikku":

---

24 *Ibid.*, 55.

I ask for nothing,
       he tells me, except
              to be freed from
all desire.
       No wonder
              his voice shakes:
even Lucifer's
       desire was less
              insatiable than that.

This isn't lyric poetry of self-discovery and metaphorical inventiveness, or reflective poetry allowing for digressions and shifting tones, but it has a strong character of its own, rooted in precedents as diverse as Zen poetry from centuries ago to Stephen Crane's briefer verses. As is so often the case with Nowlan, the creation of a voice through exact word choices and careful pacing helps make the poem dramatic, not merely a bald statement. Look at the ways the arrangements and breaks of the lines emphasize "except" (what humour in that word), "all desire," "shakes," and "insatiable," and how that final word's strong *s* echoes the many *s*'s in all the previous three lines.

Whereas "The Bhikku" is witty in questioning the impossible, in-human ideals of those who crave total transcendence over their wants, "The Atheist, Praying" casts irony over the poem's speaker, begins with a strong qualifier, and emphasizes similarity rather than difference. It, too, is paced in a way that makes it a poem perhaps better suited to silent, private absorption than to public consumption:

Perhaps the voice
       cannot create
              anything beyond itself

and the act alone
       is nothing more. Yet
              it is good to share a thing

so human: this
       reaching out
              in fear or gentleness.

This poem might appear straightforward, but thinking so undervalues the key effect of the seemingly paradoxical title, the idea of a voice making nothing "beyond itself," the wondering if prayer is self-sufficient, the recognition of "a reaching out" as "so human," and the implication that "fear or gentleness" could also be described that way. "Hymn to Dionysus," "Greatness," and "The Pilgrimage as Worship" are other clear but not simplistic poems of epigrammatical force, and concise poems such as "The Traveller" and "Exile" use glimpses of narrative in archetypal situations. In "The Traveller," Nowlan offers the image of "destination" as a "trunk, half as long as a coffin," in a poem that could be mistaken for a translation from Han-shan (the eighth-century Chinese poet also known as Cold Mountain).

ooooo

Alden Nowlan is among many things a great poet of fear. Again and again his poetry recalls the fears found in childhood. Three times the early poem "Communion: 1946 and 1962" uses the italicized line *When I am a man I will not be afraid.* One poem simply begins, "I being twelve and scared" ("Letter to My Mother"), and another concludes a description of walks in the pitch blackness this way: "it wasn't until tonight / almost twenty years / later I began to realize / how much I was afraid" ("The Mosherville Road"). As often as not in Nowlan's poetry, literal darkness is implicitly associated with psychic or metaphysical darkness. For a much briefer poem than "The Mosherville Road," he borrows the title of a childhood rhyme, "Star Light, Star Bright," admits that at the age of forty-six he still recites it, and adds, "you're like me: silly / and afraid of the dark." That he speaks for more than just himself and his reader becomes obvious in the poem's final three lines: "Bend closer. / I know a far greater secret: / everyone else is too." This brief poem is one of Nowlan's that can be heard as addressing a single reader (and as indicated in "Bend closer," even *whispering* to you, whispering to me), yet it also concludes by looking far past the isolated reader to "everyone."

In Nowlan's early poems inspired by his youth in rural Nova Scotia and in Hartland, the fear of weakness—especially of showing affection or sympathy—is found in the lives of several people who appear in the poetry. "Cousins," sharp and bemused, describes the poet's male cousins as men "who are not frightened / by boots or tire-irons / behind the dance hall in Bennington," but who are "so afraid / of weakness"—in particular of showing loving emotion for their wives—that they are "scared into hilarity and contempt by kisses." Likewise, in "Poem for the Golden Wedding of My Puritan Grandparents" Nowlan depicts an old couple who refrained from all expressions of love; if the grandfather called his wife "darling" in his "annual drunkenness" at Christmas, the grandson imagines, "her lean lips / would have recoiled as when she tasted milk / that had gone sour." In Nowlan's first chapbook, one remarkable juxtaposition of two poems is that of "Whistling of Birds"—a quiet piece reminiscent of haiku but longer, addressed to bird voices heard near dawn—and "Child of Tabu," a stark poem about bullying told from a bully's perspective. The first poem offers a lyric sensibility in contrast to the hard-heartedness recalled in the accompanying poem. On other pages of his early work, Nowlan captures moments when fears of appearing vulnerable, unmasculine, or sympathetic are momentarily overcome when someone reaches out to another with gentleness. It wouldn't be quite right to say that Nowlan has mastered the poem of kind gestures, because what he depicts aren't mere gestures but acts that spring spontaneously from wellsprings of compassion.

In his later poems, Nowlan continues to describe moments when we break through repression, hesitation, and convention to be honest and unguarded with each other, while he also goes on recognizing the guardedness central to many of our interactions. At the ending of his best-known poem of Saint John, "Britain Street," he reports that in nine months he hasn't heard a gentle word in his new neighbourhood, but that "I like to tell myself / that is only because / gentle words are whispered / and harsh words shouted." Two reasons those lines aren't sentimental is that they end with a reminder of the "harsh words shouted," and they acknowledge the wishfulness of the feeling described; "I like to tell myself" qualifies the assertion of gentleness, stops short of stating it as a definite thing. How different this poem would be, how much less credible its ending, if the final stanza simply read: *But harsh words are shouted / and gentle words whispered.*

The words "lonely," "loneliness," and "lonesome" appear just as often in Nowlan's lines, especially in the early poetry, as the word "fear." In his chapbooks, we find them in "A Night Hawk Fell with a Sound Like a Shudder" ("I was suddenly lonely and cold / sitting there on the fence"), "Sparrow Come in My Door" ("pound at the glass you do not know imprisons / you in your loneliness and me in mine"), and "I Knew the Seasons ere I Knew the Hours" ("I was once six and so damned lonely / I called love Rover, he had two sad ears, / a black-white checkerboard of a face"). In contrast, Nowlan also admits in later poetry the virtues of solitude, and in "Friends" he humorously fantasizes about keeping a convenient couple stored away in the basement or a clothes closet, willing to stay there while the poet is working, sleeping, or simply "happier alone." Yet the couple are easily prompted into action when he calls, "Hey! Wake up! / I'm lonesome." The differences of mood and feeling between those early poems and the ironic "Friends" indicate one of many ways in which Nowlan's poetic treatments of basic human situations vary widely.

ooooo

Though his poetry is unflinching in its recognition of fear, loneliness, pain, grief, and death, it would be difficult to find any poet who expresses more than Alden Nowlan does sheer gratitude for being alive. In *The Mysterious Naked Man*, "On the Stairs" imagines a boy "for the first time aware / how strange it is to be himself, and here," and a poem with the spacious title "Alpha and Omega" speaks of "a childish wonder at how mysterious it is / that I am looking out through the eyes / of a certain body and this body is alive, / here and now." In such passages Nowlan concentrates on the strangeness or mysteriousness of being alive, but gratitude is explicit in poetry he published later. In the penultimate poem of *I'm a Stranger Here Myself*, Nowlan comically imagines having a dialogue with a contented great bull walrus, and concludes that "not being born is / the only tragedy / that we can imagine / but need never fear." Another poem in that collection describes stray cats at dusk lying in the warm ashes at a city dump, and concludes by addressing the cats, agreeing "it is good, / very good / to be alive" ("The Fire Is Not Quenched"). Those concluding lines are echoed in the title of the concluding poem of *Smoked Glass*, "It's Good to Be Here," a moving, fascinating retake on the much earlier poem, "Beginning" ("From that they found most lovely, most abhorred, / my parents made me"). In "It's Good to Be Here," he imagines his parents' clenched dialogue after they learned of his conception; their moods move from worry, frustration, and anger to quiet and difficult acceptance. While the body of that poem is in the past tense, the title is in the present, and it's no mere tag but a sentence that adds a great deal; a reader's eyes easily return to it after finishing the poem. I recall one day in August 1975 at the Yeats Summer School in Sligo, Ireland, when in casual conversation over pints of Guinness a participant who had just seen "It's Good to Be Here" in its magazine publication praised its emotional frankness and its mix of rawness and poise.

Gratitude for life is expressed openly in the poems just mentioned, and at the ending of "My Beard, Once Lionheart Red," in which Nowlan describes himself as a survivor of cancer as "fortune's child"; but we shouldn't forget that thankfulness for the good things of life—including love, friendship, food, art, and the presence of other creatures—is suggested and dramatized in many of his poems without being declared.

On Nowlan's tombstone in the Forest Hill Cemetery in Fredericton, these words are carved:

REST LIGHTLY ON HIM O EARTH.
HE LOVED YOU SO.

ooooo

In a discussion much longer than this introductory essay, many other dimensions of Nowlan's poetry could be honoured in detail: explorations of selfhood, including our propensities to keep secrets, nurse self-flattering fantasies, and mix together the angelic and the demonic; sympathy for outcasts and underdogs ("Shouting His Love to Strangers," "Partnership," "Rehearsal"); reflections on class, including questions aimed at blinkered bourgeois views of the proletariat; incorporation of Biblical motifs, Greek myths, and regional legends; references to Canadian and European history; satirical pokes at pomposity, hypocrisy, and professorial pretence; dramas of friendship, hosting, and hospitality; appearances of nightmares and curious dreams; poems of escape from the confines of normalcy, such as those beginning *Bread, Wine and Salt* ("I, Icarus") and *The Mysterious Naked Man* (the title poem); passages or whole poems recording the voices of Maritime Canadians ("Language," "Land and Sea," "The Red Wool Shirt," "From the Memoirs of Tom Long," and "Ypres: 1916" with Private Billy MacNally and an old vet on TV); sympathetic views of animals, often seen as beings in themselves, not merely symbols (cat, dog, squirrel, bitch fox, bucking bull, belled deer, moose, deer, tiger, porcupine, skunk, phoebe, sparrow, wasp, blackfly); and expressions of love, love of many kinds. (Geoffrey Cook has offered a helpful list of elements in Nowlan's poems of love: "moving declarations and eroticism; furious lust and terrible shames; graceful compassion and heroic evocation; loneliness and longing; selfishness and bitterness; comic and tragic portraits of 'deviation,' the politics of marriage and family."[25])

---

25 Geoffrey Cook, 68.

A comprehensive appreciation of Nowlan's poetry would also look at its connections to his short stories, his novels, and his many non-fiction works, including his hundreds of newspaper columns. (Some of the columns have passages you can imagine being reworked to become Nowlan poems; some of the poems have a voice like one of the many found in the columns.)

In a letter written in 1981, Nowlan told Irving Layton that if he were to write an autobiography, he could call it *The Wine of Astonishment*, borrowing a phrase from Psalms 60:3: "Thou hast made us to drink the wine of astonishment."[26] In reading the hundreds of poems Nowlan wrote during a life that was cut short at too young an age, we find that the sense of his astonishment merely at being alive is inescapable, despite the suffering, sorrow, and difficulty that underlie many of the stories he has to tell. In the year after *Bread, Wine and Salt* was published, Nowlan wrote in a letter that, after thinking of himself as some sort of romantic, "I discover to my own astonishment that I'm really a classicist.... Simplicity, relatedness to reality. Like old Catullus, I even discover that the virtues I endorse instinctively are the old Greek virtues — courage, honesty, compassion."[27] Courage, honesty, compassion: those are qualities found often in the poems of this man. Patrick Lane and Lorna Crozier wrote in the introduction to their volume of Nowlan's selected poems: "often we have heard students say that in their studies of the classic Canadian anthologies it is Alden's work that stands out, his poems they remember and take into their lives."[28] David Adams Richards has witnessed the responses of strangers to his recitations of lines by Nowlan. "I would quote his poems and watch, in Sydney, Australia, or Brisbane, or Virginia, or New Orleans, or London, people's faces light up for the first time at the man's genius — recognize themselves in him, and hear... some great eternal wisdom."[29] Many readers will experience that lighting up, that recognition, and that wisdom during hours spent with this giant gathering of an incomparable poet's work.

26 Cook, *One Heart*, 310.
27 *Ibid.*, 202.
28 Lane and Crozier, xi.
29 Richards, 121.

SOURCES

Bartlett, Brian. "Nights in Windsor Castle: Remembering Alden Nowlan." In *All Manner of Tackle: Living with Poetry*. Windsor, ON: Palimpsest, 2017.

Bly, Robert. "For Alden Nowlan, with Admiration." In *Playing the Jesus Game: Selected Poems*, by Alden Nowlan, 5-10. Trumansburg, NY: New Books, 1970.

Cook, Geoffrey. "Alden Nowlan: Selected Poems." In *Alden Nowlan: Essays on His Works*, edited by Gregory M. Cook, 64-69. Toronto: Guernica, 2006.

Cook, Gregory M. "Alden Nowlan: A Rising Young Canadian Writer Talks to *Amethyst*: An Interview by Gregory M. Cook." In *Alden Nowlan: Essays on His Works*, edited by Gregory M. Cook, 32-45. Toronto: Guernica, 2006.

———. *One Heart, One Way: Alden Nowlan: A Writer's Life*. Lawrencetown Beach, NS: Pottersfield Press, 2003.

Lane, Patrick, and Lorna Crozier. Introduction to *Selected Poems*, by Alden Nowlan, xi-xix. Don Mills, ON: Anansi, 1996.

Metcalf, John. "Alden Nowlan Interviewed by John Metcalf." In *Alden Nowlan: Essays on His Works*, edited by Gregory M. Cook, 46-63. Toronto: Guernica, 2006.

Milosz, Czeslaw. Foreword to *Miracle Fair: Selected Poems of Wislawa Szymborska*. Translated by Joanna Trzeciak, 1-4. New York: W.W. Norton, 2001.

Neilson, Shane, ed. *Alden Nowlan & Illness*. Victoria, BC: Frog Hollow Press, 2004.

Nowlan, Alden. "Growing Up in Katpesa Creek." In *Double Exposure*, 15-24. Fredericton: Brunswick Press, 1978.

———. "Something to Write About." *Canadian Literature* 68-69 (Spring-Summer 1976): 7-12.

Pedersen, Jon. "An Interview with Alden Nowlan." In *The Wanton Troopers*, by Alden Nowlan. Reader's Guide Edition, 261-97. Fredericton: Goose Lane, 2009.

Richards, David Adams. "I Went to Meet Alden Nowlan." In *Alden Nowlan: Essays on His Works*, edited by Gregory M. Cook, 120-32. Toronto: Guernica, 2006.

Toner, Patrick. *If I Could Turn and Meet Myself: The Life of Alden Nowlan*. Fredericton: Goose Lane, 2000.

The Rose and
the Puritan

The Brothers and the Village

The neighbours, in a Sunday meeting mood,
Would roll sweet bits of pity on their tongues
And wonder gravely how the honest Browns
Could breed so little virtue in their sons.

For Jimmie whimpered when he saw a crow
Come down in answer to a classmate's rock,
And fondled roses like a foolish girl,
And quoted school-book poets when he talked.

And Tom shaped women with his pocket knife
From bits of wood, beneath a lazy tree,
Or frightened village maids with silly tales
About the beauty of love's ecstasy.

And John, the eldest, once as mad as they,
But now subdued with children, farm and wife,
Threw all his earnings into books and rum—
And cursed the bitter pointlessness of life.

A Night Hawk Fell with a Sound Like a Shudder

A night hawk fell with a sound like a shudder
        and I was suddenly lonely and cold
sitting there on the fence. Because some rabbit
        or likelier a mouse could not grow old?

No, though in any hunt I'm with the quarry
        it was no mouse's agony that I
felt when I heard the rush of a hawk's wings
        fall without warning from the harvest sky.

A Poem to My Mother

I being twelve and scared, my lantern shook,
shrunk to string my stomach knotted,
breathing the sultry mustiness of hay
and dung in the cowbarn,
and the heifer calving.

Ours was a windy country and its crops
were never frivolous, malicious rocks
kicked at the plough and skinny cattle broke
ditch ice for mud to drink and pigs were axed.

Finding the young bull drowned, his shoulders wedged
into a sunken hogshead in the pasture,
I vomited, my mother, yet the flies
around his dull eyes vanished with the kiss
your fingers sang into my hair all night.

Mother, O gentler Christ, O warmest bed,
hearing the wind at bay your heart was milk;
under the crazy quilting of such love,
needles of adoration knit
bandages for my babied eyes; I slept.

A Letter to My Sister

Dearest of strangers: in your separate room
no smoke intrudes, nor howling from the stable;
the bats make crazy circles in the night—
you smile, adjusting napkins on the table.

The haltered horses scream and flaming shingles
come down like bombs upon the yard and yet
even the heat that cracks these windows shall
never disturb the table that you set.

Running with buckets between barn and well,
seeing so little done by all we do,
my gentle love, I cannot quite decide
whether to pity or to envy you.

Hens

Beside the horse troughs, General Grant
swaggered and foraged in the dry manure,
that winter we had twenty-seven hens
graced with white feathers and the names of heroes.

Cock of the walk, he took the choicest fodder,
and he was totem, stud and constable
until his comb and spurs were frozen, bled,
and then the hens—quite calmly—pecked him dead.

Sparrow Come in My Door

Sparrow come in my door, and at the window
your wings, hysterical, shall pound the glass
between you and the sky, invisible,
a nothingness that will not let you pass.

When I was seven in the summer kitchen
a bird flew in and all of mother's breath
escaped in one long sigh because she said
a bird invades the house before a death.

Sparrow come in my door, and at the window
be neither omen, prophecy or sign;
pound at the glass you do not know imprisons
you in your loneliness and me in mine.

All Down the Morning

All down the morning, women sprinkled crumbs
Of musty laughter, watching Janice Smith
In brazen languor smear her husband's lips
With public kisses, while he glared or blushed.

And when the Sunday village itched in church,
They thought of Janice, hot as Babylon,
Who lured her Jimmie to the porch and bared
His people's blanket-buried secrecies.

Or dancing to the snarl of feline strings,
Each Friday at the school, they leered at jokes
That made obscenities of her taut breasts
Against her startled husband's sweating suit.

For she was city-bred and unaware
That love was bordered by the rumpled quilts
And children bred from duty as the soil
Was ploughed to hide the seed and not for joy.

So taunted by harsh laughter, half-ashamed,
Enraged with rum and manhood late one night,
And shouting like betrayal, Jim came home
To bruise his knuckles on her shameless face.

The Egotist

A gushing carousel, the cock
Revolved around the axeman's block.

Sweet Christ, he kicked his severed head
And drenched the summer where he bled.

And terrible with pain, the scream
Of blood engulfed his desperate dream—

He knew (and knowing could not die)
That dawn depended on his cry.

Two Strangers

Two strangers, one of whom was I,
who heard another stranger cry,
when walking in a hunted wood
were frightened into lonelihood.

For one, the sheepish blat of death
re-echoed in his lifted breath;
He drummed his heart for that which dies
and (ritualistic) wet his eyes.

For one, the threshing thing in pain
unloosed wild horsemen in his brain;
he tasted in his rearing will
the salty savour of the kill.

And flank to flank in mist and trees,
they burned with their identities —
two strangers thralled by evil art
to seldom meet and never part.

Weakness

Old mare whose eyes
are like cracked marbles,
drools blood in her mash,
shivers in her jute blanket.

My father hates weakness worse than hail;
in the morning
     without haste

he will shoot her in the ear, once,
shovel her under in the north pasture.

Tonight
        leaving the stables,
he stands his lantern on an over-turned water pail,
turns,
        cursing her for a bad bargain,
and spreads his coat
carefully over her sick shoulders.

Cattle among the Alders

Cattle among the alders
on the hill among the scrub spruce,
cattle black as leather with white
splashes like milk on their shoulders,
feeding in the khaki grass.

The boy shall come for them
the blue legs of his pants
stroking one another with the sound
that leaves make in the wind and he in love
with all the girls in the world
whistling.

And I know him as though
we had wrestled together in the womb,
and his mother
who is like homemade cider
that goes over the tongue like soapy water
and then is warm and comfortable
in the stomach,

And his father
who laughed when the boy got drunk

on fermented molasses
and whipped the pants off him when he forgot
to water the cattle.

Whistling of Birds

Little bells
under the dark water,
ringing in the dark water,
as the tide moves you;
it is near morning
when I hear you,
shivering like flowers,
little bells in the dark water.

Child of Tabu

Shouting the name our parents whispered,
we circled him in the school yard,
winking at one another complacently
when we found we could make him weep.

It was not strange that we hated him,
who was conceived so casually by strangers
in the soft hay and the high noon.

Begotten furtively in the marital night,
beneath the crush of blankets
and the long shame,

we avowed our ancestry
with the ruthless simplicity of children,
offering our gods
a dripping handful of his heart.

Shouting His Love to Strangers

Shouting his love to strangers,
rumpling the hair of deformed children,
shaking the grimy hands of beggars,
whistling at the ugliest of girls
and stopping an evil old woman
to admire her eyes...
        ...this was the madness of my brother.

I was not surprised when they came for him,
pinioning his arms in canvas...
        ...rebuking the gay gush of his laughter
          with the terrible sanity of their faces.

When Like the Tears of Clowns

When like the tears of clowns the rain intrudes
Upon our ordered days and children chant,
Like repetitious birds, their sexless shrill:
My heart crawls lean and lewd, a shrinking thing,
To haylofts where, when I was ten and whipt,
Tall horses swore fidelity and drummed
As wolf-thoughts howled within my punished wrists.

There in the seasoned hay's unsubtle tang
The lash of fleshly pride unleashed my lips

And in a dream I saw the meek bequeathed
Their deep and narrow heritage of earth.

The Rose and the Puritan

He said, the panthers rendez-vous tonight
outside my cubicle, and beasts with wings
are mauling their tremulous meat. I hear
the blatant bellies of ogres, the clack
of rats — a leper peels his putrid hands
of meaningless fingers, giggling. Praise God
for shelter, even such as this.
                                    She said
nothing. He spoke again and louder, hear
the girls in silken sins and jostled hair
who tempt me with castanets, see the lights
that naked boys have aimed from grape-grown hills,
and, listen!, the wily old cannibals
have thought to lure me to their pots with chants
of freedom. Luckily these walls are sound.

And rose said nothing, nothing at all. God
is my refuge, he whimpered suddenly,
even this lightless tomb, this cell, this cage
is preferable to that which shrieks outside —
the world is wind, the winged wind with claws,

But God is there, not here, said rose,
then mute again she turned the key and smiled.

A Darkness
in the Earth

Hymn

O God of Hainesville, Mattawa and Bath,
feted with raisin juice and leavened bread,
my bare knees bent like boomerangs of wrath
to you, the wind, the knuckles of the dead.

Think for the moment of one blind from birth,
there was just such a darkness in the earth.

O God, only the passionate profane
express such humours as I shared with you,
boxing with my own body, gone insane,
O God only the passionate profane.

Think for the moment of one blind from birth,
there was just such a darkness in the earth.

I saw the crows they hanged to spook the corn
on Sundays, and a girl with yellow hair
whose belly was accursed; and she was torn
by tongs of talk until her bones were bare.

Think for the moment of one blind from birth,
there was just such a darkness in the earth.
Boxing with my own body gone insane,
O God only the passionate profane.

In the Hainesville Cemetery

Not all these stones
belong to death. Here and there
you read something
like
> John Andrew Talbot, 1885–1955
> Mary, his wife, 1887–

and on decoration day
Mary will come here
·and put a jam jar of water and tulips
on her own grave.

       The Talbots are people
       who make the beds before breakfast
       and set the breakfast table
       every night before they go to bed.

Sacrament

God, I have sought you as a fox seeks chickens,
curbing my hunger with cunning.
The times I have tasted your flesh
there was no bread and wine between us,
only night and the wind beating the grass.

About Death They Were Wrong

About death they were wrong, the ancients
   who painted him terrible on the walls of Eridu;
Old John walking on the island with his
      skull-faced cavalier,
believing every twig broken to be the step of Christ;
the gray-eyed men crying
      death   death   death
whenever they thought of their gods;
poor, filthy wonderful Francis
smiling
      welcome my sister death,

for not the sneer
but the snicker of death
makes death unbearable:

the fact that for every boy
who stabs himself for love
or starves himself for poetry,
a hundred thousand die
disputing the right of way,

and for every old man
beaten to death by the secret police,
a million succumb
to economic ulcers and cirrhosis of the liver.

The Gunfighters

They die so young and yet evaded death,
These stunted boys with hot, consumptive eyes,
The final centaurs of the final west,
Who live in children's games as Achilles
Once lived when boys with staves reconquered Troy.

It is too easy for the old to smile
At such unlikely heroes or defame
Their myths with truths inane and pitiless:

Theirs was the honour of the eldest gods
Who left mere mercy to the womanly,
And notched their triumphs on archaic guns
That never shot a city or a back.

In Awful Innocence

Machines in awful innocence ordain
The decalogue of static certainties;
Like Newton's universe and Persia's gods
Assume the changelessness of laws.

Listen, I saw a surging thing of steel,
Convinced three cycles always meant a chair,
Inhale a child and twist its pretty neck,
Then sprinkle varnish in its bloodied hair.

After the First Frost

After the first frost,

resting in the cool shadows,
the undisciplined lilac bushes
a green web around her,

old woman in brown stockings,
smelling of wintergreen
a clean burn in my nostrils,
sipping hot milk and ginger,
among the dead lilacs.

Her daughter I knew as a legion of whispers:
how she lay three summers in the hen house,
rocking her simple baby.

And the old woman swept out the hen house with
        spruce boughs,
and built her a hammock from a crazy quilt,
till the baby's head grew
unnatural and huge, and he died.

And the old woman pried him loose from her arms
and laid him on a board between two chairs,
and clothed him in velvet trousers
and a shirt bleached out of flour bags,

and went out to wait in the shadows,
the tilting branches closing around her.

Go

Elizabeth, in your shoes with tartan laces,
gather your books and go,
running so fast your pony-pig-tail bounces.

Soon all the corridors are dusk, the classes
dismissed. The janitor
mingles with crooked shadows as he passes

through the incredible emptiness and silence
like an abandoned one.
Run, Elizabeth, run!

Blue Ballad

When Janet saw her sister's lips were blue
She came to me and said, if sister sleeps
What is this arctic mood of hers that creeps
Across her cheeks and leaves her kisses blue?

And Janet thought and thought of polar blue,
Of skies when rinsed with rain, of summer seas,
Of Alice gowns, new skirts, and whispered, please
Why does my sister sleep with lips of blue?

And I was loath to think of polar blue,
Of Alpine ice that holds its prey for years
Preserved as if in mockery of tears—
I lied that sister's lips were never blue.

Flossie at School

Five laths in a cotton dress
was christened Flossie
and learned how to cry,
her eyes like wet daisies
behind thick glasses.

She was six grades ahead of me
and wore bangs; the big boys
called her "The Martian,"
they snowballed her home,
splashed her with their bicycles,
left horse dung in her coat pockets.

She jerked when anyone spoke to her,
and when I was ten
I caught up with her one day
on the way home from school,
and said, Flossie I really like you
but don't let the other kids know I told you,
they'd pick on me, but I do like you,
I really do, but don't tell anybody.
And afterwards I was ashamed
for crying when she cried.

I Saw My Daughter's Mercy Spare

I saw my daughter's mercy spare
The fly that tripped a spider's snare;
I watched her hold the rescued mite
And touch its wings in rapt delight.

And touch its wings in rapt delight,
Embrace its weakness with her eyes,

Caress its foulness with her might,
Like a pig-tailed god of flies.

Like a pig-tailed god of flies,
As she pouted in surprise
At its tickling tries at flight
Before she crushed her fingers tight.

Only the Lazy Boy

Only the lazy boy whose lax guitar
Idled through dusty summer saw her go

With wind in skirts and grasses to the fence,
Over, into the croaking swamp below.

Only the lazy boy was spared the dark
Rumours of how her final day was spent,

And strange in one whose ways were slow with sleep,
Only the lazy boy knew why she went.

Parakeet

The Pentecostal parakeet who speaks,
Like Peter, tongues he cannot understand,
Sits lisping on my thumb, repeats, repeats
With high fidelity, bewhiskered damns.

He says profane, profane, profane and tweet,
Consigns my soul to hell and shakes the flame
Of fire-blue feathers, as a bird might laugh
If birds were laughers; I caress his beak

With tenderest perversity as one
Will pat a small boy's bottom, perhaps, or lift
A cat by furry nape—I say "how can
So small a bird contain so many damns?"

He glares at me from sullen slits that throb
With hate that only dwarfs and caged things know,
And silent suddenly he pecks and pecks
With rage so mad it tickles in my hand.

Atlantis

No waves ten storeys tall and terrible,
abrupt and hissing as a severed vein,
erased this city. First the rivers spilled
across our outer provinces, and then
there was some talk of dams, but most of us
approved of irrigation, anyhow
the peasants need a bath sometimes, we said,
and later when the swamps began to swell
and gulls were white against the misty sky,
the ancients said almost the same occurred
often when they were young, and so of course
we were ashamed to mention things like drips
we heard at night, and someone always laughed
when little men at parties claimed that pools
were rising slowly, slowly in their cellars.

Wind in a
Rocky Country

Marian at the Pentecostal Meeting

Marian I cannot begrudge
    the carnival of God,
the cotton candy of her faith
    spun on a silver rod

to lick in bed; a peaked girl,
    neither admired nor clever,
Christ pity her and let her ride
    God's carousel forever.

Baptism

Along the river, women sing of sin
and girls in dripping dresses dry their hair,
and giggle in the water, half-afraid
of thoughts as high and marvellous as prayer.

The preacher's hands are certain like his faith,
and sweep reborn devotees from the womb
of cleansing water where they hymn in praise
of Him who rose who broke a stronger tomb.

And when they wade, enwrapped in towels, to shore
the girls like damp young angels stop to greet
their younger sisters, whom they bless with tears
and kiss — with new and womanly conceit.

Our Brother Exalted

A hardware salesman, potentate and priest
of Arab brothers, he displays the chain
of sheikdom, ruling all the Mystic East,
encompassed by the hall on Fifth and Main.

Each Monday night he lifts the sacred sword
and orders grocery clerks to drain the blood
of interlopers found without the word
that marks each lawful wearer of the hood.

And when, in arcane ritualistic prose,
he orders closure of the occult tome,
their carpeted Sahara seeks repose,
and they play nickel poker and go home.

Summer

It's summer yet but still the cold
coils through these fields at dusk, the gray Atlantic
haunting the hollows and a black bitch barking
between a rockpile and a broken fence
out on the hill a mile from town where maybe
a she-bear, groggy with blueberries, listens
and the colt, lonesome, runs in crooked circles.

Partnership

Aliens, both like the last survivor
of some lost tribe, the old man drunk
on lotions, his breath like a brothel, the boy
half-certain he's seen a star
fall like a hawk and roll in the dooryard—

each practised
in talking to himself, the weather
or anything else that listens:

the old man teaches
the boy about mermaids;
the boy filches
bay rum and tonics —

the crippled monkey
on the blind dog's back.

Neighbours

Bitch fox stealthy
but the grass betrays you
shivering with impatience;

it is my duty
being neighbourly
to kill you —

my uncle the deacon
questioned God's purposes
in creating you,
chicken thief.

John Sproull
would spit in my eye
if he could see me
wishing you well at his henyard.

Street Corner Idler

His tragedy is that he seems to wait—
idlers should swagger in and entertain!
the tramps in mother's kitchen always paid
mouth organ tunes and stories sad as plays.

They had unfaithful sons and cheating wives
and when they left us it was strangely pleasant
to think of them, full of our beans and bread,
turning beside the gate to thumb their noses.

To Sylvia on Her Fourteenth Birthday

Suspicious of the customary oughts,
        the peevish algebra of argument,
I too am pricked by quint-thorned senses, share
        your brittle joys, your skittish discontent.

All royal questions lead to wharves of where,
        zig-zag through seas of why to farther riddles:
philosophers ransack the violin
        until they doubt that anybody fiddles.

Life being various, Goliath falls
        prey to the stone-propelled tribute of love,
sometimes; such singular plurality
        affiliates the tiger and the dove.

To traffick with reality involves
        the risk of shrinkage—shrinkage is to know,
say, that your patron saint was half a rogue
        and, knowing, crow.

Sylvia, truth is vast and more
than two and two are firmly four,

for two and two sometimes will be
an atom of infinity.

You, in your bicycle pants,
torero tight around
the April slenderness of boy-girl legs;
you, whose ambition
is to have sixteen years
and a boy with a motorcycle,
what can I add who love you
neither as father nor lover
but with a love greater
and less than theirs,
being almost impersonal?

At the Fair

Terry and I at the Fair
won everything —
    we filled the car

with green-eyed bears,
black jackasses with red-lined ears
and one old tiger with horsehair
whiskers that tickled

    my neck, there was barely room
    left for us:

we got drenched,
running to the car,
and sat there,
laughing crazily among our queer beasts,

    as the empty Ferris wheel
    went around
    and around
    in the rain.

Clarence Carle

Though Clarence Carle inherited a basement
sufficient for a college or a convent,
he never built upon it, pitched a shack
behind the cellar wall. When I went back
to talk with him he'd tell me how his place
was equal to his means, he was content,
he said, and planned to fill the hole
with dirt and plant potatoes as a fool
could see that that was practical. And yet
his eyes were tortured with an old regret.

I Knew the Seasons ere I Knew the Hours

I knew the seasons ere I knew the hours;
the Christmas cactus blossomed anytime
after December first and scarlet flowers
fell patiently, in patterns like the blood
from shallow wounds, in mother's russet parlour.

I was once six and so damn lonely
I called love Rover, he had two sad ears,
a black-white checkerboard of face, a nose
for venison, he stole my uncle blind,
was caught and shot and buried in the pasture.

For months I sprinkled daisies over him,
sucking my grief like lemons. Stephanie
shredded the daisies when she punished me
for being born her brother and we wrestled,
crushing the grass like lovers, till our mother
whipt us apart. Eventually the flowers
were laid less for my grief than for that struggle.

Pussywillows in March

Pussywillows beside the full ditches
blossoming in the season
when the last snow
is more soot than crystal,

there are such curious conflicts
in you, joy and sadness,
and a strange loveliness
in your mud-coloured stalks
and the little blossoms
in their leathery pouches
that are exactly
the colour of an old white shirt
that doesn't look clean
no matter how often you wash it.

God Sour the Milk of the Knacking Wench

God sour the milk of the knacking wench
with razor and twine she comes
to stanchion our blond and bucking bull,
pluck out his lovely plumbs.

God shiver the prunes on her bark of chest,
who capons the prancing young.
Let maggots befoul her alive in bed,
and dibble thorns in her tongue.

Poem for the Golden Wedding
of My Puritan Grandparents

Their love was sister to the starving deer
and brother to December. Had he called
her "darling" in his annual drunkenness,
(for he got drunk at Christmas) her lean lips
would have recoiled as when she tasted milk
that had gone sour or observed a girl
in little breeches. So he always spoke
of her as the "old lady," "ma" or "Maud."
And in their fifty years they never kissed.

But when he withered of the fanged disease
that ate his vitals till he lived on slop
and sat in silence louder than a groan,
we children marvelled how she sometimes sat
for hours simply staring at his face,
and how before they closed the box she bent
with awful eagerness to pat his hand.

Poem

for Helen and Martha Knox, Hainesville, New Brunswick
Missionaries to Kenya, 1910–40

The sisters Knox were thirty years in Kenya—
Christ in a cedar chest brought out to smother
bare-naked men, bull gods, eccentric weather,
demented vegetation, the hyena:

Wesleyan gentlewomen having ices,
humming and hemming in a manse rose garden.
Hush, dung-flanked Africa—no serpent jargon!
God has his merciful, if daft, devices.

For Nicholas of All the Russias

Wind in a rocky country and the harvest
meagre, the sparrows eaten, all the cattle
gone with the ragged troopers, winter coming,
mother will starve for love of you and wrapping
newest and least accustomed leave him squalling
out in the hills beside the skulls of foxes,
it cold and snow in the air.
                              Stranger, knocking,
(now in this latter time even the poor
have bread and sleep on straw) what silly rumour
tells me your eyes are yellow and your lips
once rose trout-quick to suck a she-wolf's teats?

Our Lord, his peaked heir and hawk-faced daughters
are gone, although they say one severed finger
was found after the soldiers cleaned the cellar.

Under the Ice

A Poem for Elizabeth Nancy

Emptied from Eden, I look down
into your eyes like caves behind a torrent,
into the blue-green valleys where the cattle
fatten on clover and grow drunk on apples;

into the house asleep and all the curtains
skittish and white as brides (even the wind
meeting their silence, whispers) and I come
into the house with hands that stink from milking,

into this house of candles where my feet
climbing your stairs like laughter leave me standing
before your door, knowing there's no one there,
knowing your room is bare and not much caring.

Beginning

From that they found most lovely, most abhorred,
my parents made me: I was born like sound
stroked from the fiddle to become the ward
of tunes played on the bear-trap and the hound.

Not one, but seven entrances they gave
each to the other, and he laid her down
the way the sun comes out. Oh, they were brave,
and then like looters in a burning town.

Their mouths left bruises, starting with the kiss
and ending with the proverb, where they stayed;
never in making was there brighter bliss,
followed by darker shame. Thus I was made.

Gypsies

Jessie, my cousin, remembers there were gypsies
every spring, cat-eyes in smoky faces,
hair like black butter on leather laces.
Mothers on the high waggons whose babes sucked
flesh on O'Brien Street, I'd be ashamed.
The men stole everything and damned if they didn't
shrug if you caught them — giving back a hen
filched from your own coop like a gift to a peasant.
The little girls danced, their red skirts winking,
their legs were lovely, greasy as drumsticks.
And they kidnapped children. Oh, every child
hoped secretly to be stolen by gypsies.

Refuge at Eight

Darkness, the smell of earth, the smell of apples,
the cellar swallowed me, I dreamt I died,
saw both blind parents mad with guilt and sorrow,
my ghost sardonic. Finally, I cried.

Aunt Jane

Aunt Jane, of whom I dreamed the nights it thundered,
was dead at ninety, buried at a hundred.
We kept her corpse a decade, hid upstairs,
where it ate porridge, slept and said its prayers.

And every night before I went to bed
they took me in to worship with the dead.
Christ Lord, if I should die before I wake,
I pray thee Lord my body take.

To Jean

So cold that any house seemed like a fire,
I snapped the lock that was less lock than symbol.
It was a rivet and a twisted wire
and I was seventeen and scared and nimble.

You twenty miles away and with a lover
I broke your empty house and stole its heat.
The stove all cold I pulled a jacket over
my shaking shoulders, slept and found sleep sweet.

Background

Where I come from, the kick of love
recalls the laughter in the throats
of boys who knocked the privy down
before the teacher could get out.

The Belled Deer

There used to be wild deer across the river,
one of them wore a bell and no one knew
its origin and so the legends grew;
grandfather thought no natural brute was ever
as swift as that one was or half so clever.
Though every fall the hunters sought her, told
of bell-sounds like the touch of ice on gold,
they said that mortal hand would kill her never.

Nobody hunts there now; a tracker's snow,
a windless afternoon were once enough
to sweep the orchards with a rifle screen.
They wanted meat, of course, for times were tough,
but there was not a man who had not seen
the belled deer in his sights and let her go.

The Coat

My grandmother's boy is dead,
his skull fractured he did not speak
as she knelt down on the dirt road
and wept on his face, her hand under his head.

My grandmother's boy was wild
as the blackbirds in Minard's clearing.
He stood up on the pedals, yodelling;
the wind too seems to ride toward death.

My father took the corduroy coat
of my grandmother's boy and hid
it behind a beam where she found it and came
weeping with it hugged to her breast,
walking slowly under the clothes line
down the pathway beside the woodshed.

There were bloody stains and the stains of mud
almost indistinguishable on the coat,
and her black dress with its red flowers
came like a ghost berating
my father as though he'd killed.
When he took the coat from her
he was so gentle I was amazed. Afterwards
he cursed and poked the coat viciously,
using a stick to crowd it
into the kitchen fire.

Cousins

My cousins, the kind
of family who in another time
and place took to brigandage
for the hell of it,

so violent they go logging
or harvesting their meagre acres
as if they were going on a raid,
work twelve hours, then hitch-hike to a dance
in Larchmont or Bennington,
get drunk as a fiddler's bitch,
roostering for skirts and fist-fights;

and when one of them
gets a girl in trouble,
which is inevitable,
he marries her,

it's a point of honour
with them to treat their wives
like whores, they talk about bedding
them as they talk
about going to the privy,

they are so afraid
of weakness, my cousins
who are not frightened
by boots or tire-irons
behind the dance hall in Bennington
are scared into hilarity and contempt by kisses.

My Father

My father never takes
anything for granted —
food, shelter, sleep,
he is always grateful.

He lives alone now,
when he opens the pantry
he always acts amazed
that there is bacon and flour.

He eats slowly
surprised there's enough
finishes wiping
his plate out with bread.

He is seldom happy
but I never saw a man
so content with small comforts:

wife, children gone
there is nothing left—

I know he could curl up
in his mackinaw
on his own barnfloor
and sleep thankful
at being allowed to rest there.

Testament

If I am sentimental
curse me, it is my inheritance,
what I bequeath
is laughter to the young lovers
of this country where summer
is tense always, a lull between storms,
where even in August
I can sense the snow clouds.
I would have it
so the first time
you are frightened, but not much,
and afterwards when the old janitor
gone crazy with religion
sweeps the snow off the steps
of our three churches, being most careful
with his own, you come awake slowly
and lie quiet for a long time
in the warmth of one another's arms.

Bone Dry and at Jimmie Kelly's

Five dogs, bitch-crazed in the dying mustard,
challenged my car and a black goat
chewed most mournfully at a black coat
drying upon the fence. I said the word

appropriate to such a place and thirst
and Tommy went in quickly and came out
hiding a bottle. Jimmie Kelly cursed
all bitches generally and kicked the goat.

Father

Father, she says, was handsome as a Spaniard,
rode a bay stallion in the Depression
and fed it better than he fed himself.
He was a strict and pious gentleman.

He called me princess even when he paced
his study with the black hypnotic tongue
of the whip licking at his riding boot.
There's not one man like him among the young.

Poem

A silence like a lizard on the tongue,
      quiet that is not peace stalks through the mind,
searching for words in all the empty rooms,
      birds that no wicker cages have confined.

Grim is the shadow of wanton despair,
      icy the rooms where not a bird is crying.
Stop at the window, motionless as mute,
      even the hawk may come, when you've ceased trying.

Baptism

In summer-coloured dresses, six young girls
are walking in the river; they look back,
frightened and proud; a choir and a cloud
of starlings sing; in rubber boots and black
frock-coat the preacher bends them separately
under; since the up-rushing stream expands
their skirts as they go down he closes them
each time with gently disapproving hands.

Saturday Night

Every five minutes they turn,
with their tires like sirens,
tusking the dirt up on the creek road,
and drive back through town —

>   slowing down on Main Street, manoeuvring
>   between the farmers' cars, hooting
>   at girls on the pavement who reply
>   with little hen movements, laughing, waiting.

The boys sport leather jackets and Levis,
but that's their underwear,
the car is their real clothing:
at Taylor's Corner they turn again,
their Hollywood mufflers
making sounds furious, derisive, vulgar —
like a bear growling and breaking wind,

>   and roar through Main Street again.

Sunday Afternoon

In the next house they're punishing a child.
Violently too: the boy is being whipped
with something limber that thwacks like applause,
water that's stoned or cotton when it's ripped.

All three are yelling. Though the boy
uses no proscribed idioms, it's plain
he's cursing manfully. But also begging—
defiant yet obsequious in pain.

The mother's inconsistent too, she wants
the boy whipped, obviously, but she hates
the man for beating him. So she exhorts
the son vindictively and still berates

the father's harshness. He a normal man
playing a role he loathes, a prisoner,
expresses his abhorrence of the whole
mess by applying himself to it harder.

The Lodge

Kneeling with fastened wrists before the skull
that's flanked with lamps of salt and alcohol
men are ennobled in fraternity,
swear to submit to sundry mutilations
should they betray the awesome secrecy
that hides the First Truth like a tasselled curtain:
life is what is but death is fairly certain.

That solemn preface done the new-made peers
undress blindfold and march in bare feet that
have been first drenched with water on a mat
wired for electricity, the cheers
of their new kinsmen roaring in their ears
as they prance goatishly and buck and bleat.

Homebrew

Molasses, oranges and yeast
purchased with promises and mixed at night,
the keg buried in steaming dung
to hasten fermentation, then the wait
for some excuse to fork it out
(a rainy day, the mill not running);
the men in their sawdust-covered denims
sitting on blocks of pressed hay in the barn
and drinking from a single mug, their thumbs
spooning out shreds of hay and frequently
flies and then bolting it, holding their breath,
and spitting afterwards, grunting their pleasure.

At the Lunch Counter

A girl, fifteen perhaps,
licking her finger-tips,
smoothing splotches
of butter and salt
off her blue pants,
cheek muscles rippling.

Nathan who is blind
sidles to the stool beside her.

They talk, he pompously,
she making faces
he can't see,
telling the boys she isn't serious.

I'm Barbara, she says,
blowing her cheeks out,
wrinkling her forehead,
Fred Ward's Barbara.
I have red hair!

She giggles
since her hair is brown
with aluminum
fishes at the temples.

But he can't see.

Then,
she stiffens and frowns
wanting us to go away
so she can be kind.

Rehearsal

So old that every ghost's a friend, he sits
propped up with canes, pelted with schoolboy teasing,
here in our little street and plots his funeral
down to the last amen and finds it pleasing

to choose again the six mane-tossing stallions,
the six pert dandies with their silver handles,
the girls to pitch the hymns like rose-white doves
out of their mouths, over the blessed candles.

The Fynch Cows

The Fynch cows poisoned:
they'd torn the fence down,
gored one another for the befouled weed;
next day they bloated
and their bowels bled,
and they staggered crazily
around the miserly pasture —

John Fynch crying
as he stumbled after them,
with his rifle.

Jack Stringer

Jack Stringer kissed his mother twice a year,
when he came home from Calgary and when
he left again and every year the time
between the kiss of greeting and the kiss
of farewell became briefer, and he went
farther to show his love for her—like going
with her to the Free Baptist Church and smoking
cigarettes in the porch, being polite
to all her friends and smiling gently at
her ignorance; recalling with each kiss
why that first great escape had been such bliss.

Rosemary Jensen

Rosemary Jensen died, to death's surprise,
she'd fought so long to wrench the burning coal
he'd buried in her from her sullen soul,
and there was so much hatred in her eyes.

And all the neighbourhood remarked how hard
Tom Jensen took it; gathered at the grave,
ashamed, faintly disgusted, heard him rave,
were slow to leave him when they reached his yard.

But he went in the house and locked them out
and for the only time in thirty years
drank whiskey in the kitchen, dried his tears,
tumblers of laughter cracking in his throat.

Alex Duncan

He's wanted to go back
since that first fall:
1920 and the frost
rending the crops
with its cold and passionate
Canadian hands.

There's never been enough.
The army worms ate up
the first fare home,
floods took the second,

and the bitch cancer
that he half imagines
to have been some animal
native here, gobbled the third,
eating the woman's breasts.

Four decades away from home
his Scottish tongue
grows broader every year.
One looks for heather
to spring up between his toes.

Sheilah Smith

Awakening as people do in dreams
naked upon the mayor's lawn, not sure
whether the crowd had come to see the fire
or take the sacraments, but certain her
presence was an embarrassment, she first
wept and embraced herself, and then, unable
to make them understand, threw up her arms
and danced—extravagantly—on the table.

Andy Shaw

Three generations (and he loathed them all)
     bought meat from Andy Shaw who clerked for Etter,
working six days a week for thirty years,
     hating his job and looking for a better.

He never married and he blamed his wage,
     never went more than twenty miles from town;
and every year came earlier to work,
     cursing the butcher shop that tied him down.

When Charley Etter died his son came home
     to run the store, so Andy got his pay.
Some claim the old man cried, offered to work
     for less — or nothing — if they'd let him stay.

Charlie

For twenty-five cents
or, if properly approached, a dime
he'll chew up a razor blade
crack it between his teeth
and grin at the same time.

Usually, it's the kids
who hire him,
a gang of them
chipping in pennies — their applause
pleases him

as he swallows
thinking how much
blood there is in a dollar.

This Woman's Shaped for Love

This woman's shaped for love, one thinks each breast
might have been grown to fit in a man's hand,
her mouth moulded by constant kisses, and
her legs devised by an evangelist.
She promenades as if her feet were headed
toward an elopement; through the plodding town
her rich posterior lilts up and down—
surely a girl begotten to be bedded.

So boys ache after her and men of age
wish they could have a little while it lasts;
young girls sniff and go home to imitate
her every motion, like enthusiasts.

And nights—her husband kneads in fists of rage
flesh that no human touch can animate.

Warren Pryor

When every pencil meant a sacrifice
his parents boarded him at school in town,
slaving to free him from the stony fields,
the meagre acreage that bore them down.

They blushed with pride when, at his graduation,
they watched him picking up the slender scroll,
his passport from the years of brutal toil
and lonely patience in a barren hole.

When he went in the Bank their cups ran over.
They marvelled how he wore a milk-white shirt
work days and jeans on Sundays. He was saved
from their thistle-strewn farm and its red dirt.

And he said nothing. Hard and serious
like a young bear inside his teller's cage,
his axe-hewn hands upon the paper bills
aching with empty strength and throttled rage.

Steve Johnson's Daughter at His Death

Of course she's sad
still it's a great adventure:
her father dead.

Everyone tries
to say the right thing
and nobody complains—the wet wreath on the door
says this is a special place; death's wings
touched her, but like a caress, death is no angel:
the old man went down like a cat
with a hen on its back.

The neighbours all come
and look at him
lying down in his serge suite—as if he'd ever
lain down in his suit, even sitting
he'd pull the cuffs up to keep the press;
it's one of the things that doesn't matter now.

They look at her too,
she knows it—last night
she refused to come in from the barn,
lay in the haymow listening
to all the people pleading.
Oh, she was sad,
but it was a fine feeling.

Carl

Nobody has ever seen Carl
when he wasn't smiling.

He grins at cats and hydrants
and a huge, wet, collie-like smile
lights up whenever anybody, no matter who,
speaks to him.

When he's hurt
his smile shrinks a little,
pulls its corners in snugly,
but it doesn't go away.

Georgie and Fenwick

Georgie and Fenwick Cranston,
in their thirties and unmarried,
Hainesville calls them old bachelors,
live with their parents on a potato farm,
six miles north of town —
they're afraid of girls.

> Saturday nights,
> in front of the Farmers Store
> some of the girls,
> their little posteriors
> gift-wrapped in Christmas-coloured
> short pants, always stop
> to tease them.

Cecelia Cameron, pressing
so close to Fenwick his overalls
scratch her bare legs, whispers,
Fenwick, do you still love me?

When she backs away
her breasts ripple
under her striped blouse,
she puts her fists in her pockets,
tightening her pants,
tugging them up her thighs,
she says, Georgie
do you want to take me home tonight?

And everybody laughs,
except Georgie and Fenwick,
who say nothing,
their mouths open,
their eyes half-shut,
blushing, rocking back and forth
in their gum rubbers. They look
like rabbits frozen
with fear of the gun.

Carl Spicer

My earliest ambition was like Cain's:
to be another and acceptable.
One from my mother's womb spewed out his brains
between my boots, as in the parable.

The Young Rector

The young rector,
an Anglo-Catholic,
is perfectly scrupulous,

but the shepherd
gets lonesome

talking to sheep
even when he loves them,

so he confides in me:
these people are dead,
all they need is someone
to throw dirt over them.
Passionless, stinking, dead.

These thirty minutes
he is the cub lion
tearing at its lamb
making violent gestures
with teeth and shoulders
until he exhausts himself

and can go back
and love them again.

A Duty Call on Paul McCullough
His Fifth Year Bedfast

Paul who endures
the weight of a coffin
without its brass splendour
or cushions, astounds me—

his facial skin
looks removable, one imagines
it on the tray
with his dentures
when the skull sleeps.

But he smokes, talks
politics and scandal, and

his wife assures me
eats like a bear.
She chuckles,
eyeing him resentfully.

I wonder if he understands.

Birth

I've seen Christ born, a stranger in the wind,
coughing in an old coat, cornered and blind,
playing the mouth organ; I saw his pay
was nickels and that only if the songs were gay.

Patricia Grey

Somebody loved Patricia Grey enough
        to carve an angel that's stood ninety years
over her grave though cattle and wild deer
        pasture upon her now and no one cares.

This afternoon I stopped to look at her
        among the purple thistles and it seemed
natural that I stooped and kissed her lips
        as though they were not stone but only dreamed.

A Phoebe on the Ground

The heart torn out
encased in feathers
pounding in the hot dust:

this small and smothering
bird overcome
by the smouldering weather.

The Homecoming

They'd never been so long apart before.
So they weren't sure of what to say. He said,
I guess there's not much news, the kids are well.
She nodded. Shyly, they went up to bed.

Blossoms

Reticent and subtle, lovely and full of light,
but sinister too as if a cat's eyes dangled
down from these tawny stalks, this is a weed
—one that does men no good, drawing its life
out of the soil that won't discriminate—
torn up, ploughed under, rooted out, incinerated,
but never beaten, never exterminated.

Walking Home from Work

Ahead a girl
in blue linen shorts,
small beads of sweat
rolling down the backs
of her legs, leaving gray stains
on her wrinkled socks.

On her thigh
a mud-coloured mole

full of moist hairs
keeps time with her step.

It is so hot
I notice every detail
yet have not decided
if her legs are beautiful or not.

John Watching Television

The room is empty except for his mind
which stands on the table like a radioactive platter
pulsating in the impossible confinement
of a mahogany picture frame.

A miracle consists of a violent solution
to an insoluble problem.
The mind absorbs such miracles—love stories
end in a permanent kiss, and crimes
are committed only by criminals,
but the central fact
is that any knot can be untied
by a knife or a pistol shot.

It is not surprising—
any of the great contemplative
saints would understand it perfectly—
that the body is so quiet
in the midst of the miraculous.
He lies still enough
to be asleep, his capacity
for violence filled
by the mind's projected, incandescent platter.

The Gift

"My son sent it," she says. The man-shaped stone
stands in its broken wrappings on the table,
defying measurement: six inches tall,
perhaps, but monstrous too, a brutal bulk
sensed in its attitude. Too starkly human.
"Esquimaux carve them," she explains. Her son
wrote her from Resolute. She laughs. "He says
it's like walking into a geography.
He always dreamed too much." The soapstone man
says nothing, though it's not impossible
that he might speak, having decided to,
since he appears ruthlessly objective
enough to be the image of some god.
If so, the old and unambiguous
kind who had hooves and buttocks. She won't say
what she thinks of this gift, except such things
as one must say of gifts from sons. It's plain
this hard and intimately squalid thing
shocks her. I see its gradual ascension
into the attic to be kept, forgotten.

Hitch Hikers

A thin spring rain tonight, the asphalt cold,
I passed six hitch hikers, each one alone,
rigid and melancholy by the road.
Even their upturned thumbs were still as stone.

Not one moved in petition when I came
or in derision when I passed, I thought
of Monmouth's men. The royal warning signs,
these piked devisers of some wistful plot.

In Esdraelon

In Esdraelon, twenty miles from here—
dirt road, spruce, balsam fir and poplar
and a porcupine sometimes
making you stop or steer around him—
the adults still stop
and stare after the cars of strangers,
suspiciously. But the kids
playing in dooryards and ditches
wave both hands and yell
as if they were welcoming you home.
That's strange too,
because if you stop
and try to talk to them
they act scared and cagey
and pretend to be mute,
as if they'd been caught
doing something shameful.

Purple Trilliums

These tough flowers
half-hidden
under spade-shaped, heavy leaves,
stinking like a wet cat—
so much at home
here by the lurching road.

They are not the kind
of flower one gives
to a girl, although
—aside from their stink—
they are full
of a tremulous loveliness.

But one can hardly imagine
them being picked
and put in a vase —
they belong here.

Driving to Moncton

A child turned suddenly and leapt upon
the road. My brakes shrieked out. He tumbled down
unhurt but crying wildly, with his eyes
knocked out of focus. As I drove toward town,

this troubled me, who am not heartless: fear
had been an acid in my throat, a pool
of searing bitterness. Scared witless, I
had for an instant hated that small fool.

Fireweed

Summer is not a season here;
August by the dirt road
ferns and the leaves of bushes brown as beer,
all dead, curdle the blood.

Driving Sunday through woods, I found
one stalk of fireweed, which
was the only live flower in the ground
along twelve miles of ditch.

Old Man on a Bicycle

An old man on a bicycle
      searches the ditches for beer bottles,
wearing a mackinaw in the hottest weather.
He piles the dusty green bottles
      in his knapsack, in a carton
      tied to the rear mudguard,
before he goes back he fills his pockets
if it is a good time — in the spring
or the day after a holiday.

But he doesn't complain
if it is a bad day,
if there are too few in twelve miles
to fill his knapsack.

When he finds a bottle broken
(and if there is even a crack they're no good)
he curses to himself, disgusted
with the fools who don't even know
how to throw a beer bottle
out of a car window without smashing it.

Christ

Aloft in a balsam fir I watched Christ go,
two crows in that same tree made human laughter.

He clambered over the log fence and crossed
the orange-yellow field, his purple skirts

swishing the grain and I could hear that sound,
so close he was, and separate the hairs

in his red beard. He passed beneath me, never
once looking up, and having reached the gate

to the hill pasture shrank smaller and smaller
becoming first a fist and then a finger

and then a fleck of purple on the hillside.
At last, at the edge of the wood, he vanished
     altogether.

Hunters

Hunters, Americans in scarlet breeches,
stopping their car here, one of them goes back
to check the network of new rope that hitches
the dead black bear atop the luggage rack.
He tightens knots, looks self-conscious and proud,
even a little boyish, though it's plain
that he's not young. One senses how this cowed
and squalid beast enlivens him — its pain
and cornered anger squelched in the dark wood
that ornaments his world. It's like a child
sprung from the violent act but tamed and good,
decoratively. He can't see it wild,
alive in its own element. He might
as well have bought it and perhaps he did:
guides trap and sell them out by weight
to hunters who don't want to hunt. The dead
beast-thing secured, the car starts homeward. There
bear skins are rugs, a den is not a lair.

Grass Fires

Grass fires burn and the relentless dusk
smells like a sacrifice; the dead blades burst
open and flower as they're touched by flame,
and then are as explosively submersed
in the dark elements: the creeping ash

that always overtakes. One thinks the ram,
restless behind his wire, understands:
faggots and basins and the asherim.

The Jackers

On Christmas eve, we killed the doe,
parted her dazzled eyes, punctured her throat,
and left small scarlet trenches in the snow
where her warm blood ran out.

A thumb of brightness gouged her eyes,
a leaden hammer split her dainty head.
Grace gone, she floundered down and did not rise,
sprawled there, undone and dead.

Grief was like spoilt bread in the mouth, I bit
the pillows, though I would not eat;
lonely as God with pity for her, yet
dogged by the sweet smell of her frying meat.

Flies

Squalor is fixed in the relationship
between these flies and me, this one returning
with crazy single-mindedness to the same spot
in the precise centre of my left wrist,
feet greased with God knows what, vomit and dung,
decomposing garbage, mucus from the eyes of dead cats,
all this and worse — brushed off in gathering fury
and whirring back, making idiot, insistent
sounds with its wings, always coming back
to the one place on my flesh. Stung into anger
as if this fly had the same conception

of our relative positions as I,
I watch for my chance and kill him.

A small bead of my own blood
bursts from his smashed body
and glistens evilly on my stinging wrist.

Bear

At Easter we went out to kill the bear
who stole the lambs; the dogs encircled her —
our rifles stuttered, blood burst from her flesh;
her death was thunderous.

Outside a roadside diner since, I've seen
a bear cub fastened with a shining chain
whose occupation was to fascinate
stray tourists looking for a place to eat.

Two Strangers

Two strangers, one of whom was I,
shook with a rabbit's queasy cry
suppressed by the quick hangman's hood
in the forest of gallows wood.

For one the child-like scream of death
resounded in his tightened breath,
he knew only the air had cried,
the voice itself had died, had died.

For one the ghostly cry brought back
the exultation of the track.
He tasted in his rearing will
the salt of the climactic kill.

For that breath's space there in the trees
they burned with their identities.
Then finding every echo gone,
still saying nothing, they walked on.

The Anatomy of Angels

Angels inhabit love songs. But they're sprites
not seraphim. The angel that up-ended
Jacob had sturdy calves, moist hairy armpits,
stout loins to serve the god whom she befriended,

and was adept at wrestling. She wore
a cobra like a girdle. Yet his bone
mending he spent some several tedious weeks
marking the bed they'd shared, with a great stone.

Looking for Nancy

Looking for Nancy
          everywhere, I've stopped
girls in trenchcoats
and blue dresses,
          said
Nancy I've looked
     all over
     hell for you,
Nancy I've been afraid
that I'd die
before I found you.

          But there's always
          been some mistake:

a broken streetlight,
too much rum or merely
my wanting too much
for it to be her.

Hunter, Beware

Hunter, beware this wood
    where every branch is frozen stiff for stinging.
I in my innocence thought love was peace,
    a drowsy drunkenness, a quiet singing.

Exploration: to Therese

We two exploring this, the oldest country,
the chariot afire, its foaming horses
racing each other in the same harness,

find it is not the same with us: the first
pair stumbled into it and God's eunuchs
scabbarded their blazing swords, they daft with
    wonder. He

gave them centuries to discover it,
being more patient then; for us the journey
crosses a beach between the tides, and ends.

Poem for Elizabeth

Not even God, you said, could be so cruel
as to ignore our innermost desire:

that to escape the fixed impermanence
of all passionate things from ice to fire.

Warning to Any Woman

Bluebeard, like any lover, locked one door
within the towered house he gave his bride.

My love, to make the moral clear, recall
how love became too curious and died.

Love Is a Rose

Love is a rose they said. And me reborn
out of a love as arrogant as horn?
Not woman only blesses, being torn
out of herself, her time. Love is a rose is thorn.

Politicians

Miracles are physical solutions
to unembodied problems. Politicians
perceive all locks are opened with one key:
the lady's buckle broken, all the doors
breached in her lord's still room and treasury.

Therese

Therese is so small a flame
I have to cup her in my hands. Even then
if there is a wind from the north
she trembles, shrinking
down in my palms. And I'm afraid
of being burnt and dropping her
on the ground where she'll go out.

Nancy

Nancy was the smoking tines,
        the distant strawstack's blaze at night
when from my window all the dark
        closed darker on that light.

Nancy was the cool beneath
        the bridge where we were forty thieves.
Cars went over, gravel came down
        Nancy was this; and please

show me what Nancy is, I said,
        the part that can never be me.
And Nancy naked was Nancy clothed
        in denser mystery.

Biography

Out of the sea I took you, laid my mouth
against your mouth and fed you with my breath
Sea lark, imaginary girl
who now insists on being real.

Down River

In cities the embittered ones are cunning;
anguish sharpens their wits, I've seen the eye
glint in whoresons and beggars, its approach
quick and malicious as a common fly.

But here persistent misery endures;
growing thick-headed like a cow, it chews
thistles in mute protest against the rain
of innocence it cannot lose or use.

Abandoned House

The mice have left this house and swallows breed here,
flying with their peculiar jerky grace
in through the highest windows that still hold
odd glass that on clear evenings reflects
the sunset, turning all its colours lonesome
and strangely cold. And small, pink roses, once
covered with bags against the cold and patterned
around the porch, grow wild in every corner
of lawns so deep and snarled a car might cross
and not be seen. Only the smaller boys
enter this house if dared and leave on finding
everything that it's fun to break is broken.

April in New Brunswick

Spring is distrusted here, for it deceives—
snow melts upon the lawns, uncovering
last fall's dead leaves.

The Smelt Run

Smelts rot on the riverbank
there are so many
some of the men
comb them out with rakes
to prove it can be done.

They build fires
on the mudbanks at night
and get drunk fishing
with nets and jig-hooks.

They fish half the night
emptying their scoop nets
in the mud by the fires
laughing at one another.

Some of the fish
are eaten, not many,
they are small and full
of tough bones — mostly
they rot on the bank
but every night
the men come back for more.

The Deacon's Cross

The deacon's cross amid the ripened grain
sports an old coat, and cotton ribbons rain
down all around it like a festival.
The blackbirds worship there. I wish them well.

The Old People

"Next summer if I live..." they say,
the old people, not with dismay,
for they might add: "I'll come again
tomorrow, if it doesn't rain."

These Are the Men Who Live by Killing Trees

These are the men who live by killing trees—
their bones are ironwood, their muscles steel,
their faces whetstones and their hands conceal
claws hard as peavy hooks: anatomies
sectioned like the man in the Zodiac.

These are the trees: alive, the sluggish light
stationed in their moist hearts; they do not fight
the axe-blade, though they'll break an axeman's back
and look benevolent. The centuries
have made a violent marriage here, the men
wedded by violation to the trees,
so they reflect each other, taking in
strange qualities. The men assume at length
the stubborn stance of trees, their dogged strength.

St. John River

The colour of a bayonet this river
that glitters blue and solid on the page
in tourist folders, yet some thirty towns
use it as a latrine, the sewerage
seeping back to their wells, and farmers maddened
by debt or queer religions winter down
under the ice, the river bottom strewn
with heaps of decomposing bark torn loose

from pulpwood driven south, its acid juice
killing the salmon. August, when the stink
of the corrupted water floats like gas
along these streets, what most astonishes
is that the pictures haven't lied, the real
river is beautiful, as blue as steel.

Homecoming

Walking all night and always toward the wind,
thought of this house sustained me. Now I find
the porcupine-sunk porch and a wild bird
flying from room to room with cry most weird,
and all the windows blind.

New Brunswick

All breath is crystal spinning in the air,
the only warmth that strokes this friendless cold,
and winter is the season that we share,
shut out and young or shut away and old.

The very dung behind the cattle freezes,
the wind insults the face like a sprung branch,
who can condemn the exile if he seizes
an icicle and thrust it like a lance

into his heart? Oh, Christ our faith is strong
that winter lasts forever, being long.

The Things
Which Are

Write the things which thou hast seen,
and the things which are.
   —The Revelation of St. John the Divine

Party at Bannon Brook

At the dead end of a road twisting snakelike
as that out of Eden, in a hunting camp, the hoarse creek crawling
through the closed door like the wet ghost of some drowned Adam,
coughing water on the floor, I sprawl on a straw-filled bunk
and drink rum with strangers:

> The chef in his tall white hat
> and apron embroidered
> with ribald slogans,
> spears steaks with slivers
> of white pine, roaring.

Beside me, in the leaping shadows
next the rough boards of the wall, her head
resting on a calendar from which all the months
have been ripped away, leaving only
the likeness of a woman
with orange skin and a body that might have been
stretched on a rack in the dungeon
of Gilles de Rais, it has such perverse,
blasphemous proportions, a girl sits, swaying
in time with the chef's song, her sweater
pulled out at the back, my circular arm
stroking the soft fat
of her belly — not because I love her
but because I am afraid. If we could do what we wish,
always, I would tell them I understand:
this is the season
when the bobcat is not driven away
by smoke, and the eagle
makes reconnaissance from the coast.

> But they will not listen.
> And they could do worse: tomorrow
> the chef will be cashiered, kill eight hours
> sending bills to debtors and this girl

sit at a desk, addressing letters
to the brains of dead men, each a packaged pudding
shelved in cold storage, and I

in whom despair
has bred superior cunning
will escape only by long study
of how the silver beads turn to gold, falling
by my employer's window, the icicles
stroked by an amorous sun.

The Terror of Thinking Myself No More a Poet

If I came in
no more a poet

because the crows
that continually press
had at last eaten up
every seed in my field
every scrap of my flesh,

I'd die, I said,
I'd cut with a knife,
I'd cut off the wick
with a blunt knife.

You'd live, she said.
You'd want to die,
you'd not kill yourself.
I know you too well
you like lager beer
and abhor Jack Knife.
And besides
you'll have me
for the rest of your life.

Ugh! Writing poems
I've smoked two cigarettes at once!
Would you want to lie
by a skeleton, every shred
of my flesh licked off by the crows!
I'd live, she said.

But bones in your bed!
White bones, and later
yellow bones in your bed!
Such bones as would scratch and tear
and a skull for a head, I said!
An eyeless, noseless, earless, hairless, brainless
skull in your bed!

Then we'd wear my flesh.
I don't know about poetry.
But I recognize everybody
in every one of your poems, she said.

Disguise

This is the amazing thing
that it is so easy
to fool them —
the sane bastards.

I can talk
about weather, eat,
preside at meetings
of the PTA.
They don't know.

Me foreign as a Martian.
With the third eye in my forehead!

But I comb my hair
cleverly so it doesn't show

except a little
sometimes when the wind blows.

Black Thread

My sister sewed her hand,
the soft flesh of her palm,
black thread under the skin,
the starbright needle
pricking her skin
so that I itched
wherever it went in.

She broke the thread in her teeth
and laughed in my face. The thread
dangling down from her flesh.
I shut both eyes with my fists
counting each stitch in her flesh.

Counting each stitch in her flesh
while she laughed and laughed like a witch.

Salvation

"Are you saved, brother?"
asks the Baptist preacher.
"Are you saved, like me?"

Ah, my poor brother!
I would touch your eyes with my spit,
if you were strong enough
and if that would open them.

I had no choice.
Sometimes, I even wish
He had let me go —

flowers spring up
where the blood pours from my side,

but I have nightmares
in which I relive
those days and nights in the tomb.

Strange Flowers

These flowers are beautiful enough.
Soft-eyed and moist
on their wiry bush.

But I don't know their name...
and some bushes burn!

Sheepish, I stand
at the fence and look.

Fire

The fire runs as fast as a man.
The swift beasts run ahead:
rabbit and deer and fox and lynx.
The lumbering ones are dead.

Smoke travels slowly, yet it came
into town weeks before the flame.
Now the beasts enter, frantic feet
racing the fire down the street.

The fire slows. Concrete and stone.
Beasts stop. They breathe again:
rabbit and deer and fox and lynx
within arm's reach of men.

Drunk: Falling

Everybody sees
the drunk lose his grip
on the wet black bricks,
the soggy mackinaw
slide over his head,
limp knees
slipping through
oil-scummed puddles
to the sharp pavement.

But look again.
You'll notice
the terrible dignity
with which he prolongs
his descent:

Saul dying,
Achilles to Lycaon:
ah, friend, seeing thou too must die
why thus lamentest thou?

The Mark

The mark is on me.
As I approach the liquor store
the winos emerge from the alley
thrust out their quivering palms,
like cripples accosting Christ.

And I give them money:
a quarter for a pint of beer,
ten cents toward a shot of rum.
"You know what it's like," they say.
"You know what it's like."

Imagining the taste,
the cool of it on the tongue.
Oh, God, the first
little glimmer of warmth
in the stomach, and then

the stones softening, the flutes,
the incorruptible body,
Marsyas challenging Apollo—

yes, brothers,
I know what it's like.
I know.

Novelty Booth

I'd gotten under the canvas
to get out of the rain
but I had to buy something

so I grabbed the first thing
I saw—a glass flower,

the kind they sell
at cheap carnivals
from here to Florida.

I picked mine apart
with my fingernails

and inside
there was a tiny cup
like a thimble

full of pus and blood
(I thought I must be going crazy)

and when I poured it out
(this is the part
you'll never believe)

there was another flower!

And this one
was
made of rubies
and diamonds
and all the jewels
whose names I'm
too poor to remember.

I should have stopped there.
But I pried it open
and the pieces rolled under
the feet of the crowd
waiting for the freak show, and

there was nothing left
except a smaller thimble

and when I spilled it
a flower like the first;
you could buy a dozen for a nickel.

The rain has stopped. The crowds are gone.
"The show's over, Mac.
Be a good fellow and go home."

It is almost morning.
I stand here shredding flowers.
My hands stink,
drip pus and blood.

November 11

There was blood.
"His buttons shone
like six little suns
of polished brass.
Under the heels
of his looking glass boots,
little red flowers
sprang out of the grass."

No, there was blood.
"And Reverend Death came like a padre
and laid his hand
on his shoulder and quoted—"

No. There was pus—don't you understand?
On the third day my belly bloated
and the other guys
couldn't stand the smell
and—"The sky was as blue
as the plumed helmet
of a grenadier.
All firing ceased.
The only sounds
were the sad choirboy voice of a bugle
and the whisper of the air."

The Bull Moose

Down from the purple mist of trees on the mountain,
lurching through forests of white spruce and cedar,
stumbling through tamarack swamps,
came the bull moose
to be stopped at last by a pole-fenced pasture.

Too tired to turn or, perhaps, aware
there was no place left to go, he stood with the cattle.
They, scenting the musk of death, seeing his great head
like the ritual mask of a blood god, moved to the other end
of the field, and waited.

The neighbours heard of it, and by afternoon
cars lined the road. The children teased him
with alder switches and he gazed at them
like an old, tolerant collie. The women asked
if he could have escaped from a Fair.

The oldest man in the parish remembered seeing
a gelded moose yoked with an ox for plowing.
The young men snickered and tried to pour beer
down his throat, while their girl friends took their pictures.

And the bull moose let them stroke his tick-ravaged flanks,
let them pry open his jaws with bottles, let a giggling girl
plant a little purple cap
of thistles on his head.

When the wardens came, everyone agreed it was a shame
to shoot anything so shaggy and cuddlesome.
He looked like the kind of pet
women put to bed with their sons.

So they held their fire. But just as the sun dropped in the river
the bull moose gathered his strength
like a scaffolded king, straightened and lifted his horns

so that even the wardens backed away as they raised their rifles.
When he roared, people ran to their cars. All the young men
leaned on their automobile horns as he toppled.

Comparison

Comparing pigs with cattle, Jack the butcher
says he likes cows and understands them. They
go where they're sent and stand until they're struck
by his great hammer, then bleed drowsily.

Pigs, on the other hand, disgust him: running,
darting and leaping and befouling him
with blood that spurts out of their backs because
they won't accept the axe like gentlemen.

The Cat

On a cloth mat
under the crackling stove,
the cat loafs on his belly,
laps milk from a china plate.

Beads of blue snow
from the other side
of the frozen river
still cling to his fur.

At intervals, the wind
rattles the storm door
and he stiffens
and shies away,
one eye bright, the other
a hideous crust of blood and pus.

The Shack Dwellers

Most of them look
as though their bodies were boneless.

Every animal
has its own defense:
theirs is plasticity.

Kick them in the face
and nothing breaks.
It's as if your boot
sank in wet dough.

But sometimes a trick
of hunger or heredity
gives one small bones
like an aristocrat's,
transparent skin
and delicate, blue veins.

You'll see one of the lost
Bourbons or Romanoffs,
dirty toes protruding
from the holes in his sneakers,
a hint of the old
hauteur in his hawk nose
as he tries to talk the grocer
out of a roll of bologna
and a loaf of stale bread.

Stoney Ridge Dance Hall

They don't like strangers.
So be careful how you smile.

Eight generations
of Hungerfords, McGards and Staceys
have lived on this ridge
like incestuous kings.
Their blood is so pure
it will not clot.

This is the only
country they know.
There are men here
who have never heard of Canada.

When they tire of dancing
they go down the road
and drink white lightning
out of the bung
of a molasses puncheon.

But they never forget
to strap on the knuckles
they've made from beer bottle
caps and leather

and there are sharp spikes
in their orange logging boots.

The Gift

Like the spluttering wick
of a dry coal oil lamp,
the day begins.

Hump-backed with cold,
the shack woman gathers
fresh twigs—the gift
of last night's raw,
wall-piercing wind.

Francis

A wool stocking-cap and a flannel-lined
windbreaker,
the buttons all different,
fastened up to his throat,

        and the sun
        like slivers of dry wood
        in the flesh, this
        third week of July—

Francis laughs at me, his teeth
so yellow and blunt
he might chew roots
like a bear, laughs in my face,
Ha!
what keeps out the cold, she'll keep out the heat, he says.

The East Brighton Road

Horseflies at suck in moist yellow sores
on her sunk back, the raw-boned mare
tugs at the clattering waggon, stuck
in the tenacious clay, a weakness
more stubborn than any strength
driving her clay-caked neck
into its ruptured collar.

The old man,
whose body might have been hewn
out of cat spruce with a dull axe,
squats in the box, intent
on her struggle, but not
interfering, his eyes half-shut,
unmoved, the reins lax
in his left hand, his tongue
solemn around an ice cream cone.

Money

My sister writes from Halifax.
"Dear Bruddie..."
Sure enough, she wants money.

Money! Why she and I
had been reared naked
were clothes money—
teeth coins ours had been knocked out,
eyes dollars hers and mine
snipped off with a razor.

Breakfast was dollar bills
sprinkled with ground dimes
washed down with melted pennies

brown as coffee, but richer, sugared
with silver—if we had any.

As I remember it, our house
was roofed in banknotes woven together.
Rain blew in on my bed. The roof leaked.
Father said: there's no money.

"Dear Bruddie..."
Sistie wants money.
She and I
write baby talk about money.
"Don't be silly, we wore
gold, azure and purple underpants
because papa stole
that cloth from the cotton mill,
flour bag shirts and madeover pants and dresses.
We ate beans until they came out of our ears
and mama saved even the salt from her tears.

But, p.s., I need money."

Fired

At five, convinced to fire meant to throw,
I saw The Company affix steel dogs
and chain men's legs and winch them up like logs
for heaving from the millyard. Then they flew—
across the sawdust dunes and lumber racks,
over shrill saws, stunned men and startled horses,
over the roofs of boxcars, till their courses
ending, their legs released, they fell in stacks.

The Stenographer

She long ago
gave up
dreaming
of freedom.

But, sometimes,
when the boss is out,
she closes her eyes
for a moment
and imagines

the office overrun
by Circassian slavers.

They strip her naked.
Her chains and collar
are of solid gold.

And the auctioneer
whose whip counts
bids on her buttocks
looks exactly
like Errol Flynn.

The Grove beyond the Barley

This grove is too secret: one thinks of murder.
Coming upon your white body (for as yet
I do not know you, therefore have no right
to speak of discovering
you, can address myself
to your body only) seeing the disorder
of your naked limbs, the arms outstretched
like one crucified, the legs bent like a runner's,

it took me less than a second to write a novel:
the husband in the black suit
worn at his wedding, the hired man
in his shirt the colour
of a rooster's comb and, in the end, you
thrown here like an axed colt.
Then I saw your breasts: they are not asleep,
move like the shadows of leaves
stirred by the wind. I hope you do not waken,
before I go; one who chooses
so dark a place
to lie naked
might cry out. The shadows quicken,
I wish you a lover,
dreams of sunlit meadows,
imagine myself a gentle satyr.

At the Drug Store

The hands of the boy kneeling at the magazine rack
do not sweat or falter though one almost touches
a thigh and the other reaches slowly for a naked breast.

Her answer is always a pout of anticipation.
She poses no nervous riddles, no sharp surprises,
will refuse him nothing, ask for nothing he cannot give.

Eyes incredulous, as at the first crest of passion,
he stirs but will not look up as, half on purpose,
girls, full-fleshed and whispering, brush awkwardly against him.

Canticle

May-white, the young girl's legs appear
stark, and unnaturally bare.
Six months estranged, the naked sun
feels curiously alien,

and the spring wind that makes the grass
caress her heels, libidinous:
however hoydenish the stride,
the limbs of an embarrassed bride.

In time, like a long-married man
the sun will rest his hand upon
this flesh habitually, seem
to think of something else, or dream.

And soon the wind-blown grass will rise
familiarly, to stroke her thighs.
But, for the moment, these address
themselves to their own nakedness.

Flesh as vulnerable as snow
and as unseasonable, aglow
with eagerness and yet afraid
in its athletic masquerade.

For all I know, her mind may feel
no more than the mechanical
rhythm of muscles and take in
only the climate of her skin.

Child of her time in gabardine
shorts and no Shunemite May Queen.
Of this I'm sure: the body knows
itself exposed from hips to toes,

shrinks back, attempting to withdraw
from weather masculine and raw;

its secret, in these vernal streets
revealed to everyone it meets.

All this will pass with the Maypole,
the self be comfortably whole.
In the meantime, she leaps, expels
unease in adolescent yells.

Porch

Immersed in night, my senses sharpen, hear
the nervous splash of water that can't stop
falling, but hesitates before each drop
breaks in a porcelain basin and the ear.

Moonlight flows through the oilcloth, a sheen
upon each grain of dust descending from
the fuliginous ceiling, platinum
stars woven in the window like a screen.

Our bodies touch, each meeting separate:
her arm, distinct and compact, like a cat
soft on my shoulder, while both ankles strain
against mine, bone to bone, her drowsing breast
crowding me toward the wall, passion at rest—
and the dull pressure of beginning pain.

October Snow Storm

The fallen snow
is green, because of the grass.
It is as though I walked
through the crystal
of an emerald.

There is so much
on the leaves
of the Manitoba maple,
its limbs bend
like foam from a fountain.

And the purple dahlias,
all but their faces
hidden,
lay their heads
on their shoulders and grieve
like flowers in a fairy tale.

Nightpiece

Like all the people whom I know
        or most, at any rate,
tomorrow I shall wake and go
        out to a job I hate.

This is November and I wish
        I were a simple bird,
could live on fruit white as the flesh
        of the thrice-risen Lord.

From my window across the street
        mornings at work, I see
a lawn where sparrows pluck and eat
        the winterberry tree.

The Execution

On the night of the execution
a man at the door
mistook me for the coroner.
"Press," I said.

But he didn't understand. He led me
into the wrong room
where the sheriff greeted me:
"You're late, Padre."

"You're wrong," I told him. "I'm Press."
"Yes, of course, Reverend Press."
We went down a stairway.

"Ah, Mr. Ellis," said the Deputy.
"Press!" I shouted. But he shoved me
through a black curtain.
The lights were so bright
I couldn't see the faces
of the men sitting
opposite. But, thank God, I thought
they can see me!

"Look!" I cried. "Look at my face!
Doesn't anybody know me?"

Then a hood covered my head.
"Don't make it harder for us," the hangman whispered.

Explanation

My best poems
don't get written,
because I'm still scared.

Don't laugh: the reports of people
who've seen the Cherubim
differ, but all agree
they're terrible beasts: part ox, part eagle, part lion;

yet even Leonardo
was afraid to paint them
as other than
quaintly winged babies.

Fruit of the Hurricane

Above the rain, above the roar of the wind
come rampaging from the Caribbean,
between the times when limbs crack like pistol shots,
we can hear the apples, thousands of them,
hitting the wet floor of the orchard as hard as hooves.

Here, sheltered, it would be pleasant to think of them:
a rain of apples, apples so sweet and moist
we might quench our thirst if water never fell again;
great heaps of apples, yellow and red,
apples rolled along the ground by tomorrow's wind.

But, in the morning, we will have to begin to gather them,
quickly, before they rot. We will need all our strength.

Better we go to bed.

The Genealogy of Morals

Take any child dreaming of pickled bones
shelved in a coal-dark cellar understairs
(we are all children when we dream) the stones
red-black with blood from severed jugulars.

Child Francis, Child Gilles went down those stairs,
returned sides, hands and ankles dripping blood,
Bluebeard and gentlest saint. The same nightmares
instruct the evil, as inform the good.

The Chopper

His axe blade nearing
the red pine's heart,

the chopper strikes harder,
doesn't hear or see

the hysterical squirrel
on the topmost limb

running nowhere and back
faster and faster.

Trans-Canada Highway

The black girls run with their pails of hot coals
because it is raining hard and if they don't get home soon
they'll have nothing but soggy cinders—

rain ricochets like tracer bullets in a newsreel;
as they sprint over the hills,
mushrooms of steam
burst from each swinging pail.

The Drunken Poet

Sometimes, when he got drunk and came back late,
he stopped a moment before every door
in the dark hallway of the boarding house,
like an intrusive saint, or murderer.

And he knew everything that those within
slept with, they laughed and whimpered in their sleep,
and he had half a mind to blackmail them
and half a mind to cover them and weep.

Later, in his own room, he seized a pen
and paper, set down everything he knew,
and re-united God and devil, since
he shared all secrets common to the two.

Each time he laughed he tasted salt. Each tear
tickled him till he howled. He went to bed,
the papers in his hand, awoke too sick
to go to work and burned them all, unread.

Voyeur

Each night in his dark furnished room, he kneels
opposite an open window till she comes,
haloed, under Orion and reveals
herself in gold and young chrysanthemums.

Or so he phrases it; seeing her bare,
remembers Swinburne and the two Rossettis;
winces observing that she's had her hair
shortened again, deplores her vulgar panties.

The Eloi and the Morlocks

At the edge of the field
behind the tarpapered shacks,
grow wild roses so delicate
their petals are jarred
loose by the lightest step.

The field stretches
to the end of the earth:
in the west its golden green
joins the silver blue of the sky.

Golden green? Silver blue?
When one can't walk without trampling
orange or purple flowers
and the sun is blinding red?
On so bright a day
one daren't look
at more than one
colour at a time.

The squatters
venture no farther
than their murky doorways.
Against the darkness, I see white hands
shielding white faces.

And the moles
burrow deeper
in fear of the sun.

The Idolator

Perhaps, we should not know our God too well.
They say a man cut his own face in stone,
then set that idol up and bowed him down,
while God walked every day in Israel.

And God, roaring with anger, called him out
and slew his sons and his camel and daughter,
powdered the idol and mixed it with water
and dog's blood, poured the message down his throat.

God's fingers opening his mouth, God's breath
panting into his face, he swallowed stone.
And all the people watched, paler than death,
then left to make them idols of their own.

Aleister Crowley

In my boy's cave of dreaming before sleep,
a ladder dangled in a darksome well,
and, at its foot, doors opened to a keep
where the concordances of daytime fell.

King of Two Sicilies and Priest of Thoth,
I bested pythons and the shambling dead,
swaggered barefoot on naked Ashtaroth,
was flagellated, love-chained to her bed.

Keats speaks of it, young Gilbert Chesterton
returned with sketches, later burnt; most men
stop all the doors with dirt; the moonstruck Crowley
fed live birds to a skeleton and cut
himself with actual knives till, having brought
it up, he purchased bricks and built an abbey.

Sometimes

Sometimes, not often, I wish there were only
the clean rapture of the body. I wish I could go
into a strange place, an amnesiac, and find that she too
had forgotten history.
                        Oh, love is good
but it reaches out
to take in the stars,
runs backwards and forwards. Sometimes I wish
for a world no bigger than the coupling bodies
of two clockless strangers.
                        But when I seek it,
she makes some small gesture—puts her hand to her hair—
        and I can tell
she has not forgotten herself, that she tries to please me
for some purpose of her own, and I almost weep; or she murmurs
some private word, and I curse myself and berate her.

Bird of Prey

All secrets spoken, her ravenous mouth
whispers "I love you," this over and over,
pleads as before that cold refuser, death,
that I put on the body of her lover.

Each repetition is more desperate,
starved beyond tenderness for self or me,
with every word of adoration, hate
attacks this object more ravenously.

"I love you," she says and each syllable
claws at my back, its black wings pitiless;
"I love you" and again the scalding, cruel
beak thrusts and tears, maddened and murderous.

"I love you" and because it is not I
she loves, would torment me and have me die.

Love Poem for Therese

We asked too much
of one another,

broken, looked
to the broken for wholeness.

That truth we shared today.

And this also: perhaps, there is no one.
Perhaps all are broken: three billion dolls
leaking sawdust. Heat, light and power
shut off in the forgotten warehouse.

No wonder, you threw yourself in my arms and wept!
No wonder, I whispered all
the old love names as I clung to you.

Waiting for Her

Waiting for her,
rain on the windshield,
cars passing,
their tires hissing
on the black pavement;

one minute the rain
pounding the car roof
as drummers
must have pounded
their drums at old executions,
with their fists,
not wanting to hear the screams;

the next minute
so quiet
I can hear my cigarette
burning when I inhale.

I listen
for her, I know how
she walks at night
and in the rain, with a different rhythm.

I brace myself to pretend
if she comes I was sure she'd come,
if she doesn't that I don't care.

Dancer

The sun is horizontal, so the flesh
of the near-naked girl bouncing a ball
is netted in its light, an orange mesh
weaving between her and the shadowed wall.

Her body glistening and snake-crescendoes
electric in her lighted muscles, she
pauses before each pitch, then rears and throws
the ball against the darkness, venomously.

The interlocking stones cry out and hurl
the black globe back, all human purpose stript
from its wild passage, and the bounding girl
bolts in and out of darkness after it.

Stumbling in the shadows, scalded blind
each time she whirls to face the sunlight, she
at last restores the pattern of her mind.
But every ball's more difficult to see.

Fall

Young boys in white hoods
hurl handfuls of the first snow

at the few rust-coloured leaves
still clutching the tip
of the highest limb
of the sugar maple.

Picking Raspberries

Noon.
But it is twilight
here
inside the
raspberry thicket:
green-black leaves
dull the nail-tipped
arrows of the sun
so they caress.

We won't feel the thorns
for hours yet;
tonight,
I will bathe
the hot scars
on her back and legs
with cool liquids. Now

the sweet berries
break
apart
on our tongues.

Moon Fear

One of the secret thoughts that go as soon
as they're put into words: I saw the moon
rise from a valley on the other side
of the black hills and burn with orange fire
over rockpiles, gaunt spruces and barbed wire,
and thought I'd never seen a moon so wide
or bright or low; for an instant, I went
back into childhood, fearing that it swelled
with God's wrath or an evil element,

shivered with horror until I expelled
held-breath in laughter, curiously glad
of the brief and unworldly fright I'd had.

Jane at Two

Lifted to the night window, Jane
(mark how detached, yet curious, her eyes)
starts at quickgold created in the pane,
grabs for the moon—and misses it—and cries!

Three Choices

Having been flogged with belts, not short of bleeding,
badgered by books and flayed by tongues like nettles,
I had three choices: madness, death or verse,
each of which asks more questions than it settles.

Closing Time

Night falling, the all-day rain
turns to hail, the puddles to slush,
yet the sober drunks
without even enough
for one last beer
gather opposite the liquor store
to watch the blue-smocked man
whose hand's on the bolt
of the fluorescent door.

The ice pellets beat
at their up-turned faces
as their eyes, with his,

follow the electric hands
of the clock suspended
above the shelves
of sparkling bottles.

Storm

This is the wildest
night of the winter.

But the cat lying,
paws folded under,
on the open verandah rail,
doesn't seem to notice

except she half-closes
her eyes each time
the howling wind
throws sleet in her face.

In Peace

"It is not death that frightens me," she said,
turning away to watch a waterfall
of moonlight drench the marble. "No," she frowned,
"it is not death, it is not death at all."

What then?
            "You'll laugh at me."
                            I never laugh.
"Don't ask me to put things for which no words
have been discovered into other words."
Without such trickery, we could not talk.
"We talk too much," she said, shaking the moon

out of her hair, one finger following
the marble lettering:
                    "...in peace."
                              In peace.
All of our lives are spent in seeking peace
and when it comes we fight like jig-hooked eels.
"You said you never laughed."
                         No words again!
"I don't feel quite right about laughter—here."
Is that part of the secret thing you fear?

"Perhaps, but it's no secret really. Only
I don't think we should seem so happy..."

Because they'll hate us?
                    "You make it sound—"
Because they'll hate us?
                    "Yet, I suppose that's it."
Listen, before we go, I'll curse you, then
you can lie down and weep so that they'll hear!

"You're mocking me!"
                    Just being helpful.
                              "No,
I heard the rhythm of your words. You know
how when you listen to one instrument
within an orchestra the others fade
as though the listener played all by ear.
I heard your hatred then. You have a way
of hiding whips in jokes."
                         And you're a fool
or maybe looking for some way to make
your hatred enter me so you can have
hate's satisfactions and love's vanity:
a woman's favourite trick against a man.

"I want to go now."
                    Do you still think they'll hate us?

"I want to go now."
                    Wait for a moment and we'll watch the moon
walk like a ghost trailing its dead-white shroud
up that great silver ramp to the black cloud.

"I want to go now."
                    They're taking the ramp up,
see how it's hauled into the cloud as if
the cloud were death's ship taking back a spy.
Did you ever mark how many qualities
the moon shares with a ghost?
                            "I want to go now."

Psalm

Through a kaleidoscope of spray and sun,
a hose whirling on the lawn, a circle of children
in rainbow swim suits, making their own music,
heads thrown back, chanting, light streaming from their bodies!

Wishing I could join them, I think of the laughing Jesus
of the Acts of John, how he linked the hands
of his disciples, made them dance in circles.
"You who dance not, know not what we are knowing."
"Dance, dance, thus, thus, whole and happy for Our Lord St. John."

Daisies

We walked a mile from the road, and with every step
she broke off a daisy, till she held thousands
in a great bunch against her chest,

till they covered her face and her red-gold pigtails,
till the top of her head was the eye of a daisy;

she sniffed of them, tasted their petals and pulp,
felt their heads and stalks with her cheeks and fingers.

That soil was rich, had we walked all day
she could have kept counting her steps with daisies:
running back to the car, she threw open her arms
and her body burst like a fountain of flowers.

Canadian Love Song

Your body's a small word with many meanings.
Love. If. Yes. But. Death.
Surely I will love you a little while,
perhaps as long as I have breath.

December is thirteen months long,
July's one afternoon; therefore,
lovers must outwit wool,
learn how to puncture fur.

To my love's bed, to keep her warm,
I'll carry wrapped and heated stones.
That which is comfort to the flesh
is sometimes torture to the bones.

from Five New Brunswick Poets

Communion: 1946 and 1962

Through the forest path on the ridge,
down the dug road to the swamp where the herons rest,
a young hostage prince sketched by El Greco
in denim shorts and a sweat shirt. He squats in the grass,
dreaming of Peru, watching the great birds and the river
winding to the west where steam roars from its cataracts
spilt on the sun, squats there and waits for me
to stir in the hill cedars and the hot cells
of his palpitant body....

> *When I am a man I will not be afraid*
> *of the stirring in the cedars, the heat in my body.*
> *When I am a man I will come into my kingdom.*
> *When I am a man I will not be afraid.*

Oh, little one, my lost Dauphin,
my Czarevitch, my last of the Bonapartes;
I followed mirages and was all but maddened
by thirst and the tittering skulls.
They offered drink, and I stopped.

> *What if the man I will be came from the cedars?*
> *I would flee, crying. What if the river*
> *Extinguished the sun?*

Little one, I would weep
for you, but that were self-pity.

> *I will go home now.*
> *Night birds I cannot name*
> *Make evil sounds in the cedars.*
> *When I am a man I will not be afraid.*

The Walking Dead

The dead rise and shuffle toward me, reach out for my hand,
greet me with that faint sneer, that stare of disbelief
with which men meet death; I have come to expect this,
no longer cringe or cry out, though I watch for hours
in the stink — no, not of disintegration, but of chemicals,
alcohol, formaldehyde — grip the claws of thousands,
all dead, all cheating death of its only beauty:
decay, and the final cleanliness
of earth, air, fire, water — their only passion,
fear of the morticians who'll wrestle them, screaming,
into their element-proof lead coffins.

Anti-Narcissus

My own face —
bloated and green
but my own face
pulsating like a
Lovecraft god in
the salt grass under
this muddy water!

I can't tear my eyes away.

Christ, but I wish
I knew the direction
a man had to take
to keep from meeting
himself.

This spring
it's gotten so bad
I see my own

bitter lips and eyes
growing into
the Buddha face
of the moon.

Night of Storm

After each silence, I hear the storm
gather its strength in the snowbound thicket
northwest of the river (in the dark, sleepless
I time it to daytime things), hear it howl
over black-white ice, bound the open fallow,
clamber the ridge, thrash, falter and stammer
in a tangle of beech, yellow birch and maple,
break free and attack this house, lunge at these doors
till they almost give, then, as if on signal
sink under the sills and whimper, shrink to a groan
on the porch steps, die at the cellar windows —
where the breath pauses in my throat and chest
as though (and this amazes me)
I were ready to pity the wind.

Railway Waiting Room, Truro, Nova Scotia

I don't even know what language he speaks,
but since 3 a.m. he's given up trying
to make the cop understand
where he was going,
and he can't find his ticket,
if he ever had one. Getting hotter and louder,
the cop names cities:
"Montreal?" "Regina?" "Winnipeg?" "Toronto?"
and the little round foreigner
only cries harder.

The Migrant Hand

For how many thousands of years, for how many millions
of baskets and waggonloads and truckloads of onions,
or cotton, or turnips has this old man knelt
in the dirt of sun-crazy fields? If you ask him,
he'll put you off: he's suspicious of questions.
The truth is that Adam, a day out of Eden,
started him gathering grapes: old Pharoah
sold him to Greece; he picked leeks for the Seljuks,
garlic for Tuscans, Goths and Normans,
pumpkins and maize for the Pilgrim Fathers,
has forgotten them all, forgotten all of the past, except
the last ten hours of blackflies and heat,
the last two hundred barrels of potatoes.

Wasp

A wasp on the wrong side
of my parked car's windshield — a thorned phallus
stuttering like a machine gun, black and golden —
striped on the passive pane. In sudden pity
for him, myself and every other being
beating at unseen walls, and fearing his
sting like a sizzling awl, since I've been stung,
I try to rescue and expel him, not
certain which aim is paramount. A book
threatening to break his back by accident,
I swish a leafy, resilient alder branch
after, over and under him, conceiving
he fears it as a man instinctively
fears giant winged things. Though that things fly
shouldn't astonish wasps as it does me.
But he jumps sideways and drops out of reach
inside the defroster, yammering!
His beautiful, masculine body gone

crazy with pitiless confusion.
Motor and fan switched on, he's
blown back still stubbornly probing
the windshield, his fish-scale wings roaring,
his head held down like a drill.
I scoop with the alder,
once, twice, a hundred times. Still he eludes me—
as the glass eludes him. What can I do with him?
Ignore or kill him? Accept defeat?
Suddenly, now, it's ridiculously important
that this bug escape his predicament
and not escape me. Holding my breath,
I grab him with my bare fingers and hurl him out—
out through the open door! Like a hot coal
grasped in the naked hand!
                            Foolishly happy,
exhausted, licking my sore paw like a dog,
I sit here, thinking of glass
and the jokes it plays in the world.

Edna

She's got the right eyes
and the separate laughs,
the silly, on-purpose one
she gives to adults,
the wise, just-happens one
she keeps to herself.

Too bad God
in letting her be eight forever
didn't remember
to stop all the clocks
at the same time

so that instead of
those mildewed ropes

bursting out of
elastic stockings

she had hopscotch legs
that go in all directions
at once,
and the funny kind of beauty
we try to meet
with gentle laughter.

Bread, Wine and Salt

I, Icarus

There was a time when I could fly. I swear it.
Perhaps, if I think hard for a moment, I can even tell you the year.
My room was on the ground floor at the rear of the house.
My bed faced a window.
Night after night I lay on my bed and willed myself to fly.
It was hard work, I can tell you.
Sometimes I lay perfectly still for an hour before I felt
        my body rising from the bed.
I rose slowly, slowly until I floated three or four feet
        above the floor.
Then, with a kind of swimming motion, I propelled myself
        toward the window.
Outside, I rose higher and higher, above the pasture fence,
        above the clothesline, above the dark, haunted trees
        beyond the pasture.
And, all the time, I heard the music of flutes.
It seemed the wind made this music.
And sometimes there were voices singing.

Suppose This Moment Some Stupendous Question

Suppose this moment some stupendous question
such as they asked of Lazarus. The dead
are secretive; they act like strangers
we ought to recognize but don't; and all
the secular accounts of resurrections
are horror stories. Grandmother recalled
how her grandmother prayed for seven nights,
cut off by grief, that she might see her dead
daughter who went blue-tongued and choking walk
into her bedroom, and maintained it happened
—though twice-great-grandmother was never certain:
she jerked the quilts over her head and screamed,
with every light gone out, the door blown open.

Long, Long Ago

It seems I always saw the Indian woman
the instant she became visible,
and never took my eyes off her
as she lugged her many-coloured pack,
three times as big as herself,
down South Mountain,
across the Little Bridge,
up North Mountain
and into our kitchen
where she undid a knot
and flooded the entire room with baskets
—cherry-coloured baskets,
cabbage-coloured baskets,
baskets the colour of a November sky,
each basket containing
another, smaller basket,
down to one so tiny it would hold
only a hank of thread and a thimble.

Sailors

Nobody younger than eighteen or older than twenty
ever combs his hair quite so neatly, nobody else
except maybe a boxer has that feverish, watchful
look when he's waiting
for a light to change, or an elevator.

This shouldn't surprise me: already, at twenty-nine,
I've learned one of the most disturbing
things about getting older
is that every year
there are more kids in the world.

Why shouldn't sailors
look like little boys

dressed in the folk costume
of some strange country?

Oh, but in Halifax, in the last war, I held my breath
like Jim Hawkins in his apple barrel, and watched them stride
down all the sidewalks, tall as Joe Palooka,
stronger than Tarzan, wiser than The Shadow,
and brave—brave as the Swiss in my Grade III reader,
brave as Thermopylae, brave as Dieppe,
        their very boots
pronouncing *Dunkirk* each time they struck the pavement.

Small Town Small Talk

How intense, my neighbour and I,
discussing the weather—

jumping with both feet
into every pause in the conversation,

almost as if I'd surprised him
in my room
and he wasn't quite sure
I'd seen him closing my diary.

And He Wept Aloud, So That the Egyptians Heard It

In my grandfather's house
for the first time in years,
houseflies big as bumblebees
playing crazy football
in the skim-milk-coloured windows,

leap-frogging from
the cracked butter saucer

to our tin plates of
rainbow trout and potatoes, catching the bread
on its way to our mouths,
     mounting one another
      on the rough deal table.

It was not so much their filth
as their numbers and persistence and—
oh, admit this, man, there's no point in poetry
if you withhold the truth
once you've come by it—
     their symbolism:
     Baal-Zebub,
god of the poor and outcast,

that enraged me, made me snatch the old man's
Family Herald, attack them like a maniac,
lay to left and right until the window sills
over-flowed with their smashed corpses,
until bits of their wings
stuck to my fingers,
until the room buzzed with their terror...

And my grandfather, bewildered and afraid,
came to help me:
     "never seen a year
     when the flies were so thick"
as though he'd seen them at all before I came!

His voice so old and baffled and pitiful
that I threw my club into the wood box and sat down
     and wanted to beg his forgiveness
as we ate on in silence broken only
by the almost inaudible humming
of the flies rebuilding their world.

Foye Buckner of Hainesville, New Brunswick, Recalls His Service with the Connaught Light Infantry, 1914-1918

They told us afterwards we'd been in France;
hell take that place, it rained continually.
The Northrup girl who hears but cannot speak
squawks like a German and as shamelessly.

London was where we vomited, the beer
warmer than piss, the girls like carpeting;
and once, astonished that he looked so small
on his high balcony, I saw the king.

The Cinnamon Bears
for Mr. and Mrs. Charlie Shaw of Hartland, New Brunswick

The cinnamon bears!
And the Eye-talian
grinding his organ
while they danced the Lancers
back of the Orange Hall
in 1910, or was it 11?

Oh, you should have seen them
cutting their capers,

waltzing on their hind legs
as pert as you please

and the Eye-talian
changing his tune
with a snap of his wrist!

The cinnamon bears!

And the man who told fortunes!
From Syria he was, an Assyrian

with a red silk scarf
tied around his head
and ear-rings —
I'd almost forgotten the ear-rings!

And the Jews
And the Gypsies
And the Chinamen and the Greeks!

But best of all
were the cinnamon bears!

Why people walked
twenty miles — all the way from Argosy —
just to see them
cutting their capers!

Daughter of Zion

Seeing the bloodless lips, the ugly knot of salt-coloured hair,
the shapeless housedress with its grotesque flowers
like those printed on the wallpaper in cheap rooming houses,
sadder than if she wore black,

observing how she tries to avoid the sun,
crossing the street with eyes cast down
as though such fierce light were an indecent spectacle:
if darkness could be bought like yard goods
she would stuff her shopping bag with shadows,

noting all this and more,
who would look at her twice?
What stranger would suspect that only last night
in a tent by the river,
in the aisles between the rows
of rough planks laid on kitchen chairs,
before an altar of orange crates,

in the light of a kerosene lantern,
God Himself, the Old One, seized her in his arms and lifted her up
    and danced with her,
and Christ, with the sawdust clinging to his garments and
    the sweat of the carpenter's shop
on his body and the smell of wine and garlic on his breath,
drew her to his breast and kissed her,

and the Holy Ghost
went into her body and spoke through her mouth
the language they speak in heaven!

Husband and Wife

Desire is spent,
but the sharing
remains: it is beautiful to hear them
bickering, knowing the hurt will not last,
all will be forgiven, all has been accepted,
yet the sparks fly
when, as he puts it,
they rub one another
the wrong way —
it is beautiful to watch them,
knowing their forty years
in the same house
have not solved the mystery,
have not extinguished
the last spark of passion.
It is beautiful to think
how, after we are gone
and cannot see or hear them,
they will make their peace
like two proud old warriors.

Purest of Gifts

The old man at the door
brings gifts to our sick,
places them gently,
one by one,
in my hands.

And I bet he made sure
they were the two finest oranges
in the bin:
golden, burning-sweet,
fragrant and healing.

Purest of gifts:
those that consist
only in giving.

Midnight of the First Snow

Midnight of the first snow.
In the open pasture
the cattle pause,
lift up their heads
with a little stir of wonder,
then go back to grazing,
getting every blade within reach
before taking
another sleepy step in the darkness.

First Impressions
for Fred Cogswell

At first, I thought you were one of the good men who appear briefly
in the novels of Sinclair Lewis:
calm, middle-aged, boyish, respectable men,
admirable for reasons the author was never ready to explain
or, perhaps, didn't fully understand:
your biography confined to a paragraph
in *Cass Timberlane* or *Arrowsmith*
because, like the rest of us, Lewis was never quite prepared
      to make his peace with his real heroes.

But I shouldn't make too much of this, because later I saw
      who you really were:
one of Rider Haggard's or A. Merritt's astonishing narrators,
pipe-smoking, bookish men who settled down comfortably
at colleges as quiet as this
to write of their descent into The Moon Pool
or of following Ayesha, She Who Must Be Obeyed,
into The Place Of The Spirit Of Life in the caves of Kor.

Britain Street
Saint John, New Brunswick

This is a street at war.
The smallest children
battle with clubs
till the blood comes,
shout "fuck you!"
like a rallying cry—

while mothers shriek
from doorsteps and windows
as though the very names
of the young were curses:

"Brian! Marlene!
Damn you! God damn you!"

or waddle into the street
to beat their own with switches:
"I'll teach you, Brian!
I'll teach you, God damn you!"

On this street,
even the dogs
would rather fight
than eat.

I have lived here nine months
and in all that time
have never once heard
a gentle word spoken.

I like to tell myself
that is only because
gentle words are whispered
and harsh words shouted.

Secret Life

WONDERFUL things
        happen to YOU
when you learn
        to play the piano...

DO YOU HAVE A SKIN PROBLEM?
        Many girls are scarred inside for life
        because they're afraid to face people.
                If you have this problem—
                        read on...

(At his place and two girls
   that he used to go out with
      came up to the apartment...
         I just want to cry my heart out,
            He has never touched me and he says he won't.)

I CRIED myself to sleep!
I'll kill myself if she does it again!
(In fact the awful mess I'm in
   is because I kept trying
      to AVOID trouble!)

WITH NO WARNING A BLINDING LIGHT
fell on my face! Later the police said
they'd been watching for ten minutes.

Broad Street

The eyes of the asters are like the eyes of dead squirrels.
The burdocks are shrunken heads
fixed on stakes in a brown jungle.
Only the leaves of the thistle have retained their greenness
even in the grave: they remind me of men,
poor, ignorant, wise, who only shrug
at each new effacement of history.

On the pavement, motor oil and melted ice
the colour of a pigeon's throat, dog shit and broken bottles
marked *Canadian Sherry*, a glove, a child's rubber ball
like garments abandoned on the road
after an accident,

and, above all,
the good clean stink of the earth,
rising from the ditch like a drunkard
to breathe garlic and beer
in the shrinking white face of the snow.

For Jean Vincent D'Abbadie, Baron St.-Castin

Take heart, monsieur, four-fifths of this province
is still much as you left it: forest, swamp and barren.
Even now, after three hundred years, your enemies
        fear ambush, huddle by coasts and rivers,
the dark woods at their backs.

        Oh, you'd laugh to see
how old Increase Mather and his ghastly Calvinists
patrol the palisades, how they bury their money
under the floors of their hideous churches
lest you come again in the night
with the red ochre mark of the sun god
on your forehead, you exile from the Pyrenees,
        you baron of France and Navarre,
you squaw man, you Latin poet,
        you war chief of Penobscot
and of Kennebec and of Maliseet!

        At the winter solstice
your enemies cry out in their sleep
and the great trees throw back their heads and shout
        nabujcol!
Take heart, monsieur,
even the premier, even the archbishop,
even the poor gnome-like slaves
at the all-night diner and the service station
will hear you chant
        The Song of Roland
as you cross yourself
and reach for your scalping knife.

A Picnic in Times Square

Once there was a city here, he said.
We learned its name in university.
London, I think it was, or perhaps Madrid
—I was never any good at history.

O

the boy resting by the sepulchre,
oblivious to the questions
of dark, imaginative children,
how will we tell him
it is too soon for the resurrection, and

the gunners concealed in the olive grove, how
does one explain to them
the quivering of the earth
over yesterday's enemy, and

the women who are almost content
with memories, what

will we say when they
refuse to open the door,
        and what will the vultures eat
        or the worms,
and there were stars, perhaps,
where will we go
when they burst from the caves of not?

In Those Old Wars

In those old wars
where generals wore yellow ringlets
and sucked lemons at their prayers,
other things being equal
the lost causes were the best.

Lee rode out of history
on his gray horse, Traveller,
so perfect a hero
had he not existed
it would have been necessary to invent him—
war stinks without gallantry.

An aide, one of the few who survived,
told him,
Country be damned, general,
for six months these men
have had no country but you.
They fought barefoot
and drank blueberryleaf tea.

The politicians
strung up Grant
like a carrot,
made him a Merovingian.
They stole everything,
even the coppers from Lincoln's dead eyes.

In those days, the vanquished
surrendered their swords like gentlemen,
the victors alone
surrendered their illusions.
The easiest thing to do for a Cause
is to die for it.

In Our Time

The newspapers speak of torture
as though it were horseplay.
This morning a picture of a Congolese rebel
being kicked to death
was captioned *the shoe is on the other foot*
and a story from Saigon
told of a Viet Cong prisoner
who complained of thirst
being *overwhelmed by the hospitality*
of his captors
who cheerfully refreshed him
and also his memory
by pumping a generous quantity of water
through rubber tubes into his nostrils.

Report from Ottawa

The Prime Minister has been kidnapped,
together with the Leader
of the Opposition,
and their places taken
by a professional comedy team
who are going mad
because the audience
doesn't get the joke
—unless we laugh louder
they'll start throwing bombs
across the floor
of the House of Commons.

Think what a nightmare it must be
for the straight man with the lisp
who aspires to be Stan Laurel
or Bud Abbott
to keep getting mistaken

for Sir Austen Chamberlain,
what torture must be suffered
by his partner, the funny one,
when he is hissed
for doing the very things
that won applause
for Oliver Hardy and Lou Costello.

The Nation's Capital

The first thing you learn here
is that the country
bears the same relationship
to the government
that outer space
bears to the earth.

The second thing you learn
is that nothing is unimportant.

Take the mystical air
of the Member of Parliament
sipping a dry Martini
in the Chateau Laurier.

Note how importantly
his Adam's apple
bobs as he swallows,
with what care his finger
taps against the glass.

Pepin, Mayor of the Palace.

He must measure his sips
and time them perfectly
or there will be couriers

from the Hill:
"The government may fall."

Ah, Mackenzie King,
I think I understand you:
how easy to commune with the dead
in a city wholly divorced from reality.

Verbal Transcription
at the Legion Hall in Hartland, New Brunswick

There were hundreds of them, lining both sides of the street
of that little godforsaken village, singing their national anthem
    like crazy,
when along came three open trucks loaded with Jerries,
prisoners, the SS, and a platoon of Yanks with machine guns;
hell, those Jerries just sort of glared and, would you believe it,
all of a sudden, that whole damned crowd was too scared to sing!

A View from the Bridge

When the movie opens, a machine is lowering lumber
    into the hold of a ship.
We see a great raft of boards swinging from a cable
    high overhead;
and we know at once that the cable will break,
    as it has broken in every movie we've ever seen,
and the boards will fall like a bomb, as they always do,
    and a man will scream,
and, almost before the screaming has stopped, we will
    hear the sirens,
then the running footsteps,
and the camera will zoom in and we will see the face
    of the longshoreman,
and if it is a face we do not recognize, chances are

he will be dead,
but if it is the face of Kirk Douglas or Burt Lancaster
        or John Wayne
he will open his eyes slowly because stars never die
        before the end
of the last reel—knowing all this,
knowing almost the exact moment
when the cable will snap (a second after
the last credit line flashes on the screen)
it is curious we are all of us so tense and silent
        until it happens—
it is almost as if we were afraid of being cheated.
Perhaps this is a foreign film, a documentary,
even Red propaganda—
what if the cable holds?
But, of course, it never does:
in another moment we will hear the steel snap,
see the boards fall—
and almost everyone in the theatre
will breathe a little sigh of relief
as he settles back
to enjoy the show.

The Fresh-Ploughed Hill

The fresh-ploughed hill slopes down to the sky.
Therefore, the sower,
broadcasting his seed, runs
faster and faster.

Bounding like a stone
the skirts of his coat
straight out behind him.

See how he falls, clawing
at the earth—
nor will let go

but still clutches
dirt in his fists, rolling
into the bright depths of the sun.

Sleeping Out

Strange how the body
accepts the hardness
of the earth,
the dampness
of the grass.
The sharp stones
under my shoulders
hardly disturb me
and here
where there is no
defence against
the night,
I am no longer
afraid of
the dark.

The Spy

My child cries out in his sleep.
I bend close, try to make out the words.
Though it fills me with shame,
I spy on his dreams,
try each word like a key
to the room where he keeps
things too private to share
even with me.

The Changeling

Today he told me the story again.
This time the parents lived in the next county.
He gave me their names. Last time they were movie stars.
Never think it to look at that yellow hair of hers.
Once or twice, they've been royalty.

She is always as blue
and golden and white
as the longest day of the summer.
She didn't know it herself until they showed her the baby.

And afterwards she goes mad
and drinks Lysol or shoves her head in an oven.

Temptation

The boy is
badgering the man
to lower him down the
face of the cliff
to a narrow shelf
about eight feet
below:
"Your hands are strong,
and I'm not afraid.
The ledge is wide enough,
I won't hurt myself
even if you let go."

"Don't be a fool.
You'd break every bone
in your body.
Where in God's name

do you get such ideas?
It's time we went home."

But there is no
conviction in the
man's voice and
the boy persists;
nagging his wrists,
dragging him nearer.
Their summer shirts
balloon in the wind.

While devils whisper
what god-like sport
it would be
to cling to the
edge of the world
and gamble
one's only son
against wind
and rocks
and sea.

Manuscript Found in a Bottle

Drunk in Christ's Egypt Land
I part from myself, my time,
I who have lived all day
with few thoughts worthy of a man.

The beast is an ass, balky,
lurching stupidly in the rocky places.
I have heard that when floods come
he'll know if the bridge is out, stop
and refuse to go on. I doubt it.

The important thing
is to get away, withdrawal;
every god has departed
disguised as a babe, perhaps,
into the dark continent:
rum is the only Africa
a man can carry—the portent is repeated
over and over, this escape into a strange country.

Footsteps in the Dark

Each night he comes nearer; now his footsteps stop
opposite the gate; even the black elm, even the grass
seem to hush while he listens, then cover his tread
with their whispering, as he goes back.

As he goes back to the darkness, the boundless, teeming
darkness of the blind, as you strain to hear,
strain to perceive the faintest stirring in the shadows
closest the window, strain though you know when it happens

it will be loud and quick, though you know he will come
like Christ with his bleeding hands to the disciples,
who backed away, half-crazed with fear, or like Jack the Ripper
falling upon a whore in Whitechapel.

The Knock

I've learned how beggars knock on doors.
Even the simplest bum
knows how to knuckle any wood
like a sensitive drum.

A trick that's harder than it sounds:
flourish and requiem,

demanding a well-disciplined fist
and a delicate thumb.

Begin with vigour to be sure
the house can't help but hear.
But soften quickly lest your faith
offend the answerer.

Remembrance of Things Past

Nobody talks fast enough to describe a cloud,
    especially when the wind's
                hellbent for Ireland
or wherever the sea ends, and even the trees
don't want to stay here,
              and the poor old man
down the street with his shirtful of bread
    tears off stale hunks as bribes to strangers
who won't tell him how to get back
    to the house where he's lived
              too long to remember.

The Dark Companions

All the physicians say his blood turned black
because in a certain mirror there are laws
that condemn those judged guiltless to go back
to the real world, and break them clause by clause.

Myself, I've dreamt of a great funnel, and
a thousand corpses dump-trucked down its throat,
woke whimpering for light, yet marked the bland
clockwork as one by one it spilled them out.

And I can comprehend how the young boy
in all the papers, watched the stars and thought
of dark companions, his curious joy,
studying his friend's face before he shot.

The Sleepwalker

Zeno of Elea said an arrow doesn't move:
it is always at rest
at one of a series
of points: so it is with a sleepwalker

who always seems to know where he's going
without knowing where he is,
the body saying
"no" to its own
movements, and the eyes
focused on something so far away
nobody can see it
without going blind
to everything between;

and when he wakes up
in his own house
in the world
where he's lived
all his life,
he says:
where am I?
how did I get here?

while the vision
darts like a fish,
signet of Christ,
cymbal of wisdom,
into the swirling
depths of his eyes.

July 15

The wind is cool. Nothing is happening.
I do not strive for meaning. When I lie on my back
the wind passes over me, I do not feel it.
The sun has hands
like a woman, calling the heat
out of my body.
The trees sing. Nothing is happening.

When I close my eyes,
I hear the soft footsteps
of the grass. Nothing is happening.

How long have I lain here?
Well, it is still summer. But is it the same
summer I came?
I must remember
not to ask myself questions.
I am naked. Trees sing. The grass walks.
Nothing is happening.

Revelation

This plane does not always travel between Toronto and Vancouver,
      via Edmonton.
Nor do its passengers always wear Chamber of Commerce
      mustaches and expressions of unfathomable boredom.
Sometimes it disappears on mysterious errands,
to Tibet and the Middle East, its comings and goings
uncharted even by the International Aeronautics Administration
—though there are rumours, hints in certain old books,
that it was this plane, or another like it,
that landed in Stockholm in 1757
and carried Emanuel Swedenborg
twenty thousand feet into the sky

where he and his fellow passengers
(including that epileptic Arab and that old rabbi from Patmos)
mistook these clouds for an encampment of angels
and the naked sun for the New Jerusalem.

On Hearing of the Death of Dr. William Carlos Williams
for Sandy Ives

I am glad I did not read of his death
until after a friend telephoned
from another country
and told me, drunkenly:
"The old man is dead
and I wanted to talk
to someone who would understand."
I am glad, too, I was drunk enough
that the two of us could sit,
side by side, on the cross bar of a telephone pole
midway between
Orono, Maine, and Hartland, New Brunswick,
dangle our feet in the sky
and drink to the memory
of an old man who took too long to die
because he had never learned
how the trick was done.

A Mug's Game

At the party that followed the poetry reading,
one girl kept telling me how thrilled she was to meet
someone who hadn't gone to university, and another said
I reminded her so much of whoever it was who played
in *Bus Stop* she kept expecting Marilyn to walk in, and the hostess
extending three bite-size salami sandwiches
and a glass of warm whiskey and ginger ale

smiled at me like Li'l Abner's Aunt Bessie
welcoming her nephew to Toronto.

The man from the CBC, who said: "Of course, you're staying
at the YMCA" and thought he was humouring me
by acting impressed when he found out I wasn't,

explained: "The purpose of such readings is to give writers
from unlikely places like Hartland, New Brunswick,
the chance to communicate
with others
of their own kind."

The Hollow Men

They tell me they have never aspired to be poets.
Their jobs, when they were young, were more demanding than mine.
With their sweetest smiles: "Nothing great was ever accomplished
by writing before breakfast; to create a man must be free."
Someday, perhaps, they'll live in Mexico or Italy.
Meanwhile, they endure as they must...
Then hand me the poem
they've preserved since their last year
in university.

Ancestral Memories Evoked by Attending the Opening of the Playhouse in Fredericton, New Brunswick

Government House,
summer, 1861;
the Prince of Wales,
bearded, with those mask-like
Hanoverian eyelids;
an address of welcome
in heroic couplets

delivered by the Most Worshipful Grand Master
of Freemasons, on behalf of the lieutenant-governor;
fifes, drums and bagpipes;
rural deans in gaiters;
a guard of honour commanded
by Captain Julian Tempest-Stewart,
late of Her Majesty's Punjabi Rifles:
"Better a raggle-taggle mob of coolies
than these dem barbarians
chewing tobacco in the ranks.
Hell take militiamen!"
And on the riverbank
under the stars
a roasted ox
and three hogsheads of beer:
one for the lower orders,
one for the Frenchies
and one for the sly and treacherous Indians.

A Treaty to Be Signed with Guests

If you like,
I will concede
that you are learned,
wise, charming
and beautiful.
You do not have
to convince me.
Now, perhaps,
we can drink
together.

Every Man Owes God a Death

I owe my landlady seventy-five dollars and fifty cents.
To understand this better,
read Tawney's *Religion and the Rise of Capitalism*
and reflect
we belong, both she and I,
to the race called Calvinists.

(Interpolation for those who've ignored
the preceding instructions: Calvinists are Jews,
one of the lost tribes, who circumcise
elsewhere to deceive the Gentiles.)

In short
she cannot let me escape
yet is almost as ashamed as I:
every morning at breakfast
it is as if
I saw her look at me strangely
and suddenly realized
I'd forgotten to zipper my fly.

Eating bacon and eggs,
going farther into debt,
I talk as fast as I can:
feed her every scrap
of gossip I can think of,
invent small lies
about the sex lives of the neighbours
—when, during the day,
I happen across
some juicy morsel
I glue it to my brain:
Mrs. Scott will want to know that.
If I tell her
the Ransom girl is pregnant
and her mother
under heavy sedation

I'll get out the door
before she thinks
to ask for the money.

Knowing all the while,
I can't really cheat her:
she collects my stories
like dividends
on an investment,
compound interest
on an overdue account.

A Dog Barking at Night

I hear you, dog,
barking in the moonlight,
and, if I were sure I'd find you,
I'd get out of bed
and tramp across the fields
to bring you home;

or, if you wouldn't come,
I'd lie beside you,
out there in the hills
until the sun came up.

But I bet if you saw me
before I saw you,
you'd hide in the bushes
until I went away —

and, anyhow,
who am I to say
you want company?
Could be you're scaring hell
out of a porcupine;

could be you think
you've got the world by the tail.

You don't know me, dog.
And I don't know you.

Full Moon

Full moon above
fields of ripe grain,
dark woods on either side,
a mile from the border
we drink the last
American beer,
throw the can out
the car window
into the grain,
where it glints
in the moonlight...

The Masks of Love

I come in from a walk
with you
and they ask me
if it is raining.

I didn't notice
but I'll have to give them
the right answer
or they'll think I'm crazy.

The Knife

I do not know
where this knife began
nor how many times
it has travelled over the world.
But this I know, my love:

Earlier today I was not applauded
by a man whom I hate and this because
I bungled a job I neither
wanted nor understood.

And a man plucks out
steel from his own flesh,
even when he knows
this blade goes
always from breast to breast.

I am not always brave
enough to keep
such knives in my body.
And so now I stab you, my love,
drive it in hard,
twist it in deep.

The Sceptic

"I know I'm ugly,
but please don't taunt me."

She presses both hands
against my mouth:
"You talk too much."

In a moment
we will quarrel
and all because I told her
that she is beautiful.

The Word

Though I have the gift of tongues
and can move mountains,
my words are nothing
compared with yours,
though you only
look up from my arms
and whisper my name.

This is not pride
because I know
it is not
my name that you whisper
but a sign
between us,
like the word
that was spoken
at the beginning
of the world
and will be spoken again
only when the world ends.

This is not that word
but the other
that must be spoken
over and over
while the world lasts.

Tears,
laughter,

a lifetime!
All in one word!

The word you whisper
when you look up
from my arms
and seem to say
my name.

Day's End
for Anne

I have worked since daylight in the hayfields.
We walked home at dusk, following the horses.
For supper, I ate hot bread and spiced ham,
    onions and tomatoes.
Now I kneel over a basin of cold water
and a woman washes my hair —
a strong woman whose knuckles rake my scalp.
Her hands smell of soap, I am naked to the waist,
    she leans her weight against me;
laughs huskily when I seize her wrists
    and try to push away her hands.
I am young and strong but a great weariness is upon me —
I would be willing to die now if I were sure that death is sleep.

Down Shore

Since I am a man and never wholly removed from man's echo
    and reflection,
I hear the sea marching against the continent, the pained
    laughter of gulls,
the boulders, hairy with seaweed, are the humps of
    slain mammoths —

a tale for children untouched by violence who smile
      in their sleep when they dream of war.

My young son, laughing at the tide and his mother's fears,
the waves like great dogs hurling themselves against him,
beating their wet forepaws against his chest;
and my wife, salt spray in her hair, still as the gulls
who stand motionless for what seems like hours,
time falling around them like the shadow
of a single cloud crossing the sun —
fancies of a man never at peace with the inhuman:
heir of Greeks and Jews whose gods were men and conquerors.
The Son of Man ate honey and fish,
I, a man, have tamed even death.

The Loneliness of the Long-Distance Runner

My wife bursts into the room
where I'm writing well
of my love for her

and because now
the poem is lost

I silently curse her.

For Carol

A bus-stop in the rain,
the three of us: night, Carol and I,
a little drunk, hoping the bus will be late.

Carol says
      bus stations are so lonesome
      why is it

we always think
of the people left behind
isn't it the going that matters?

And I say Carol
listen to me, death matters if I think
the crows will pluck out your eyes.
I can kiss them here
because we're dead, all of us,
and to the dead
love is all that matters.

Not money, she says
or what people think
or Bolivia? Carol is
beautiful
when she laughs because she's sad
and doesn't understand,
which is when most of us laugh
—the hardest anyway.

Carol I say don't go,
don't leave me. And she says, don't you think
it's the earth that dies,
when you're dead
it's the end of the world—the trouble
is that each of us
lives in a separate world...

Carol I say I love you.
She says, what you mean
is you don't want to die.

The bus leaves
and I stand in the rain
wanting a drink or anybody,
even a fool, to talk to.

The Last Waltz

The orchestra playing
the last waltz
at three o'clock
in the morning
in the Knights of Pythias Hall
in Hartland, New Brunswick,
Canada, North America,
world, solar system,
centre of the universe —

and all of us drunk,
swaying together
to the music of rum
and a sad clarinet:

comrades all,
each with his beloved.

A Boy in a Red Loin Cloth

He waited for the men to come, and the beautiful white horse
he would ride into the jungle. They would stop by a spring,
where he would bathe and change into a red loin cloth,
and the pygmies would suddenly emerge from the trees
and lead him down the secret road to the city,
beating drums, blowing curious little horns, like fifes
or piccolos — and he would be their prisoner,
(perhaps they would even blindfold him) and there would be elephants
and a great pit full of lions and a sun so big
he could not circle it with his arms, and a house of children
who'd make him their brother, though he was always stronger;
and in time he would leave there, but by then he would know
so many singular arts all men would be awed by him,
        and whenever he wished
he would summon the beautiful white horse and ride back to the jungle.

The Wickedness of Peter Shannon

Peter had experienced the tight, nauseous desire
to be swallowed up by the earth, to have his blue
eyes plucked out of his fourteen-year-old head,
his arms sliced off, himself dismembered and the
remnants hidden forever, his shame was so unanswerable.
Oh, God, God, God, it was so he could take any part
of Nancy Lynn O'Mally and lie open-eyed and stark
in the darkness with it—her lilting backsides
in the candy-cane shorts—and bring his thighs together
like pliers, muttering, and it was like the taste
of peach ice cream and the smoke of leaves burning
and the wanton savagery of a pillow over his face,
breaking him, until he swung out over the seething
water and the limb went down and down and down and
the rain was a thousand horses urinating on the
fireproof shingles and he whispered... ohhhhhh,
Jesussss... mad as a turpentined colt among the rockpiles
in the north pasture; what are your breasts like
Nancy Lynn O'Mally, how is it that no matter how much
I'm ashamed I don't blush, except in company... my cheeks
burning as though Christ slapped them!

Rivalry

The nurse, who is neither young nor pretty,
warms the cold lotion with the friction of her palms,
massages my flesh as though coaxing a tired lover,
leans so close I can tell her belly is without fat,
        her breasts firm and, perhaps, beautiful

and smiles mysteriously across my naked body
at my wife, who holds my hand in both of hers,
her own smile becoming tighter and tighter.

Suddenly, a Stranger

Fear in my young son's face
entering my hospital room
for the first time
since the operation

eyeing the door
as though ready to bolt
should this bandaged monster

spring from its horrible bed
to chase him.

In the Operating Room

The anesthetist is singing
"Michael, row the boat ashore,
Hallelujah!"
And I am astonished
that his arms
are so hairy—
thick, red, curly hair
like little coppery ferns
growing out of
his flesh
from wrist
to shoulder.
I would like
to reach up
and touch
the hairy arm
of the anesthetist
because it may be
the last living thing
I will ever see
and I am glad

it is not
white and hairless
—but if I reached up
and wound
a few wisps
of his hair
around my forefinger
as I would like to do
they would think
their drugs
had made me silly
and might remember
and laugh
if I live,
so I concentrate
very hard
on the song
the anesthetist
is singing—
"The River Jordan
is muddy and cold,
Hallelujah!"
And soon
everything
is dark
and nothing
matters
and when I try
to reach up
and touch
the hair
which I think of
now as
little jets
of fire,
I discover
they've strapped
my arms
to the table.

Morning of the Third Operation

Thinking,
just as I
blacked out:
what if all
the evidence
is wrong,
what if
the dead
look on
but can't
make us
understand,
what if
I die
and go home
and Claudine
is crying:
will she know
what it means
even if I
have the strength
to knock
a pencil
off the table.
Listen, Claudine,
look at me!
I'm alive!
Don't be
so damned
stupid, woman.
I'm here
beside you.
But she keeps on
crying
and then
a friend comes
and takes her away

because it isn't good
for her
to be alone.

Escape from Eden

When I was near death,
these little nurses
stripped me naked
and bathed me.
When it appeared
I would live,
they covered
my loins
with a sheet.
When I learned to sit up
and drink consomme
through a straw,
they somehow managed
to wash my back
without removing
my pajama jacket.
Now that I can walk
to the sink and back
without falling,
they knock loudly,
pause,
before slowly opening
the door
of my room.

The Mysterious
Naked Man

The Mysterious Naked Man

A mysterious naked man has been reported
on Cranston Avenue. The police are performing
the usual ceremonies with coloured lights and sirens.
Almost everyone is outdoors and strangers are conversing
    excitedly
as they do during disasters when their involvement is
    peripheral.
"What did he look like?" the lieutenant is asking.
"I don't know," says the witness. "He was naked."
There is talk of dogs—this is no ordinary case
of indecent exposure, the man has been seen
a dozen times since the milkman spotted him and now
the sky is turning purple and voices
carry a long way and the children
have gone a little crazy as they often do at dusk
and cars are arriving
from other sections of the city.
And the mysterious naked man
is kneeling behind a garbage can or lying on his belly
in somebody's garden
or maybe even hiding in the branches of a tree,
where the wind from the harbour
whips at his naked body,
and by now he's probably done
whatever it was he wanted to do
and wishes he could go to sleep
or die
or take to the air like Superman.

The Bhikku

I ask for nothing,
        he tells me, except
                to be freed from
all desire.
        No wonder
                his voice shakes:
even Lucifer's
        desire was less
                insatiable than that.

Brandy of the Damned

His fears are those that no man dare confess
except in jest; only the powerless
harbour ambitions high as his — my brother
who, drunk as a lord, tells me how another
hyena followed him today, its breath
stinking against his neck, it came so close
before he turned and strangled it to death,
braiding his girl's long hair into a noose.

Sweetness of wine or bitterness of beer.
"Little brother," he says, "you need not fear.
You will see no hyenas in the street,
and every nun and traffic cop you meet
will nod or wave and measure you for mayor,
sheriff or member of the Legislature.
Why, had we not been twins like Eng and Chang,
Senate and House of Commons might have sung
your praises, high school history classes ring
with your name, coupled with Mackenzie King's."

He sits upon by bed and tells me this,
laughing his elder brother laugh, and throws
a sunburnt hairy arm across my shoulder,

warns me the army worms are growing bolder:
last night he woke to find a great white veil
like those they leave on roadside bushes, lying
across his face — here laughter is the wail
of wind in alder leaves sucked dry and dying.

4 a.m., April 4

"Wake up. You're having a nightmare. You've been
     whimpering in your sleep."
Because the people at the end of the long line shuffling
     toward the crematorium
don't realize they've become invisible
to the armed guards lining the road.

Hymn to Dionysus

The trick is to loose
    the wild bear
        but hold tight
to the chain,
    woe
        when the bear
snatches up
    the links
        and the man dances.

Absolution

Father it seems
    I am condemned
        to forgive
you,
    having looked
        into my own mirror
so many times
    and seen your face.

In the Park

Two old women
    sitting side by side
on a green bench,
    a bottle of amber
wine between them,
    arguing religion
at the top
    of their voices:
"To hell with your Guinea pope!"
"I'll kiss the arse of no Limey queen!"
Like two old alley cats
    ready to fly
at one another's
    throats —
but having
    the time
of their lives:
    they take turns
drinking
    from the same
precious
    beautiful
        bottle.

Greatness

I would be the greatest poet the world has ever known
if only I could make you see
here on the page
sunlight
a sparrow
three kernels of popcorn
spilled on the snow.

From *The Confessions*

All secrets spoken, her relentless mouth
whimpers "I love you," this over and over,
pleads as before that cold refuser, death,
that I assume the body of her lover.

Each repetition is more desperate,
starved beyond tenderness for self or me,
with every word of adoration, hate
attacks the object more ravenously.

"I love you," she says and each syllable
claws at my back, its black wings pitiless;
"I love you," and again the scalding cruel
beak thrusts and tears, maddened and murderous.

Two Dreams

Last night I dreamt of you and seemed to wake;
dreamt that you slept, your body pressed to mine,
and that I woke and found you there, no sign,
weightless as fog and moonlight, but an ache
in my embracing and imprisoned arms.

Country Full of Christmas

Country full of Christmas,
the stripped, suspicious elms
groping for the dun sky—
what can I give my love?

The remembrance — mouse hawks
scudding on the dykes, above
the wild roses; horses and cattle
separate in the same field.
It is not for my love.

Do you know that foxes
believe in nothing
but themselves — everything
is a fox disguised: men, dogs and rabbits.

The Arsonist

The arsonist awoke, afraid
at finding nothing changed (he'd prayed).
Sane, yet condemned to talk alone,
confiding in a man of bone:

I lost my kindling in a storm
and burned my oil to keep me warm.
God stript me of all save desire,
my burning need to start a fire.

Christ man, the man of bone replied,
I've used no matches since I died.
Why whimper for the fun or fire?
I dance although my marrow's wire.

Another Parting

Is this what it's like to be old?
To have endured so many partings
that this time I scarcely feel
the throat's tensing for the blow,
the sick pendulum in the belly,

feel only my pain
flowing into
an all-encompassing sadness

like the sound of that high plane,
full of people I don't know,
people I can hardly imagine,

breaking the silence
of this dark room
where I lie sleepless.

The Last Leper in Canada

Deep in the woods of Restigouche,
so legends say, a leper lives,
the last in Canada. He fled
from the white nuns of Tracadie.

And every spring, they say, he drives
a cart drawn by a blinded horse
into a village near the woods,
his coming signalled by the bells
of every church along the way.

Women who hear the bells run out
to fetch their children in, and men
bring out moosemeat and venison,

baskets of onions, flasks of wine
to leave beside the gate for him.

Then all curtains are drawn, all doors
bolted, all the inhabitants
kneeling before a crucifix,
praying in silence so they'll hear
those hoofbeats die away again.

A Paradox

Minutes ago
alone in a warm bed
my hunger for her
kept me awake;
I lay in the dark
and sulked at the north wind.

Then the telephone rang.
I ran out of the house.
And now
bent double by the weight
of a Canadian December,
my hair frozen and white,

I find myself wishing
the silly bitch
had sense enough
to let me sleep.

Snapshot

It takes even more than this to make you cry
or laugh
    aloud
        when you are old enough
to find a forgotten snapshot of yourself,

take it up in your hands,
hold it close to the light,

discover slowly
    and for the first time

that once
    long ago
        you were almost

beautiful.

Fireworks

Fireworks are being set off
from the highest point in the city
and because explosions scare me
I sit here sullenly, bracing myself for the next one,
hoping it will be the last.
    After all, we've set off so damn many
explosions this past seven or eight hundred years
it stands to reason God must be getting sick of them.
One of these days he's going to hear a firecracker
and decide that's it, I've had it, they've gone far enough.

What a hell of a bang there'll be when that day comes.

The Mosherville Road

If a man wishes to be sure of the road he treads on,
he must close his eyes and walk in the dark.
    —*St. John of the Cross*

It is nowhere so dark
      as in the country
          where I was born.
I remember nights
      I held my hand
          an inch from my eyes
and saw nothing.
      Yet I kept putting one
          foot in front of the other
and don't recall ever falling
      into the ditch,
          though I was so aware
of it, three feet deep,
      on both sides of me
          with gravel walls
and filthy water
      at the bottom of it,
          that it seems to me now
I must have gone into it,
      at least once
          and forgotten. There was glass
from broken bottles
      and everything else
          that gets thrown from cars
in that ditch and thorn bushes grew
      on the opposite side of it,
          and there were trees .
and night birds
      and flying insects
          I couldn't see.
Usually I talked
      to myself and sometimes I sang
          as I stumbled along
and it wasn't until tonight

almost twenty years
          later I began to realize
how much I was afraid.

The Atheist, Praying

Perhaps the voice
          cannot create
                    anything beyond itself

and the act alone
          is nothing more. Yet
                    it is good to share a thing

so human: this
          reaching out
                    in fear or gentleness.

The Pilgrimage as Worship

Man needs to touch
          and be touched.
                    Therefore the pilgrimage.

And if he finds nothing
          he did not leave behind,
                    well, all the better

—then he can bring back
          everything.
                    Exiles do not know this:

the profit comes
          at the end
                    of the circle.

For Claudine Because I Love Her

Love is also
my finding this house
emptier than a stranger
ever could.

Is it the sound of your movements
enlivening the chairs
although I hear nothing, is it the weight
of your small body moving the house
so little no machine
could ever assess it,
though my mind knows,
is it some old
wholly animal instinct

that fills every room with you,
gently, so I am aware of it only

when I come home
and there is nothing here.

X-ray

Sickness is a crime.
        For habitual offenders
                the penalty is death.
In the doctor's waiting room
        we study one another
                slyly, like embezzlers.
In the hospital
        even those who love us
                seem afraid of what
we might do to them.
        (The sick have no friends.
                Here there are only strangers,
brothers and lovers.)
        Anyone who can walk
                erect without swaying
is my superior.
        Astonishing how soon
                one learns the tricks
the weak use
        against the strong.
                For almost the first time
I have become
        a credible flatterer. Next
                I will learn to whine
—already I find myself
        struggling against it.
                The orderly who sneered
at the fat bearded man
        in the Mother Hubbard—
                would I have done differently
or only been more clever,
        deceiving myself
                that what I felt was pity.

Danse Macabre

One Maccaber, said to have been a Scot, is supposed to have originated the "Dance of Death" that swept Europe during the Bubonic Plague. Whence danse macabre.

When from six centuries of sleep
     Maccaber of the drums awoke,
himself the prancing skeleton
     that he'd once painted on his cloak,
revived his orchestra (renamed
     "Mac and the Deadmen") and appeared
on television, no one thought
     it more than only mildly weird.

Child, in this century of plague
     it's fitting you've revived the dance
invented in another time
     of pilgrimage and flagellants.

In an Irish Village

I was an alien
in the village where
I was born,
three thousand miles away,
am as much
and no more
an alien here.
     But now
a nation is held
responsible:
all Yanks are a bit daft, they say.

So nobody tries to change me
or even dreams it possible
for me to behave
in any other way.

A Signboard in Soho

Often the dreams themselves
are whimsical, if it were possible
to translate them perfectly
into reality, there might be nothing
to turn away from in disgust.
            A child of ten with ringlets
like Queen Victoria's granddaughters at Balmoral
in 1885, a short frock, long pantalets
and innumerable mildly perfumed petticoats
—Lewis Carroll could have written poems to her, John Ruskin
sent her notes with delicate
pastel sketches in the margins.
            She has played croquet
and had tea and biscuits and now
her governess is undressing her.
Soon she is naked and her hair
hangs free to her waist.
            That is all that happens.
                  Or there is a boy
dressed like a Spanish prince for his first communion
or like the son
of Elizabeth Barrett Browning
and he is punished lightly
by a gentlewoman
until he cries prettily and is forgiven.
            As for those who desire
to be slaves or beasts:
Sandro has gold rings
in his ears and his penis has been pierced
in the Chinese manner
so that he may delight
his mistress with feathers.
            And the mare Marigold
carries her master The Duke
so well that he feeds her
slices of apple
from his own hand.

If the enactment were perfect
the need that created it
might be all
we'd be right to pity.

Blueberries, Strawberries, Wintergreen

1   When I rub a blueberry
   between my fingers
   it turns to black—I discovered this
   thirty years ago
   yet never tire
   of performing
   the miracle.

2   The way to eat wild strawberries
   is to pick one,
   crack it between your teeth
   and let it dissolve
   on your tongue before
   picking another.

   There are those who bring
   paper cups, in the old days
   some filled quart jars

   —barbarians!

   These are a delicacy
   that must be eaten alive.

3   When I was five
   I filled my hand
   with wintergreen
   berries:
   there is a wound in each
   where they joined the plant

like a tiny mouth
but with jagged edges
       and when I felt
       all the mouths
       of the berries
       nibbling my palm
I was afraid they
were eating me
       and threw them down.

Points of Contact

Letters unfinished or unmailed;
the characters in my short stories
who will never read about themselves
or even remember they knew me;

all the girls who've turned
my skull into a camera;

even so small a thing as my pantomime
of a drunk on an airport bus;

an old man I can't recall
ever having seen
telling his granddaughter
I am his first cousin, once removed
(a small boy with a squint
who said little and carried a pocket dictionary).

All this suggests
that I too appear in books
of which I've never heard,
written in languages I don't understand,
that I am a family joke
in South Boston or Salt Lake City
or Belfast or Nottingham

because a man I don't know
entertains his children
with tales of a bumpkin he once saw
ordering coffee in a railway station,

that a woman whose name I've forgotten
sometimes murmurs my name in her sleep.

Re-entry

He has been out of his head
but nowhere else: the diagnosis is delirium.
They have him almost convinced
until he touches
the medallion of the priestess.
        The film ends there.

Sleep is a different story.
        How I fought to keep
every detail of the vision,
a work of art that explained
almost everything!

When I wake up, I thought,
I'll find pencils and scissors and paste and paint
and get all this down
on paper so everyone will perceive
how true and beautiful it is
— a discovery!

Manuscript of an unpublished poem
with a tiny green watercolour
        in the upper right corner
and a drawing of Mark Twain's head
        in the upper left
above a picture

of Little Orphan Annie
  cut from a comic strip.

You see how
the dream dissolves:
  like a fistful of diamonds
that were really ice, after all.

Mr. Nine Lives

Woosh!
The cat is safe
and I barely have time
to ask myself what's so important
on the other side before
Woosh!
he's dodged six more cars,
a bus and an oil truck
to get back
to his starting place.

The Way to the Station

I only wanted to know
the way to the station
but the old man
snatched my suitcase,
said, I'll take you there, sonny,
I'm not doing nothing;
  so I had to run after him
  and I said, listen,
  I only want to know
  the way to the station—
he was drunk, I guess,

and he sort of
patted me
on the ass and said,
look, kid, I'm doing you a favour,
        get smart,
        shake the hayseed out of your hair.
By this time I had the suitcase
and grabbed the arm
of a man passing by
and said, pardon me, mister,
could you tell me
the way to the station?
        But he shook me off,
        said, you little punk,
        do you want to get run in!

And that started the old man
laughing like crazy.

The Night Nurse

I've never clearly seen
the face of the night nurse.
She conceals herself
behind a flashlight and besides
I don't ring for her unless
I'm half out of my head.
        She's big, I think,
        and strong
        or perhaps it's my helplessness
        makes me imagine that.
I know her voice
is husky.
It comforts me
to hear her,
though I can seldom
make out the words

and she wouldn't let me
answer
even if I were able.
      One thing's clear:
she's a tough broad.
I think that's exactly
the way to put it. I mean
the slightly archaic
flavour is intentional.
And even here
knowing I may die
and too sick
to care much
      I've fallen in love
with a woman I've never
really seen.
      And once or twice lately
I've wakened
when the drugs
were just strong enough
to soften the pain
without turning
my brain into an omelette
and I've thought of ringing
so I could tell her.
      But I haven't done that yet
because I'm always afraid
of spoiling anything
that's beautiful.

The Victim Tentatively Identifying Himself

I was standing in the lobby
of the General Post Office in Dublin
when an old woman started yelling:
      "Clean the Niggers out of Ireland!
      Ireland for the Irish!

Clean out the bloody black-arsed bastards!"
And because I'd never seen
a black man in Dublin
I wondered if she'd quarrelled
with her Pakistani lodger
or if, as was more likely,
she were out for the blood
of the black Protestants,
        and as you can see
I wear a red and yellow beard
and that day a Carnaby Street
turquoise and orange ascot,
        so I didn't want to turn around
because to look straight
into the eyes
of the insane
is to share
in their insanity.
        On the other hand, I thought,
how will I defend myself
if she comes at me from behind.
        And of course all this time
I was licking very beautiful
Irish postage stamps
        and straining very hard
to keep my face
as non-committal as possible.

The Bearded Man's Poem

Now that I wear a beard
certain small children
tend to fall silent
when they look up and see me
and a very few of them
smile at me differently
than I've ever been smiled at before.

There is astonishment in the way
their faces light up
but no fear
and some of them look
almost as though
they wanted to protect me.

First Lesson in Theology

"God is a Baptist,"
my grandmother told me
when I was three.
"John the Baptist baptized him,
so what else could he be?"

Alpha and Omega

I am awake. I know where I am. I have a name and a history.
All this is happening in Trafalgar Square, but will go on
      happening
wherever I am until I die. I boast of nothing,
each one of these thousands has created me,
is therefore my god. I am nobody,
only a childish wonder at how mysterious it is
that I am looking out through the eyes
of a certain body and this body is alive,
here and now, in the thin English sunlight,
surrounded by pigeons as though we were all saints,
staring up at Lord Nelson, who looks as if he
      were being shot into space,
eyeing the black and sinister taxis, the huge toy buses,
the young men arrayed like Janissaries
who have looted the palace of a foppish sultan,
the beautiful young women who do not dress but simply

adorn their nakedness.
It is a Sunday afternoon in August, 1967,
and there are many other places I could be
but no one else can stand
exactly where I am standing
now, thinking of Van Gogh's Sunflowers,
almost the only picture
in that giant mausoleum to reach out and touch me.

Five Days in Hospital

1 I have come beyond fear to a place where there is almost
     silence,
  except now I am all the numbers
  on all the clocks in the world:
  things are broken apart,
  I am the ruins of a crystal man
  and there are no sentences
  but only words...

2 I have discovered to my amazement
     that I am unable to believe
        in my own death.
  I know that I will die but I do not believe in it.
  Then how is it there are times
  when I am almost crazy with fear?

3 I look IN at the world
  like a ghost startled by the sight
  of his own body
  lying quite apart from him
  in this bed...

4 Where do flames go when they go out?
     They go back to the sun.
  How do they get there?

Like a flight of birds with bright feathers
        flying south through the black morning...

5   Fear of deafness has stopped my ears.
    Fear of blindness has sewn up my eyes.
    Fear of nakedness has stripped me bare.
    Fear of the desert has made me abjure drink.
    Yet even now, bad joke for a black morning,
    fear of silence has not stilled my tongue.

Police Beat

When a man is overcome by the police
there is always a moment
when he looks as bewildered
as you or I would
if we woke up out in the street
without the faintest idea
of how we'd got there
and were suddenly handcuffed.
        Soon it comes back to him
and he pulls himself together
and looks scared or cocky
as they hustle him into the car.
        But there's always that moment
when even the toughest of them
looks as if he were struggling to remember.

A Poem about Miracles

Why don't records go blank
the instant the singer dies?
Oh, I know there are explanations,
but they don't convince me.
I'm still surprised

when I hear the dead singing.
As for orchestras,
I expect the instruments
to fall silent one by one
as the musicians succumb
to cancer and heart disease
so that toward the end
I turn on a disc
labelled *Götterdämmerung*
and all that comes out
is the sound of one sick old man
scraping a shaky bow
across an out-of-tune fiddle.

The People Who Are Gone

In the days of the people who are gone — that was the way
the old people began their stories, Peter Little Bear says,
and now, well, those story tellers they've gone too.
Until the white man came we had no history
and now we have nothing else.
     But in the old days,
in the days of the people who are gone (he grins because
even though we're friends he still needs
that grin to escape through
should I suddenly betray him
and it's a weapon too that he can use
if I ask more than he's able to give).
     In the old days, then,
every one of our boys when he came to a certain age
was sent into the woods alone to talk with God.
They fasted, I guess, and I don't think they were allowed
to take any weapons. The men may even have done
things to them before they went. I don't know. But every one
when he got to be, oh, thirteen or fourteen, had to go
into the woods and wait for God to come
down from the sun or out of the trees. So every man

had spoken with God, face to face.
        —And what did he say, I ask, their God I mean?
I don't know, Peter says. Maybe they never told,
maybe he only said hello
in Maliseet. My Gosh, if God himself
spoke to you would you remember what he said
and would it matter if you did?
And, gently this time,
Peter grins again.

A December Conversation with Professor Algernon Squint

I believed in Santa Claus until I was seventeen,
says Professor Squint, I was a seminarian,
you see, and there was nobody
to tell us different.
                When I was twenty-one
I left the church; ever since then
I've fought against mumbo-jumbo.
                                Though we observe
Christmas for the children's sake,
explaining it as a quaint survival
of ancient superstition.
                On our tree
we hang the Happy Man,
our Humanist Fellowship Symbol.

Hilltop at Night

I have drunk wine.
        The empty bottle
        lies beside me
        in the grass.
Though it is night
small beasts and birds

fear to sleep
while I am here.
    I entertain myself,
    my hand outstretched
    level with my eyes:
it amuses me
to pretend
    I snuff out the moon,
    handfuls of stars.

The Ascetic

Boris has grooved in
on poverty and lives on wild grapes
whose vines have penetrated
the wide cracks around the windows
of his hut and spread across the floor
so that he harvests breakfast
without lifting his head
from the rucksack he makes do
as a pillow,
              yet so disciplined is he
by daily meditation
to the accompaniment
of sitar and tabla
that when I offer him sustenance
he will attempt no more
than a half glass of wine
and a wafer of cheese,
puts both aside unfinished when he decides
the cheese is domestic, the chianti unequal
to that he learned to love
last winter in Florence.

Circles

You keep peeling off hollow dolls
and finding another
inside: I divide into men,
fat and thin, half a dozen
boys, children and babies
of various sizes.

        I could have said it
a year ago in a Russian boutique
but it didn't happen
until tonight

        and then
there was no apparent
connection at all, so that I was startled
when I felt myself lifted off the chair
and stretched
and shaken.

Ypres: 1915

The age of trumpets is passed, the banners hang
like dead crows, tattered and black,
rotting into nothingness on cathedral walls.
In the crypt of St. Paul's I had all the wrong thoughts,
wondered if there was anything left of Nelson
or Wellington, and even wished
I could pry open their tombs and look,
then was ashamed
of such morbid childishness, and almost afraid.

I know the picture is as much a forgery
as the Protocols of Zion, yet it outdistances
more plausible fictions: newsreels, regimental histories,
biographies of Earl Haig.

        It is always morning
and the sky somehow manages to be red

though the picture is in black and white.
There is a long road over flat country,
shell holes, the debris of houses,
a gun carriage overturned in a field,
the bodies of men and horses,
but only a few of them and those
always neat and distant.
                              The Moors are running
down the right side of the road.
The Moors are running
in their baggy pants and Santa Claus caps.
The Moors are running.
                              And their officers,
Frenchmen who remember
Alsace and Lorraine,
are running backwards in front of them,
waving their swords, trying to drive them back,
weeping
          the dishonour of it all.
The Moors are running.

And on the left side of the same road,
the Canadians are marching
in the opposite direction.

The Canadians are marching
in English uniforms behind
a piper playing "Scotland the Brave."

The Canadians are marching
in impeccable formation,
every man in step.

The Canadians are marching.

And I know this belongs
with Lord Kitchener's mustache
and old movies in which the Kaiser and his general staff
seem to run like the Keystone Cops.

That old man on television last night,
a farmer or fisherman by the sound of him,
revisiting Vimy Ridge, and they asked him
what it was like, and he said,
There was water up to our middles, yes
and there was rats, and yes
there was water up to our middles
and rats, all right enough,
and to tell you the truth
after the first three or four days
I started to get a little disgusted.

Oh, I know they were mercenaries
in a war that hardly concerned us.
I know all that.

Sometimes I'm not even sure that I have a country.

But I know they stood there at Ypres
the first time the Germans used gas,
that they were almost the only troops
in that section of the front
who did not break and run,
who held the line.

Perhaps they were too scared to run.
Perhaps they didn't know any better
—that is possible, they were so innocent,
those farmboys and mechanics, you have only to look
at old pictures and see how they smiled.
Perhaps they were too shy
to walk out on anybody, even Death.
Perhaps their only motivation
was a stubborn disinclination.

Private MacNally thinking:
You squareheaded sons of bitches,
you want this God damn trench
you're going to have to take it away

from Billy MacNally
of the South End of Saint John, New Brunswick.

And that's ridiculous, too, and nothing
on which to found a country.
                    Still
It makes me feel good, knowing
that in some obscure, conclusive way
they were connected with me
and me with them.

Another Poem

Another poem: there have been so many
in the twenty-four years since I decided I'd grow up
and fool everybody by becoming
Son of God and King of Albania,
        and I keep it up for so many reasons
I won't try to list them and anyway
I'm a little afraid of sounding foolish,
to tell the truth.
                    I think of death
and of how I should leave something,
one poem, one story
that will tell what it was like
to be alive, because that matters,
and I am a little drunk
        (not a dwarf lush but a big man
        slightly inebriated)
so it seems I might do it
by putting down what happens:
        my young son's laughter,
I could never tell you
how much I love him
except in a poem
where everything is secret
and I am not myself because, mercifully,

all poets are dead,
                    that is the key to it
and the urge to abolish poetry
because it's almost all shit
          (my friend Louis Cormier
          saying he writes poems
          for the same reason
          he goes to the bathroom).
My young son's laughter and I
am Edward III at Agincourt
or Crécy, whichever it was, and
when the messenger came
crying disaster the old man asked only:
"Does my son still live?" and told that he did said:
"Go then and tell those who sent you
that while my son still lives they have nothing to fear"
and later that same day
when the Black Prince rode up to him he said:
"This day, sweet son, thou hast acquitest thyself well."
          Laugh at me no more
          than I laugh at myself.
And there was a man crying
"Groceries!" It's hot, I told him, and he said
"hot as the hinges of hell," and I emptied all
the marked bags in the freezer and stacked the cans
one on top of the other, making sure the colours
of the labels made a pretty pattern,
          and there were cucumbers
and green peppers
and pickles from Poland
and many varieties of lunch meat
and three kinds of cheese.
          Yesterday the milk spoiled
because one of us forgot
to put it in the refrigerator
so I am very careful
and feel somewhat important, a man,
provider for a family, a host
who will have bread

to break with his guests.
        Besides
I do this sort of thing so seldom
and am not good at it.
        This morning we took the car
to a service station because there is something wrong
with the steering apparatus and I was a little afraid
at intersections where there was the sound
of rubber scraping against concrete
and the wheel trembled in my hands
and I knew nobody at the service station
because we are new here, and that too
is ordinary
        and important:
it's better to have someone you like
fix the steering apparatus on your car,
someone you can talk with as he works.
        And a friend came bringing
two beautiful girls and I observed how the eyes of one
seemed to look out from inside her body,
as though there were another
girl in there, and I wished
she'd fall madly in love with me and to hell
with Leonard Cohen,
                she had such eyes,
                                but we only
played dominoes with the names of books.
        I went upstairs
and wrote a fair poem and part of a story
about the year I became a Taoist, after which
a young man who looked like a painting
of Jesus Christ came to interview me
and the first question he asked was:
"Why are you at UNB?"
"Damned if I know," I answered.
And he said he wouldn't write the article
because articles are scripts
the subject has to follow and he wanted me to be free,
and we looked at one another with understanding

which is so rare I loved him
for a second,
        and later we ate scallops
prepared with love because my wife keeps
a shaker full of love in her spice cabinet
and if you think that's funny
you should eat something she's cooked
without that ingredient,
        and she came home
from her first meeting of the Faculty Wives Club
with a card on her dress with my name on it
and the word "Poet" because everybody there
had to show what their husband was and I am a poet,
which makes sense but seemed funny as hell
for a minute and a half,
        and Gordon Lightfoot
says stupid things between songs
I suppose because he's afraid
people will know he's singing
about himself and that
scares hell out of him the way it does me sometimes
—but already I can see it's no use
to put all this down,
        it is only a fragment
of what happened today
and I have lived roughly
12,775 days—if I got all that
into a poem, shorter than this,
maybe I'd stop being afraid
        of death
or at least I might manage
a smile when I get it,
        but I've never come closer
than this sort of thing where you feel ashamed
when it's done because there's so much more
you'll never say, and the best you can do
sounds like a cheap trick when you re-read it.

Kind of a Love Poem

Don't leave me
            alone,
I think,
      for Jesus' sake,
            don't
leave me
      alone.
            But you're asleep
and the only way
I can keep you
awake is by telling
you what a bitch
you are.
      You bitch.
            And even
if I make you cry,
                  that
is not so bad
            as being alone.
                        Not quite.

For Jamil Baroody
*Saudi Arabian ambassador to the United Nations,
on the occasion of his address to the Security Council, June, 1967*

He tosses his pencil on the table
(not as a symbol of anything but simply because he is
      through with it)
and it bounces on the floor, out of reach, the first accident
to occur here tonight, and he glances down,
wondering where it fell, not because he cares
but because it is human
to glance down at things that have fallen.

He interrupts his speech, which is not a speech after all,

but the monologue of a man who, it is apparent,
has made many speeches in his time
but is old now, and, perhaps, already childish,
speaks to the Russian beside him, says something
that makes the others laugh
not because it is funny
but because it is the kind of thing
an old man says to a younger.

The Russian nods and smiles. He is a little nervous
about what the old man may say next
and a little amused and there is even
a hint of affection.
                         For the first time
I believe the Russian
really likes Chinese poetry, bow ties and pipe tobacco.
I am even prepared to believe he has laughed
until the neighbours banged on the wall
and that once, long ago,
he cried himself to sleep.

But forget the Russian. He could be replaced by a computer
programmed in Moscow, and the others are no better,
endlessly exchanging their mimeographed resolutions
while, somewhere else, drunken gods shoot dice
to decide whether or not to continue history.

Listen to this one old man, apologist for slavery,
· servant of a king who still lives in the 14th century,
one who, I have little doubt,
truly believes that his Prophet's corpse
revived, mounted a white horse
and leapt from the Rock of Abraham into Paradise;
a man as ignorant, cruel and bigoted as the rest of us.

Laid bare so innocently, even his weaknesses
possess a kind of grandeur,
as when he forgets he's supposed to leave
the table when he's finished speaking

and has trouble understanding the little aide sent to remind him,
finally gets to his feet, makes a slight but very formal bow
toward the diplomats who already are listening
to someone reading a long statement about something else
and walks away with the smile
of an old man forgiving his own stupidity.

The Backbiters

Two housewives, friends
for years, are uttering malice
against a third
who is friend to both.
　　At the office
there are those
who can scarcely hide
their restlessness
when a companion
delays his departure
and thus postpones
their parade of his weaknesses.

Pettiness, I used to say.
　　Even vileness.
Now I think I know better.
It is a purgation
that permits us
to be a little gentler
when we face
one another again,
perhaps even
in its own strange way
　　an act of love.

On the Stairs

Knuckling his temples on the shadowed stair,
the boy is for the first time aware
how strange it is to be himself, and here.

Hard knot of consciousness behind the eyes,
hot nails against his forehead as he tries
to free a truth so true we've only lies

in which to hint at it: terror, delight
and an unspeakable confusion, light,
darkness, a pebble thrown from a great height.

Blessed Are They That Mourn

Every night this week there's been a rehearsal
from the knock at the door, the boy with the telegram,
to Aunt Agnes fainting (they've debated for hours
whether she should fall in the porch or run wailing
from room to room till she drops in the kitchen)
—so their timing is flawless, each word and gesture
Balinese in its lyrical perfection.
"I'll weep for two minutes," says Cousin Arthur,
"covering my face with my hands, then I'll straighten
—like so—and take Lily in my arms and kiss her
a Jimmy Stewart kind of kiss and she'll say—"
"I'll say, 'don't cry, Arthur,
we have to be brave' and we'll help one another
to the sofa where we'll sit for a long time,
staring at the floor and thinking
deep sad thoughts about past and present and future."

The Saint's Apprentice

Not that I'm
        a saint but
                I think I can
tell you they're not
        all that
                happy about it.
Ever since I
        was sixteen
                I've been finding
myself
        alone
                with
girls so beautiful it
        made you lame
                to watch them
and eight out
        of ten as
                my hand began
to receive little
        electric
                shocks from their
thighs
        have started telling
                me how much
alone they are
        how they wish their
                husbands or lovers
understood them half
        so well and many
                have curled up
in my arms
        and cried so
                I couldn't take
down their panties
        without risking incest
                or sacrilege and later

running into me
    on the street
        have tossed me
their sweetest,
    most sisterly
        superior
little smiles.

The Men in Antonio's Barber Shop

They have the faces of jurors who have been called too often,
middleaged sergeants, foremen put there too early and left
    there too long,
men who aspired for little, attained it and guarded it well
    for the best part of a lifetime.
        They wear slacks and polo shirts
and those peaked caps that are partly athletic and partly
    military,
because this is North America, where men are expected
to disguise themselves as boys, and all their lives
these men have done whatever was expected.

They smoke cigars, but never the cheapest
or most expensive brands and, on occasion,
they drink, but almost always in moderation and with a
    certain solemnity.
They hardly ever smile, except as a stern parent smiles
at the naughtiness of somebody else's child.

And their laughter is never accidental, or too loud.
And each of them knows who would have won
if Joe Louis in his prime had fought Cassius Clay in his;
knows whether or not the World Series is fixed;
knows which team in the National Hockey League
will finish first, and if the same team will win the Stanley Cup;
knows why Pearson resigned, his secret reason that none of
    the papers dared print;

knows how much the Premier
drinks and whether or not his wife is unfaithful;
knows the names of the conspirators who murdered the Kennedys
        and injected cancer cells into Ruby;
knows what Nixon is thinking;
and what Ho Chi Minh wants; knows how to raise children,
punish criminals, produce better movies,
prevent cars from rusting,
cure a cold, avoid syphilis, keep the heart healthy,
        end employment.

Once in a while I imagine I envy them.
That's not true, of course. Still it would be comforting
to be as certain of something as they are of everything.

In Memoriam: Claude Orser (1894–1968)

Claude, if you thought about it at all,
I suppose you believed in that golden city
you'd been hearing about all your life,
although you'd never seen
any city bigger than Saint John
and no pearls or diamonds or rubies
unless there were some on exhibit
in the New Brunswick Museum
that day we took you there
and you struck up conversations
with all the tourists
and expressed your astonishment
at absolutely everything
in an accent straight from the banks
of the Main Stream in Carleton County.
But even if your spirit is still around somewhere
as that minister who talked about Gadh-thuh-Cree-eight-tor
claimed it was, the day of your funeral,
you wouldn't be happy with pearly gates and palaces;
and you'd never be comfortable with those fellows he talked about,

like Bildad the Shuhite and Abimelech, the King of Gerar.
For one thing you'd want a place
where there were a lot of broken things
you could fix—year-old toys you could make better than new
with friction tape and rivets,
pots with holes in them for you to patch,
tables and chairs you could make new legs for.
And probably there ought to be a few small holes in the roof
you could plug to keep out the rain.
But most important of all there'd have to be a replica
of Taylor's Corner in Hartland on Saturday night
where you could sit on the ledge in front of Ginson's Grocery,
you and your cronies trading the latest gossip
about everybody who walked by, exchanging tall tales
about the great things you'd seen and done,
chewing tobacco or smoking handmade cigarettes
and every once in a while
warming the walls of your belly
with a nip from a half-pint bottle
of Black Diamond Demerara Rum.

On the Nature of Human Compassion

I said to a herring gull with a broken wing:
Bird, I am sad for you.
If I could make you trust me
I'd take you up in my hands,
carry you back to the city
and hire a veterinarian to heal you.
Or if my stomach were stronger
I'd use a stone or a club of driftwood
to shorten your death.
                    And the herring gull answered:
Man, you are not sad for me,
but for yourself, so great an egotist
you can put on the body of a bird
or play Mephistopheles to a housefly,

what you call your compassion the conceit
that all living things are Alden Nowlan in disguise.

On Dreams of War

My generation,
children of war,
still dream of flying
our fathers' Spitfires,
awake to regret
we were not at Dieppe.

Once when I
was very drunk
—and drunkenness
is a kind
of dreaming
—I told a veteran
of the Italian
campaign
I was captured
at Hong Kong
and because
I look older
than my years
and have been a liar
all my life,
I think he believed me.

Another time I dreamed
the most vivid dream
of guarding the Nazis
at Nuremberg:
it was I who smuggled
cyanide to Goering,
out of a pity
I'd never felt

until his ghost
so disarmed me
that ever since
I've half-suspected
there may be worlds
as real as this
we haunt in our sleep.

A thousand nights
I've flown with Beurling,
cried out in nightmare
from the beaches
of Normandy,
sweated in engine rooms
until it seemed
my skin peeled
as from sunburn,
endured winds so cold
my teeth chattered until,
one by one,
they fell out and bounced
off icy decks
into the North Atlantic.

Hitler's War.
My war.
What epic guilt
we must have felt
the children of
my place and time
as we played
Junior Commandos
and bought
War Savings Stamps:

guilt that we were
so young,
so small,
so weak,

guilt for the very sea
with which
God or Chance
protected us.

The Blue Chair

The bright blue chair on the other side of the room
has not moved, and neither have I;
we are exactly where we were
an hour ago. Only our relationship
has changed. Yet there is more space between us.

And I am beginning to feel
more gentle toward the blue chair,
now that it does not stand
so heavily, and its colour is softened.

I have ceased to own you, blue chair.
You are no longer involved in my life.

I find myself smiling at you.
I am content to have you there

and could address these same words
to every object in this room

now that I have pulled back
into my own body and they and I
are freed from each other.

The Golden Apples of the Sun

Both as mere children see a tinsel star
(with undivided wonder) and as men

observe the ornaments they've fashioned when
their art is clumsier than their desire:
I see you, all my love, a tree afire
in the cold forests of me, and again
a tree I made from staves torn from the pen
of loneliness, and all its roots are wire.

My love, with so much hatred in the earth,
a thousand bats against the burning sky,
I think it seldom matters why the seed
of love was planted if it comes to birth.
Love is too rare to kill (though it will die)
whether it grows in you or in my need.

"Look at the Stars," They Said

"Look at the stars," they said.
"Go look at the sea."

But the stars play no jokes.
Our cries do not move the seas.

I have seen His image only in men.

Children running from a forest,
the steps of the woodcutter,
hunchbacked executioners
mad that they are not loved.

Who but a God
could have created *them*?

Blackflies

The first day you fight them,
the bloodthirsty blackflies
storming out of the steaming Devil's Island
of the swamp.
You stand it as long as you can,
then curse and throw down your axe,
yell every obscenity you know
as you smash their bodies
into bloody pulp on your forearms.

But they keep on coming.

And the second or the third or the fourth day
you realize they'll keep on coming forever,
that nothing you can do will stop them.

So by the end of the first week
you've learned to ignore them except
when you pause, wipe the sweat from your eyes
and watch one of them wriggle
under the hairs, brace his legs and wings for the thrust—

Christ, it gets so you somehow
sympathize with the bastard, even grunt with relish
as though you tasted blood
when he taps your veins
with his needle-hot stinger.

The Adam Tree

No need to stretch. Fruit bears the branches down
until leaves swish across the waist-high grass.
Kneeling an ironist could gather in
apples to last him till All-Hallowmass.

Each bite is sweeter for surprise
one always feels, expecting bitterness
from shrivelled pouches that deceive the eyes
and mind, despite the tongue's experience.

At dusk a harvester, prickled by frost,
and knowing everything would waste or die
in one clear night, went out and shook his fist
at Venus, twinkling in the cold sky.

Dream of Man, Whale and Tiger

A whale beached amidst
uprooted trees whose
black limbs are like
the arms and legs
of corpses
in a cemetery that
has been bombed
or shelled
by artillery—the whale itself
gives no sign
of life, although
it seems not
quite dead,
its huge body glossy
with black oil
from inside
itself.
          Then
                    I look back and see
a white tiger:
an albino, I think
to myself, not much
surprised at
the presence of such
a creature or

wholly afraid but
knowing well enough
the beast is
a stranger here
although why
that should be
apparent, I don't know
—this is an outlaw
planet.
            The animal comes closer
and I am not sure
if I am still the man
standing there
on the shore
with the body
of the whale
above him, because
the tiger is some
distance behind
and it is not right
that I should see
it approaching unless
I'm another
man altogether.
                Our ancestors
saw by day that
which we
see only in dreams.
                Imagine it!
A man coming
upon such
scenes without
the excuse of sleep. That
is how it was once, how
it may be again.

A Black Plastic Button and a Yellow Yo-yo

I wish I could make her understand
her child isn't the Christ Child
and didn't create the world,
then maybe she'd stop shaking
her fists in his face
and he could come out from inside
his yellow yo-yo
or black plastic button
because that's where he hides:
I've watched from my window,
unable to write because of her screaming,
and seen him flying out of his body
into the yo-yo,
where he can neither see nor be seen,
neither hear nor speak,
a Buddha smaller than my thumb,
a sleeping Krishna,
there inside that dancing yo-yo;
and if she knocks it from his hand,
why, he simply turns
the second button from the top
of his windbreaker,
a black plastic button,
turns it between
his thumb and forefinger,
focuses his eyes on it,
until he is safe again,
curled up in a ball
where nothing at all can reach him.

The Snakes

Mother, the snakes are like ice around my ankles
and I am afraid of the iceman
whose skin is like a lemon upon black velvet,
and of his son whose fingers leave bruises
on my breasts that are two small scoops
of ice cream, with their pink cherries,
even when he does not quite touch me
when we pass in the school and his black hands
crumble chalk and sprinkle
white dust at my feet.
                    Daughter,
lest the time come when you wear these snakes
        like bracelets,
father will snap them like whips till their necks
        break.
                    Sleep.

The Shaft of Light

Bent like a sprinter in my boyhood's bed,
I gaped for hours at that shaft of light
I'd fashioned, kneeling with a book, the crack
between the darknesses so measured that
I lay invisible, a Cyclops, when
my cousins moved on girl-mysterious
errands across the hall, their little feet
spanking the carpet while my belly rose
and fell as though it bore the rise and fall
of their lithe bodies. Oh, I dreamt the fire
of my ambushing spear would spread, would burn
each stitch to falling cinder so they stood
like Daniel's Hebrew children, bare, their faces
incredulous, exultant, as they reached
with timid fingers to caress the flames.

Dry Spell

I stare at the yellow paper
in my typewriter until I find myself
contemplating its texture
and even the bruises
where the machines pressed too hard
become important to me
but, above all, the blankness
is more beautiful than any mark
I could put on it today,
so I write only:
there is nothing on this sheet,
and realize at once that it is impossible
for these words ever to be true.
That is one more of the many things
I can never tell you.

One Starry Night on Winter Street

Terry speaks to
every strange kitten she sees on the street,
and strokes its head
with the tips of her fingers,
lightly and briefly,
almost the same way
as cats greet one another, except
they use their noses
—which would be good
to watch even if Terry
were a little girl, but
when I tell you
she's a woman who can set fires
in a man's body with
those same fingers, well then,
it becomes an act of holiness,
that little gesture.

The Persistent Caller

The doorbell is ringing, but
I won't answer: I'm working
and besides it's probably
only some kid
looking for Johnnie
who isn't here.
     I'll have to be quiet, though,
because hardly anybody ever
stops ringing unless
he's convinced there's nobody
home.
  Now he's started knocking
and after each little pause
knocks louder.
     Doesn't that damn fool know
when he's not wanted?
      Go away, whoever you are!
But the knocking
goes on and on and on
      because it's a kid
out there
and he doesn't know
any better.
    Of course.
      Of course.
And I'm a grown man.
     Still I keep my eye on the door
in case whoever it is
making all that noise
should turn the knob
and start to push it open.

O'Sullivan's World

Earth is three billion separate planets
and on one of them
my friend O'Sullivan
tells me there are no women
but only symmetrical
little animals somewhat like deer
that are allowed to go almost anywhere
they like just as cats and pigeons do
in my world and when a man
feels the urge he goes to one of them
with a handful of sugar cubes or if the beast is beautiful
a little ice cream or half of a chocolate bar
and more often than not it trots along beside him
to wherever it is he wants to go,
its tiny hooves beating time to the music
of the clusters of little silver bells
tied with silk ribbons
to its switching tail.

The Dream of the Chocolate Dog

Chocolate dog
    Irish wolfhound except
        in colour it
turns out I
    need not have feared you
incarnation of a friend
    yes yes I know
        that is what your tongue
writes on my cheeks
    and in the basement
        of a hotel made
from red bricks
    I sit with others
        at a table and watch

through a window above me
          the bombs dropping hear
                    the roll of their thunder and
damn fool that I've always been
          write
                    with a pencil stub on a single sheet
the horizon is ash
          and the stretcher-bearers
                    are running away
but what I need to perfect
          is the colour of the flares
                    everything
else is black
          one
                    is like a blinding green flame
and the other
          pale purple yet
                    the light of it
a razor blade slashing
          the black sky
                    what does it matter
I ask myself
          the point
                    of writing poems except
to hide my fear
          from the others
                    and even they see
my hands are shaking
          so I can hardly read
                    what I've written
how long does it last I ask
          the man sitting beside me
                    what are you writing
he says and
          we look into
                    one another's eyes
and laugh.

The First Stirring of the Beasts

The first stirring of the beasts
is heard at two or three or four
in the morning, depending on the season.

You lie, warm and drowsy, listening,
wondering how there is so much difference
between the sounds
cattle and horses make,
moving in their stanchions or halters,
so much difference that you can't explain,
so that if someone asked you
which of them is moving now?
you couldn't answer
but lying there, not quite awake,
you know, although it doesn't matter,
and then a rooster crows
and it sounds, or maybe you imagine this,
unsure and a little afraid,
                            and after a little
there are only the sounds of night
that we call silence.

The second stirring of the beasts
is the one everybody understands.
You hear it at dawn
and if you belong here
you get up.
Anyway, there is no mystery
in it, it is the other stirring,
the first brief restlessness
which seems to come for no reason
that makes you ask yourself
what are they awake for?

The Dark Whirl

Touching you tongue to tongue in the dark whirl
     of drunkenness and whispering my love
into your hair, I held another girl
     that you knew nothing of.

Out of your warmth I lifted her and she
was all of you, coupled with all of me
and all of love itself and every need
answered: from the quick, sullen greed
that wet my armpits to human desire
for mothers, nymphs and goddesses of fire.

Sober and guilty now, I say:
to deify is to betray.

The Barmaid's Daughter

Beer was my father's beverage,
the barmaid's daughter said;
a brewer's horses drew his bier,
a keg pillowed his head.

And every year, his family,
all of us, old and young,
trundle a puncheon to his grave
and there knock out the bung

that in his oaken coat, our dad,
his mouth still open wide
may taste again that foaming brew,
that rich, full-bodied tide.

Afterword to Genesis

"Let us hasten away before He changes His mind again," the
      Patriarch said as he cleaned his knife on a handful
      of leaves and grass.

And they came down to the tents as quickly as the old man's
      infirmities would allow, not looking back for fear He had
      chosen to follow them.

And later men were assigned to drag branches over the hoofprints
      of the caravan,

and to leave meat at the site of every encampment, covering
      it over with stones so that birds and animals could not
      defile it.

Yet the time came when the young man, Isaac, could not sleep
      for remembering

how he had been made less than a woman, less than a child,
      less than a slave,

how he had stood perfectly still like an animal,

how he had trembled with fear and an inexplicable eagerness

waiting to be blotted out, swallowed up, made nothing.

Communiqué

The angel of the Lord was always stopping for breakfast
or tapping a camel driver on the shoulder and asking
the shortest way to Sodom or Damascus;
my friends, Louis, Martha and Lanni
hand me their poems while the necessary machinery
of life functions around us
—Moosehead Ale, the minor problem
of finding matches for cigarettes,
a lonesome puppy barking
upstairs, Gary Cooper tugging at his hatbrim
on the silent television screen—
and their poems are so young and innocent and beautiful
that I know they have been buttonholed
by that angel I am Alone and
that angel I Love You and even
that humpbacked gnome of an angel
We Are All in This Together and
I tell them, Yeah, that's not bad,
that's pretty good,
and they smile at me
and at one another
and we say goodbye
and they walk away toward their separate homes.

New Year's Eve: 1948

It is ordained that the mad should not dance with the mad
        lest they fall upon one another, so the female
        patients embrace the guards and the male patients
        take the hands of white nurses and the frightened
        bandsmen strike up *The Blue Skirt Waltz* and
        celebrate the advent of the new year two hours
        earlier than those who have not been certified
        as mad or engaged as keepers of the mad which is
        just perhaps since we inhabit a different time zone.

Oh, Annie Laurie MacTavish, were you cut from white cotton
and starched and your eyes, nose, mouth and buttons
stuck on like the red, green and black gumdrops
of the enchanted cookie man? There are rumours
you wear no underclothes and I and a friend who
talks without ceasing of the girls of Japan and
Polynesia with whom he cohabits while they sleep,
his soul going forth like an incubus, once hid
in a tunnel to ambush and rape you — to pierce you
with our horns like the minotaur.

Because madness is a crime, Annie Laurie, and we are all
rapists, arsonists, murderers. Another of my friends
when he was free, set fire to houses that he might spill
his seed on hot ashes, yet he defends me from
the guards, devises monstrously elaborate conspiracies
against me which he upsets to heighten my affection
and when I hit him he smiles at me proudly....

Can you imagine I once posed as a murderer to win greater
respect in the laundry where I was the only worker
who had never been convicted? I was Cream and
Crippen, Brides in the Bath Smith, Saintly Billy Palmer.
When they discovered I was only a crazy kid from the
boondocks they took down my pants and threatened
to castrate me.

Let me make conversation. Did you ever hear of Aleksandar
Obrenovic, King of Servia? Or Draga Mashin, his
wife? If I live a hundred years I will write the
book of their lives. They were quite mad, both of
them. My book will tell what they remembered as
they huddled together, naked, in a closet before
the officers found them and killed them and threw
their bodies

from a window of a palace into a beautiful garden.

The Salmon Brought to Gaff

A salmon does not die as a smaller fish
dies, but much more like an animal or a man.
That is to say
it is not enough
to close your mind
against it.
If you don't want to watch
you must shut your eyes
or turn away.

A Mime for Lovers

They are facing one another
in a little clearing
in the jungle
                and have exchanged
all the words and signs
of greeting:
                he has held out his hands to show her
they are empty
                and she is very careful
not to touch a stone
or stick she could lift,
      so careful, in fact,
that he's becoming
suspicious of her motives
—why does she keep looking away
from that rock near her feet?
Has he misjudged her, after all?
His eyes narrow. He hesitates,
then decides to take a chance.
He hands her the smallest of his knives
and waits to see what she will do with it.
The blade is small. At worst she can only
scar him.

She smiles. They
                    smile at one another.
Slowly,
        so he will not misunderstand,
she takes a handful
of arrows from
her quiver and drops them
at his feet.

An Exchange of Gifts

As long as you read this poem
I will be writing it.
I am writing it here and now
before your eyes,
although you can't see me.
Perhaps you'll dismiss this
as a verbal trick,
the joke is you're wrong;
the real trick
is your pretending
this is something
fixed and solid,
external to us both.
I tell you better:
I will keep on
writing this poem for you
even after I'm dead.

Apology

I talk too much
but the manner
of your listening
calls the words
out of me.
You say almost
nothing. Yet
there would be
only silence
if you were not here.

The Sound of the Birds at Dawn

All night long
we sat on opposite sides
of the room and talked
of everything and nothing, each
becoming more and more
a part of the other.
        And I was less aware
of your body than I might have been
had we only touched
in a doorway
or on a bus.
        Even now it is not
of first importance that
my invisible hands
undress you. Besides
I'm drunk and beginning
to be very tired.
        I wish there were magic
and everything beautiful
        happened
without spoiling
anything. I wish there were perfection

such as exists sometimes in dreams
but without such simplicity. I wish
our communion of words
and little mystical gestures
did not have to stop
but could transform itself slowly
into something at once
purer and more
ceremonious. I understand now
what is meant
when the priests speak
　　　of a consummation.

Portrait of the Artist as a Sweet Little Boy

My great uncle Leo went back into the mine
to see why the dynamite hadn't gone off.
My mother used to say
she couldn't like Dutchmen
no matter how hard she tried,
because one of them
met great uncle Leo
crawling out of the shaft,
with the blood
streaming down
his face
and ran away.

It wasn't true, of course,
her not liking Dutchmen,
but she thought it
a rather romantic
thing to say.
Like telling me
to shut my eyes tight
and imagine what
it was like to be blind.

I'd squeeze my eyelids
until the tears came
because it pleased her:
"Aldie is so tender-hearted,
so much like me."

And Sunday afternoons
I'd lead the blind man
on long walks
across the fields,
guide him back, slowly,
both of us knowing
he could never
have found
his way home
without me.

Two Poems for the Nova Scotia Department of Highways

1 We sprayed the roadside with poison
   to kill the leaves
                   but later it was decided
   the bushes should come down.
   It made you feel good to look back
   at the stacks of fallen alders
   but especially because
   it was so clean,
                   like a little park
   between the fence and the road
       and each man had
   his own section, something he'd done
   all by himself
                   and it was almost beautiful.

2 And one day at noon, sharing
   eggs boiled so hard there was a purple skin
   over the yolks, but great with a pinch of salt

(we sweated so much on that job we ate salt like candy),
cold beef, bananas, washing it all down
with the boiled black tea
we drank scalding hot
as though to defy the sun,

Old Howie told us
how come he'd never cheated:

every so often he'd go home and climb in the window,
it would be dark as the inside of your hat, you see,
and his old woman would be lying there,
pretending to be asleep,

and sometimes he'd be her secret lover,
ready to jump under the bed
if her damn fool husband turned up,

and other times she'd yell
so he'd have to clamp his hand over her mouth.

Either way, said old Howie,
it was as good as a circus

and just as much fun
as having a strange piece.

A Million Years Ago

I hear
a young girl
weeping in
the apartment
        above me.
             No,
she is not weeping so much
           as wailing:

the sound comes
                    from her nostrils
and I can picture her swaying
back
        and
                forth
back
        and
                forth,
like Eve mourning
—the sound
is that old.

Floating Boxes

As if each of them took
his little box of truth
from a certain river:
in my native village
one style was favoured, another
in the town where I grew up, a third
in the city
to which I came as a man.
But none was bigger
than a matchbox
and it was impossible
to keep more than one,
they said,
and every other
was a sham.

Chance Encounter

There is something odd in the road ahead.
A man in a black coat walking a dog,
a tall man in a long black coat walking a big red dog,
or is it a black mare with a red colt.
                                    God
don't let me hit them.
                          I don't like
to be splashed by death.
                          The car stops in time
and I roll down the window.
                                There is a cow moose
standing not ten feet away
and her calf a little farther off,
neither of them knowing what to make of the headlights,
bright as lightning, solid as the light
of a full moon on a cloudless night.
Then the cow crosses over, very slowly,
not looking back
until she reaches
the edge of the woods
on the other side
and finds the calf has not followed her,
                                    but gone back
and they look at one another
across the light that separates them
and perhaps she makes little coaxing sounds I can't hear,
while I will him
not to run away where they might never find each other
but to be brave enough
to walk into the light
I don't dare turn off
for fear of humans like myself
—and at last he begins to walk
toward the road
                and after a moment's pause
enters the light
                and crosses it

in about thirty seconds,
                    a long time
when you're holding your breath,
                         and the instant
he's safely over, she runs and he
    runs behind her,
            and I drive on,
                    happy about it all,
bursting to tell someone about the great sight I've seen,
yet not even sure why it should seem so important.

from Playing the Jesus Game: Selected Poems

The White Goddess

I being twelve and scared, my lantern shook,
shrunk to string my stomach knotted,
breathing the sultry mustiness of hay
and dung in the cowbarn,
and the heifer calving.

Ours was a windy country and its crops
were never frivolous, malicious rocks
kicked at the plow and skinny cattle broke
ditch ice for mud to drink and pigs were axed.

Finding the young bull drowned, his shoulders wedged
into a sunken hogshead in the pasture,
I vomited, O Mother, yet the flies
around his dull eyes vanished with the kiss
your fingers sang into my hair all night.

The Time of the Fire

Dearest of strangers: in your separate room
no smoke intrudes, nor howling from the stable;
the bats make crazy circles in the night—
you keep adjusting napkins on the table.

The haltered horses scream and flaming shingles
descend like bombs upon the yard, and yet
even the heat that cracks these windows will
hardly disturb the table that you set.

Running with buckets between barn and well,
seeing so little done by all we do,
my innocent, I can't make up my mind
whether to pity or to envy you.

Therese

I tell Therese
I'd like to set fire
to all the haystacks,
just at dusk,
then sit on a hill and smell them burning.

I call that poetry.
But she smiles.
You'll never grow up, she says.

Then I tell her
about Dachau and Hiroshima,
although I think it blasphemy
to write poems
about pain not experienced,
and she says it frightens her
to talk of such things.
She has made me promise
we'll keep one friend
without intelligence
who'll drink tea in the kitchen and gossip.

She is a fool.
But she loves me
as we are asked
to love God:
without understanding.

Tonight, coming
to meet me,
she wore shorts
under a raincoat
and when she came near,
passing a street light,
with each step
I could see
her white thighs
glistening with rain.

Golf

My friends believe in golf, address the ball,
however bent, to an appointed place.
Newtonians, convinced no orb can fall
out of the numbered course of time and space.

But I, from clumsiness or pity, drive
balls out of bounds and into woods and traps,
my knees and wrists vindictive in their love
for dark and tangled places not on maps.

"Golf's not your game," they say. But I persist.
"Next one goes straight..." I promise. Oh, they're fooled
right cunningly by my secretive wrist
that treacherously lets the world go wild.

Let them attack the green. As for myself,
I pitch into the darkness, like a wolf.

The Dog Returned from the Woods

After three days the dog came home, a stranger,
slinking along the footpath from the hills,
drawn by a sullen truce of thirst and hunger,
his muzzle visored in porcupine quills.

The children saw him first and yelled his name
or rather the name of the dog who'd gone:
"Peter!" As if so wild a beast would come—
"Peter!" might have been "death" for all he knew.

And then they saw the difference in his walk,
a strangeness far more terrible than pain,
a wild thing lapping at the cattle trough,
his black lips oozing blood and the red stain
floating like ribbon in the water. Hurt

and baffled by his treachery they scowled,
wanting to weep, and he, his grim thirst met,
threw back his quill-bewhiskered head and howled.

Language

Whenever I'm tired I catch myself talking
like everybody else from the northeast shore
of Cobequid Bay in Nova Scotia.

Tongue held close
to the floor of the mouth,
far back from the teeth,
breath shallow and slow.

Tired, then,
is pronounced like tarred.
Balsam tar on your skin and clothes.
Hot tar in your calves
when you've knelt ten hours
peeling green logs
then walked three miles home.

A useful language
for exhausted men
saving their breath
for the next struggle.

My people say:
a man fights
for whatever he gets.

Pronounce it like an Irishman
just back from Armageddon.

Natural Child

Infant (Anglo-Catholic name
means Prince of Aragon in Spain)
considered for these nine months past
swelling and sorrow, now at last

motherless, fatherless, nameless bone
born of the act of flesh alone:
a disembodied phallus thrust,
knife-like, into the bowl of lust.

Not welcomed here. A spiteful cat
that Christians may not drown, this brat,
a traitor from the very start,
a crowing spy beneath the heart.

Who'd nurse a tumour in her arms?
Behold him at the young girl's breast —
her niplet plunged in his black maw
like the pink knuckle of a fist.

Stars

I wish I knew all the names of the stars.
But I know only the nearest or brightest, and the others
frighten me sometimes —

not you, old Orion, many-buckled hunter,
nor you, Sirius, cross-eyed hound,
nor you, Aldebaran, bloodshot eye of the bull;

I can pull you down
into the matchbox of my mind.

But I wish I knew
the names of the others.

I would say them aloud now as I walk
alone through the woods and down to the frozen river.

Beets

Swollen to bursting like a pod, her ripeness
tense as a vegetable's (one senses
something about to snap and plop open)
the young expectant mother
gathers beets in her garden.

Their stalks and smeared leaves
could have been crushed in a wound to staunch it.
The roots themselves resemble
sickening cores hung with shredded tissue,
bloody her hands as she harvests them absently,
her eyes unfocused, mouth half-open.

Coming Attraction

By the entrance to
the temple of dreams

stands the naked likeness
of a brass-skinned actress

with a monstrous vulva
in schoolboy crayon

and a red wax brassiere
stamped "Quebec Board of Censors."

Belatedly, for Carol on St. Valentine's Day, 1945

Because I hooted
at the hearts and flowers,
the dried-lily-scented
velvet and meringue
card that you gave me,
I am condemned
to recall forever
how your hands shook
as they tore that heart into shreds,
how when you turned away
your face was that of a child
asked a question he can't hope to answer.

The Palomino Stallion

Though the barn is so warm
that the oats in his manger,
the straw in his bed
seem to give off smoke —

though the wind is so cold,
the snow in the pasture
so deep he'd fall down
and freeze in an hour —

the eleven-month-old
palomino stallion
has gone almost crazy
fighting and pleading
to be let out.

Birth

It's five o'clock in the morning and the new-dropt calf
lies on the fresh clean straw while the milky daylight
softens the golden blanket the cobwebbed bulb
hung from the ceiling spreads over his small wet haunches.

I have brought you here
to share in this wonder. Do not think I trick you
though the red and white mess still hangs from her—
               this is part of the miracle.
Watch how the mother
eats from the manger, lifts up her head,
crooking her neck around the stanchion,
to stare at me or at him,
her eyes never changing
expression as they move
from one to the other.

Witness to Murder

The cameraman must be running backwards
in front of the soldiers and their prisoner
who wears black shorts and a sportshirt
imprinted with sunflowers and daisies
and has sandals on his feet
and does not look as he understands
that he is about to die.
           But we know
he would not be there on the screen
unless something horrible
were in store for him.
           And I hear myself talking
to his picture, as I haven't talked
to a picture since I was ten:
           Make a run for it! I shout.

There's a chance you'll make it.
Grab for a gun, maybe you'll take
one of the bastards with you.

                    But he can't hear me.

He keeps on walking.

A Psalm of Onan for Harp, Flute and Tambourine

When I was twelve I was kidnapped and sold as a slave
to the daughter of the Emperor:
I wore my hair long with a scarlet band across my forehead;
otherwise, I was perfectly naked except
for bracelets of gold on my ankles and wrists;
it was her whim
to hang little bells from my penis.
When she breakfasted
at a little Japanese table
facing a window
overlooking the sea,
it was my privilege to bring her
iced juice and grapes
and a single rose
on a silver tray.

When I was thirteen
I was permitted to kiss her feet.
Her cousins admired me.
The master of the kitchen
was careful not to bruise me.
When I carried
messages to her lovers
I wore sandals
made from Spanish leather.

When I was fourteen
I rode behind her
on a white mule

when she and her lover
sported with hounds and falcons.
Sometimes it pleased her
to have her wenches
play with me lewdly.

When I was fifteen
I was put to war;
and, being so brave and clever,
was made a freeman
and captain of a thousand.
When I was sixteen
I conquered a city.
When I was seventeen
the Emperor ennobled me.

When I was eighteen
I married his daughter.
Ah! How well I remember
how she cried out when
my sword of bone
plunged into her body,
how my hot seed scalded
her gasping thighs...

When I was nineteen
I became an Emperor.

How He Lost the Respect of a Friend
by Pointing at the Moon

Tonight I looked up from my work and saw the sky through
      a window of the newsroom,
a white moon drifting in a blood-red haze like a woman in a
      white dress, the ghost of a woman who died by fire,
like a goddess come back from the time when men knew their gods
      and feared them

(now there is only the nagging discomfort of being unable
        to recall a familiar name).

I turned to the man at the next desk and pointed to the window.
"The moon is beautiful tonight," I said.
He muttered one word and looked away. I could see he was
        embarrassed.
It was as though one of us was disfigured and the other,
        in his generosity,
had pretended not to see.
Now I had broken the rules of the game.
I had forced him to look.
We had become strangers to one another—
staring at a white-filmed eye, a white club foot.

The Life Wish

Twice in my lifetime
I've chosen a place for the rope—
why is it, I wonder,
I never think of poison and seldom of water.
Once it was a beam
in a sawmill: comedian even then, I imagined
men walking to work past my swinging body.
Another time a drainpipe. To think a rope
and a five inch pipe
will solve problems
unresolved by philosophy!
But I see now
what I always wanted
was not to die
but to come back to life:
as though a corpse would come alive
by breaking its neck.
                    Now when I read
how a man laid his face
by an exhaust pipe and wrapped his head

in a raincoat to make sure,
I think of a corpse
who doesn't want to be dead
breathing carbon monoxide
because he thinks
it will give him life again.

When We Danced

When we danced, we boys and girls,
the village was deserted, every house was in darkness.
There was only the moon and our orange lanterns,
for everyone came to the hall to be with us:
babies asleep in their mothers' arms,
children clapping their hands,
old men and women
stamping their feet in time to the music!

The Critic

Of the critic, let it be recalled
how at Knox College he used to keep
a chamber mug beneath his bed
lest the floors of the long dark hallway chill his feet.

The All Night Diner

The man in the next booth pleads for forgiveness.
Each time our eyes meet I read the same questions:
Who am I? How did I get here? What have I done?
What must I do to make you love me again?

And we're almost strangers. Though I've seen enough
to know he's the kind of drunk who can hold down a job
by working twice as hard as anybody else
days he's sober enough to work:
                                        his face is the same
as those of the winos who spend every day
making chin music on the riverbank
back of the Chinese laundry, but their hands are as soft
as a priest's or a banker's. Not his. After forty years
of punching stone walls to prove he's a man,
of clutching that last shred of dignity
that won't let him spill a drop of his hot pork gravy
(first food in three days) though every blood vessel
burst with the effort of keeping the spoon from shaking.
There can come a time
when holding a spoon like a man will save a man's soul.

The Actress Performs before the Wicked King to Implore Mercy for Her Lover

From the high window
of my hospital room,
I see my wife
whose name
for months now
has been
Claudine Claudine
Claudine Claudine
Claudine
—by whom

I measure
time
here
where clocks
are not
timepieces
and watches
are kept
for the dead
—see her
as a camera sees
an actress
putting on her role;
halfway across
the parking lot
she has
almost
perfected it,
her performance
could be screened
almost uncut:
a girl dressed
in her happiest colours
hurrying
good
news
to her lover.

Sweet smiling fraud
who,
if her muscles
failed her,
would slice off
part of
her lips
with a razor.

Only the Wind

A howling mad man
rattles the locked doors
of our storm-stayed car.

Don't fear, my sweet,
it is only the wind.
See —
I hold a match to the glass,

his crazed white face
runs down like tears.

I reach my hands
under your sweater,
under your wool mackinaw —
it is as though your blood
seeped through my skin,
into my veins.

We are so close
I don't know
whose pulse I feel.

Nobody knows
what is true,
what is real.

Oh, my darling, my precious, I will call you
all the timeworn names
and they will not sound stupid;

and when you leave me — even when you go
only for a little while
I say that you leave me —

I will hate myself for the times
I have been and will be cruel:

tomorrow we will meet again
in the real world
and you will utter
some idiot remark

and I will not be sly or quick enough
to disguise my disgust.

But for now,
for a moment,
I hold you safe.

Lie quiet, sweet.
It is only the wind.

Hide and Seek

When my sister
and I played
hide and seek
a thousand
years ago,

she was always
the first one
caught and I
the last;

when we hid
in the privy,
for instance,
she would
bar the door
that was never
shut except
when someone
was there,

while I
would leave
it open
and stand
behind it,
laughing to myself

—that was
30 years ago
yet when I
think of it
I feel as
guilty as when
I was five,

if I believed
in God
would ask
him to
forgive me

for being one
of those
who know
how to hide.

Semi-Private Room

"Mr. Nowlan, are you asleep?"
In the morning he will waken me with his whistling.
He may even be singing when I open my eyes,
for he sings while the nurses cleanse his wound,
hums when they bathe him:
dance tunes of the 1920s and Scottish marches.
"Time to rise and shine, Mr. Nowlan!"
Now, in the orange darkness he is silently praying
that I don't hear his voice blurred by tears,

cracked from exertion,
praying the pillows sufficed
to muffle his sobbing.
"Mr. Nowlan, are you asleep?"

Confession

Beloved, it frightens me
how all things circle and meet.

I have singled you out
from all the world.

When you lie naked beneath me
or when only our fingertips
touch on the street,
I love you so gently
I become a saint
and would preach to the birds,
had they no better music.

Yet nothing is simple:
all things circle and meet.

The man who took his pleasure
of the young girl's body
and then strangled her
and threw her in the sewer
like a used condom—

there was a moment
before he gave way
to terror
when he studied her knees
like a famished boy,

an instant when he noted
how the spring wind
played with her hair
like young deer in a wheatfield
(he too was a sentimentalist)

and I, beloved,
lightly kissing your breasts
(do you remember, my little jester,
how you told me once
to be less gentle
with the sacred grotto
between your thighs
because, darling, it won't break)

might love you less
if I did not know
that other so well
had not talked with him
far into the night.

The Fat Man's Poem

A fat man is lying on a bed in a furnished room in Pimlico.
He is writing with a mechanical pencil on a sheet torn from
        a child's exercise book.
His writing board is a magazine — at intervals he doodles
        spectacles and mustaches on Elizabeth Taylor,
        Richard Burton and three anonymous models
clad in made-in-America sweaters of washable Orlon.

He props himself up on an elbow and writes:
In those days I was as innocent as one of the legendary child-saints.
Then, after a pause: *But aren't innocence and sainthood incompatible?*

He lights a cigarette and, from habit, because he has always been poor
counts those left in the package.

He wishes he were a painter or a singer,
how he covets the hands and eyes of Paul Klee,
how jealous he is, sometimes, of applause and of money—
though he is thirty-two years old
he plays records with his eyes shut
and pretends it is he who is singing!

So this is one of those who would change the world!
He is very disgusted with himself today
because he has waited for the voices
and they haven't come
       (*pretentious balderdash* he scribbles on his sheet of paper).

Then, suddenly, he writes:
A fat man is lying on a bed in a furnished room in Pimlico.
Soon his pencil is racing across the paper;
and he forgets about cigarettes, forgets about everything,
until it is finished
and he reads what he has written
and doesn't know whether to be proud or ashamed.

The Gardens
of the Wind

The Gardens of the Wind

First Voice:
The daisies are growing through the eye sockets of the skull.
They reach up for the sun
as everything that lives
reaches up for the sun.
           (Even vegetables go crazy
in blind cellars, the paranoid potatoes
sprouting mad tentacles that grope towards a light
that can neither foresee nor remember.)

The daisies are growing through the eye sockets of the skull.

If we had discovered this sooner
we'd have gathered stones
         of a particular
shape
    and colour
and piled them one on top of the other.
We'd have played shepherds' pipes
and beaten drums.
        We'd have linked hands
with strangers
      and danced
         as flames dance,
leaping
    higher and higher.

Sound: *Marching drum beats — quick march — background for following:*

Second Voice:
The engineers have come into our fields.
They do not make paths and keep to them
but walk where they please, trampling the grain.
Their grins are lordly; they wear
mysterious hats and boots.

The engineers have come into our pastures.
They are city-bred and have never learned
the importance of gates,
                              so cattle and sheep
roam the roads.
                    Old men who give
names to the years
                          will remember this
as the year the animals
raided the vegetable gardens.
                          Yes, they will say,
that was the same year
the war started. Every sunset
was the colour of blood, they'll say,
barns were struck by lightning
and the cattle —
                    the cattle everywhere
broke out and raided the gardens.
That was the year
the war started.

Third Voice:
The engineers
have come into our yards.
They pump water and drink from our wells
without performing the small but necessary
ceremonies.
                  They do not knock at the door
and agree it is hot,
                        hotter
than it was yesterday,
                        hotter
than they hope it will be
tomorrow or the day after.
                          The woman watches them
from her kitchen window, standing
far back from the glass
and slightly to one side.

Their laughter is lordly.
They peer through their instruments
and send messages to one another
with their arms.
Their hands
are gloved in soft leather.
They drive
stakes in the earth.

First Voice:
And one old man
tears out the stakes
and burns them.
One old man.

Second Voice:
What was it the old nut kept yelling?

Third Voice:
Damned if I know. It sounded like:
Thou shalt not crucify the land.

Sound: *Judge's gavel*

Third Voice:
Oyez. Oyez. Oyez.
The charge against the said
is that he did knowingly,
wilfully and with
malice aforethought
remove and destroy
an unspecified number
of wooden stakes,
the property of
Our Lord the King—

Voices:
God save the King!

Fourth Voice:
—and did thereby
give aid
and comfort
to the enemy—

Voices:
Frustrate their knavish tricks!

Third Voice:
Hang the son of a bitch!

Fourth Voice:
—and did also endanger
our national sovereignty
and territorial
integrity, did, in short,
offend
against his God,
                  his King
                        and his Country.

Music: *O Canada—few bars*

First Voice:
The wind has no love
for the trees,
                  yet there is grass growing
in the wounds of the elm,
twelve feet from the ground. Who
but the wind
could have made such gardens?

Second Voice: *(To be read seriously, not as parody.)*
We shall fight them on the beaches
and on the landing grounds.
We shall fight them in the hills
and in the streets.

We shall fight on and on,
and we shall never surrender.

Third Voice: *(To be read seriously, not as parody.)*
If I advance, follow me.
If I die, avenge me.
If I retreat, kill me.

First Voice:
The boulder cannot see the rain
whose fingers it has directed
for so many thousands of years
that now there is a hollow
in the stone
         and there, too,
               the wind has planted.

Sound: *SIEG HEIL! SIEG HEIL! SIEG HEIL!*
    (Incidentally, the following is the Italian Fascist cheer.)

Sound: *EIA EIA EIA ALALA! EIA EIA EIA ALALA!*

Third Voice: *Hail, Caesar! We who are about to die, salute you.*

Fourth Voice:
And the Lord God of Israel poured out His wrath
upon the Jebusites.

First Voice:
One day
       so far from now
that only the most learned men
will care whether or not
our civilization
ever existed,
        one day the grass
will crack open
this rock
      like an apple.

Sound: *Military drum: quick march: background for following:*

Second Voice:
The caterpillar men have come into our fields.
Their machines are like the knives of fishermen
that slit open the bellies of trout.
The caterpillar men have come into our fields,
the caterpillar men and the dynamite men
have come into our fields,
into our pastures,
into our yards.
        The dynamite men have come into our fields;
and the glass in the windows
                trembles;
the spoons on the table,
            the knives and the forks
rattle against the plates;
            the cups and saucers
mill about,
      chattering;
         the very house
shivers almost
      as a man shivers
when his teeth
      are set on edge.

Third Voice:
The dynamite men have taken over our land.

First Voice:
The plow is husband to the earth.
The earth is a woman
        and the plowshare
             a phallus.

Sound: *Judge's gavel*

Fourth Voice:
Prisoner, what is your name?

First Voice:
I lived here before God was born,
before he called back
the innumerable separate particles of himself,
before the god-spark flew out
of everything that lived,
                    and the sky was full
of small bright bits of God returned
to rejoin his body.
                    I wonder how many
millions of eagles
it took to make his eyes, and how long he waited
for the soul of the great tree that became
a single hair on his smallest finger.

Sound: *Derisive laughter silenced by Gavel*

Fourth Voice:
Prisoner, how do you plead?

Third Voice:
There is no order
                    except that
which the mind confers:
                    the small boy exploring
the swamp,
                    tasting the mystery
of the orchid,
                    the only one
                    ever found there,
part of the apocrypha
                    of one man's life,
the miraculous
                    . infancy of us all,
the small boy
                    contemplating the orchid,
and, of course, he becomes
a prince reared by swineherds
for fear of his uncle,

the usurper,
        but there is more to it,
                much more,
the small boy contemplating the orchid
for days
      or weeks
          or months
              or years
                  or centuries
—the beginning of a myth.
           There is no order
except that
        which the mind confers.
           There is no order—

Sound: *Derisive laughter interrupted by drum roll and trumpets*
      fanfare

Fourth Voice:
Prisoner, I heartily wish it were in my power to
               sentence you
to be hanged, disembowelled and castrated—

Sound: *Vigorous applause and cheering*

Fourth Voice:
Since, unfortunately, that is impossible, it is
          my order that
you be returned to the house from whence you came,
          there to be
afflicted by the ridicule and resentment of
          your family, your
friends and your neighbours until such time as
          it shall please
God to terminate your existence—

Sound: *More applause and cheering*

Fourth Voice:
—And may God have mercy upon your soul!

Music: *RCAF march past*

Third Voice:
And now the local news.
Wednesday, January 25, 1940.
Five months ago, Michael David O'Sullivan, a
                    76-year-old
farmer battled with the RCAF and lost.
O'Sullivan removed and destroyed the surveyors'
                    stakes and at
one point threatened government officials with
                    a rifle, in
the course of his attempts to prevent the
                    expropriation
of his land as site for an RCAF Flying Training
                    School.
Ironically, O'Sullivan was buried in the family
                    cemetery,
less than one hundred yards from a runway that
                    covers what
was once a pasture for his cattle.
I have just been handed a bulletin. Marshal
                    Petain today—

Sound: *Roar of Second World War Aircraft*

Second Voice:
Yet, they were beautiful in their way, war planes.
Butter-coloured, they were, swarming like bees.

First Voice:
Or like palomino colts,
                    leaping
from cloud to cloud.

                    Yes,
they were
            beautiful.

Fourth Voice:
And they were ours.

Third Voice:
Ours.

Second Voice: *(diminishing)*
Ours.
        Ours.
                Ours.

Sound: *Planes gradually rising*

Third Voice:
We were all children.
There were Norwegians,
Australians, New Zealanders,
Poles, Frenchmen,
Englishmen, Canadians,
and wild back-thumping,
chest-punching,
rebel-yelling
Texan irregulars.

Sound: *Planes reach crescendo and out*

First Voice:
We were all children.

Second Voice:
We were all children.
                    They wore blue tunics,
the colour of the sky before a summer rain,
the wedge hats,
            and sometimes

there were pistols on their hips,
and a few of them patrolled
the tall barbed wire fences
with rifles and bayonets.
                              We
went barefoot and almost naked
during the summer.

First Voice:
We were all children.

Third Voice:
Loving them,
                    we talked in their slang.

Second Voice:
Cheerio, old chap. Keep your pecker up. Smashing.

Third Voice:
He's a good old boy, you all. Hear?

Second Voice:
We said, "hello" and "goodbye"
in Norwegian and Polish.

Music: *"Beer Barrel Polka" blended with "I've Got Sixpence"*
          cut

Third Voice:
We were all children.
                              Aching
to grow taller,
                    knowing
when we grew tall enough
that we, too, could have wings
                              and fly.

Sound: *Sound of planes*

Second Voice:
When one of the student-pilots was killed
the flag on the hangar
was flown at half-staff.
We could see it clearly
from the schoolyard,
although separated from it
by a valley and a river.
                    We pretended to grieve.

Sound: *Drum beats: Slow march: Out after third voice*

Third Voice:
We were all children.
                    We pretended to grieve.
Knowing no name but "grief"
for the wonder we felt,
tasting the memory.

Second Voice:
And, of course, we were envious.

Third Voice:
Yes, we envied them their death.

Second Voice:
In our dreams we saw them die
like lightning bolts thrown from the sky.

Third Voice:
The day the war ended,
the teacher told us
we could go home.
                    We cheered ourselves sore.
And, afterwards,
                    because the war was over
I went into the woods alone
and lay down in the moss
                    and cried.

First Voice:
Grown men go to war
less because they want to kill
than because
they desire to die.

Third Voice:
I went into the woods alone
and lay down in the moss
                              and cried.

First Voice:
There is no order
                    except that
which the mind confers.
There was the star that fell
by daylight,
              and the boy was afraid
to tell even those who sat
in the same room with him.
                              It happened that
he glanced at the window
an instant before
it struck the earth,
              a great wheel of flame
fallen
      from the chariot of heaven,
a crescendo
      of sparks
              in the backyard,
the ordinary
              backyard
where he had played
for as long
              as he could
                              remember,
and he never afterwards
looked for evidence
of its fall.

To touch the world
with the most private
parts of self,
            to find
a child's dreams
encompass history.
            That
is the lost
key to the circle.

Sound: *Buildings being wrecked behind following:*

Second Voice:
The destroyers have come
        with their Morning Stars,
                with their iron pendulums.
The destroyers have come
        with their sledge hammers and fire axes
                —the nails scream
                as they're torn from the wood.

Third Voice:
The barracks are gone.
The mess halls are gone.
The hangars are gone.

Second Voice:
The earth has made no provision
        for the works of man.
Concrete does not grow with the rain,
        nor does the sun
                        strengthen it.
Everything that lives
        is in league with the grass.

Third Voice:
In the cold,
            the crust
                    of the earth

stirs
    like the flesh
        of a woman,
shivering.

Second Voice:
The concrete gives way.

Third Voice:
The sun
    opens it
        like a flower.

Second Voice:
And grass
grows in the wounds.

First Voice:
Who but the wind
could have made
        such gardens?

Third Voice:
The daisies are growing through the eye sockets
            of the skull.

Sound: *Judge's gavel*

Fourth Voice:
Prisoner, what is your name?

Between Tears and Laughter

Intimates and Strangers

How little we know
one another, ever.
Reminders of it:
                meeting
an old friend's wife
for the first time,
sensing how different
he is with her,
hearing him use words
that don't seem
to belong to him (not
that they are exotic or,
in themselves, important),
perceiving the constraint
in certain familiar
movements, the greater
freedom in others
equally familiar,
as the two of us,
she and I, without willing it,
tug him first one
way, then the other
(for a few moments,
for an instant at the very
least, he is more a stranger
to her than I am
simply because she
knows him so much
better);
        or finding anybody
you know well in
any place where one of you
feels at home and not
the other: that is an almost
equally good example
of what I mean — my brother
welcoming me to his office,

the infinitely subtle
falsity, the smile
friendlier by
an iota than it need be.

The Moon Landing

They tell me the moon
has ceased to be mysterious.
But what mystery did it ever
present to them? How many
of them ever even looked at it?
Be honest. Were you ever once
afraid of moonlight,
of what you felt it doing to
your genitals, your spine,
the hair at the back
of your neck?
Were you ever tempted
to bathe naked in it, rolling
in the grass?
When you realized men
were about to land there
was there a moment
when you were frightened
of what might happen
when they touched?
Did you laugh at yourself
childishly wondering
if it would explode
and fragments of it
rain on our earth
while terrible things
happened to the tides?
And if the answer is
"yes," did anything change for you
when they told you such emotions

were no longer the fashion?
Their rockets changed nothing.
The moon is mysterious
still to those who have been alone with her.

Decline and Fall

I look at the rulers
of the world and see
madness in their faces.
Their eyes contain that
which makes it seem possible
they roll on the floor
like Plantagenets,
chewing the carpet, or
there is nothingness
in their eyes and they imitate
laughter as though in
mockery of all
that makes other men
laugh. At midnight
their eyes follow me
and I'm afraid.
How many of his
contemporaries knew
Caligula was insane,
or Nero, or Tiberius?
Their courtiers must
have known. Others
must have at least
suspected. But no doubt
there were many who
said, You know, I believe
the emperor is crazy,
said it without being
altogether convinced
of it as I'm saying

it even now.
The evidence is there
but the mind cannot
bring itself
wholly to believe in
a dynasty of mad men.

Friends

On nights like this
I wish I had a friend
or better yet two
friends, a man and a woman,
who knew me better
than they knew each other,
who would talk but
not talk too much,
who would make me laugh
and laugh with me,
who would say something
to surprise me
occasionally but
only occasionally,
who would not
think of conversation
as putty with which
to plug the silences
or as chess played
with invisible pieces
on an invisible board,
and who, above all,
were content in
my clothes closet or
in the basement
behind the furnace
where they'd stay
while I worked

or slept or was happier
alone;
      on a night like this
I could go upstairs or
go down and
poke my head around
the furnace, say
to them: "Hey! Wake up!
I'm lonesome."

Dead Letter

I wanted to speak, but could not.
I stood mute for so long
that I came to despise my mouth
and would have been almost agreeable
to having its silence punished
by permanence: the penances include
the ground invited to
open and swallow,
the stammering tongue
torn out by the roots.

Today at last I was able to tell you:
I love you and wish we could be together always.

I say it easily now over and over again.

And you are so pleased with it
I can't allow myself to
stop, even for an instant,
although I knew,
almost as soon as I spoke,
that I'd waited too long, that
everything had changed and
not a word I said to you was true.

Low Cloud Ceiling

The Air Canada Vanguard to Montreal
flies so low this grey morning
that it looks to me
about six inches long.

What if this were another age
would I mistake it
for a bird — no,
it resembles a fish.

It's as if I were standing
on the floor of a lake,
looking up at a trout swimming
just beneath the
surface of the water.

Accounts of Captain Cook's
first visit to Australia
report the aborigines
could not see his ships,
though they anchored only
a few hundred yards away,
could not see his men
when they rowed ashore,
although they were almost
near enough to touch,
could see nothing
out of the ordinary
because nothing
in their experience
had prepared them
for such sights.

One Night in Christmas Week

I've been waiting for somebody to ask me
where did the trees come from,
they weren't here last night.
                              I'll tell how
the brooms of a squadron
of gargantuan witches
nosedived to earth like the whistling Stukas
of my warlike childhood.
                              The eyes of the houses
are too far apart, their noses
too large for beauty. They are women
with the faces of cows, Egyptian.
As for picket fences:
hardly anybody notices
how they vanish into thin air
as soon as it's winter.
                              I see all that
by the lights of the parking lot,
and a small boy,
too young to be out at this hour,
takes off his mittens
before making a snowball,
throws it so miraculously
high and hard,
for no apparent reason at all.

Why He Wanted to Abolish Capital Punishment

When I was a boy I imagined
I was motivated by my
extraordinary compassion.
As a youth I laughed and said:
"I suppose the real reason is
I'm scared they'll get *me*."
Then I became a man and discovered

I'd always been afraid
if it didn't end
there'd come a time
when I wouldn't be able
to stop myself:
one day I'd have to go down and tell them
to forget about the fee,
I'd be hangman for nothing,
just for the fun of it,
if they'd let me.

Sunday Driver

Everybody laughs when I tell
about the man in the black Chevrolet
who wanted to murder me today
at an intersection when the light changed
and I was slow getting away.

Everybody laughs.
But I saw the hatred take his face
in its hands and twist
his jaw in one direction,
his forehead in another.

He'd have killed me if there'd been a button
marked "Death" for him to press.

Mistaken Identity

It's good sometimes
to be mistaken for
someone else, although
it usually ends
badly.

Getting down from
a bus in Boston
in 1951, when I was
seventeen, I stepped
into the arms of
a fat woman whose
breath smelled of
beer, and she kissed
me on the mouth and
said, Walter, Walter,
and I was so lonesome
that for a second I
was almost tempted
to pass myself
off as whoever she
thought I was; but
what I did was
mumble something
about there being
a mistake, and even
before I spoke she
had realized that
and was pushing
me away.
       Another time
a beautiful young girl
blew a kiss at me
from the open window
of a cab in New Haven,
Connecticut, and
shouted, Hi, Davie!
She wore a red scarf,
I remember. And I waved.
Then because I wanted
her to keep smiling
at me, lovingly, I
very quickly
turned away.

Fair Warning

I keep a lunatic chained
to a beam in the attic. He
is my twin brother whom
I'm trying to cheat
out of his inheritance.
It's all right for me
to tell you this because
you won't believe it.
Nobody believes anything
that's put in a poem.
I could confess to
murder and as long as
I did it in a verse
there's not a court
that would convict me.
So if you're ever
a guest overnight
in my house, don't
go looking for
the source of any
unusual sounds.

The House Painters

The heads and shoulders
of the men painting the house
keep appearing at windows
and I don't have the gift
of being comfortable
with them.
   I can't
feign blindness
with dignity, as they do,
am too much a coward to

close the curtains
in their faces, and
what can you say to a stranger
who assumes rights
you'd deny a friend
and begrudge a lover?

Domestic Allegories
for John and Elaine Gill

Our new friends, John and Elaine, are refugees
from the bourgeoisie. My wife, Claudine, and I
spring from the lumpenproletariat. Consider that
a preface to the poem. The four of us
have arrived at the same place, where we
seem comfortable together. I love it
that he gives her a bracelet, a bit of
costume jewellery he picked up on the rivershore;
I love it that she can show us
the gift, proudly, with that supreme
innocence that comes after, not before,
experience, and only rarely
comes at all. So I am not saddened by
continual small accidental reminders
that in our beginnings, they and we,
might almost have inhabited
different continents or centuries.
In fact it's an adventure to share
the day with them: there are so many
little allegories, so many symbols
that come alive. This afternoon
their two little boys came asking for something
to drink and Claudine, victoriously,
opened the refrigerator and proclaimed
there was cold orange, cold ginger ale,
cold chocolate milk and cold Coca-Cola,

while Elaine, having learned that too much
can be as dangerous as too little,
looked on in silence,
obviously wishing it wasn't happening.

The Beggars of Dublin

I'd rather beggars made me happy,
I'd like to think of them
as the Greeks did, or my Irish ancestors.
I'd like to wonder
if this little lad blowing
a tin whistle could be Pan, testing me,
or the Christ child
offering himself,
although even those transactions
must have resembled
what goes on
in a used car lot, the host debating
whether the chance of the bum being Apollo
was strong enough to warrant
a jar of good wine, or so slight it was stupid
to invest more
than stale bread and a slice of cold mutton.

I'm ashamed of dropping a shilling
in the tweed cap that seems to contain
only pennies: as the coin leaves my hand
I split into two men, the one a native
sneering at the bleeding American
arrogance of the other, because it is not human
to drop à shilling
into a cap to which everyone else in O'Connell Street
has contributed a total
of less than six pence without feeling
vain, the more if a shilling
is almost as much to you as it is to them.

And if I'd added only a penny
to those given or, what's more likely,
put there as bait, the other fellow would have cursed me
for a miser: in Europe the only thing worse
than a rich Yank is a Yank without money.

And three paces later a woman with eyes the colour
of the inside of a beef kidney
and carrying the kind of baby
whose face always looks as if its pants were dirty,
runs at me, not up to me or toward me, but at me,
saying, for the love of God, mister, and I pass her
two shillings and six pence as though
it were something filthy it was her job to clean up,
and of course she's the mother of the lad
with the whistle who is only a kind of signalman,
and of course she sticks pins in the baby or pinches him,
and of course I feel more of an ass than ever.

A Tiger in the Dublin Zoo

Know that I am Napoleon, the great, the magnificent tiger.
Observe how an emperor
takes possession of the ground
on which he stands, imposes his own order
on the space around him.
                    I walk to and fro,
                        and am never halted.
I stop and turn where I choose.
                    And that
is three feet short
of the end of the cage.
                    No more and no less.
Never once have I forgotten myself
        and been stopped by the bars.
I am Napoleon, the great, the magnificent tiger.

Tolstoy

When Tolstoy lay dying
in the cottage of Ozolin,
stationmaster at Astapovo,
he persisted in moving
his hands — that much
his biographers tell us.

    The truth may be
    it was his right hand only,
    the forefinger outstretched
    that crawled back and forth
    across the blanket,
    writing.

He Finds Himself Alone in the House

I talk out loud
in three different voices.
I try to swallow my nose.
I make up a song called *The Ballad
of the Itching Anus* and sing it.
I dance about
naked, my fat belly
bouncing. I play at being
Silenus, father of Bacchus,
whose statue in
the Victoria and Albert
Museum I so much resemble.
When a slice of beef happens
to fall to the floor
I snatch it up and eat it,
dust and all, my eyes rolling.
I purr like a lion.
Not because I'm drunk or drugged

but because I'm happy and there's nobody
else here, nobody not even myself to deny me
the pleasure of going crazy.

He Grows in Understanding

"Which one of you is Christ?" somebody would shout
and I'd almost always answer,
                              "That's me. I'm him."
They'd throw me down
            and drive spikes through my hands.

That hurt.

              So now I keep my mouth shut.
I'm scared
            and much more modest
            than I used to be.

Survival

The first man who ever stepped on a lion and survived
was Og
who afterwards attributed
his good fortune to his poor eyesight,
he having been unable
to see anything but claws,
teeth and a monstrous body
while his companion
stood transfixed by the indescribably beautiful
visions that he saw with his third good eye.

The Golden Pyramids of the Sun

All truths are half-truths.
     But there is a quietness
between
the condemned and his gaoler,
a quietness
        almost
like the love
between certain hard suspicious men
     doing dangerous work together.

The Iconotrophic Instant
   for Robert Cockburn

The old remember everything:
nothing is lost.
         If your lover outlives you
by half a century and when asked your name
cannot recall it, names are less important
than your falling in the snow that night,
near a bonfire or under a neon light,
and rolling in it like a child
though you were already
the mother of his children.
He never tires of telling it:
"Once, I remember, she slipped
on an ice patch, fell down and rolled over and over
like a kitten or a puppy."
Those who care for his needs
wink at one another, they do not know
he has told them the whole story
of his love for you, of your love for him.
And that old soldier
in the hundred-year-old diary
of an English curate:

Talking of wolves,
he said he remembered,
how every night they came down to drink from the river,
four or five of them, like mastiffs and as big.
The soldiers used to scare them
by snapping the locks
of their flint muskets, making the powder flash.
When the wolves saw it they went away.
They did not like to see that.
"It is nothing to write," the curate wrote,
yet he was wise enough
to record it twice in five months
during which he must have heard it
scores of times.
                    It was one man's history
of the Peninsular men who followed hook-nosed Atty,
not yet Wellington, into Portugal, through Spain,
        across the Pyrenees.

Secular Magic

You're a liar only if
nobody believes you.
                    Which reminds me
of how my eyes listen:
                    when my ears tire
of my favourite music.
I put on the records
and play them for friends,
taking pleasure
proportionate to theirs
                    in sitting slightly apart
and very quietly
studying their faces.

Reunion

Almost from
    the moment
        friends separate, or lovers,
each becomes
    somebody else,
        another
living on
    inside
        the other.

A year passes,
five years, ten.

        Something always dies
        when we meet again.

Why I Am Not More Afraid of the Dark

You are:
        windows.
                That
is the name
        for you.
And the darkness
            moving
within
and behind
        your terrible brightness
is not
    the wings
        of bats caught
in a furnace, not
something nameless
            rising, but
men

and women
behaving like humans.
Still I all but
say it aloud:
Windows.
Humans.
And am grateful
that I possess words:
charms
unknown to animals.

Epistle

Practise religion, Alden, if you must
in the same spirit as you knock on wood,
half-smiling at yourself,
and if you're caught at it,
laugh with the others.
Be ridiculous
as when you reached into an empty pocket
and found an Irish penny, then another,
another and another, until your hand
scarcely could hold them —
that was last summer
and there was an instant,
less than an instant, when you almost believed
the coins would fill the table, overflow,
cover the floor, if you only kept reaching.
You are that much a fool, old friend. Remember it.
Knuckle the woodwork, but refrain from preaching.

He Attempts to Dignify a Quarrel with His Guests

That divine malice of which
the Greeks wrote
at times possesses
me, divine not
being a synonym
for good—the Greeks knew
better, but signifying something
that comes from without and can't be
refused admittance; and malice
in this instance meaning
a kind of mad rage against
barriers. It's as though I'd
stripped myself naked or
almost so and nearly
everybody else who happened
to be present had
put on the blindfolds that
all of us carry with us
and the coveralls
we almost none of us
ever go anywhere
without, and I'd gone
after them with my
teeth and fingernails,
trying to make them
touch me, even with
their fists and boots
—that were better
than pretending nothing
had happened, which is how
most of us spend
most of our lives, pretending
nothing has happened,
so that skill in doing so
is almost the measure
of one's education:
if I tell you I've gone

crazy and am about to
turn into a lion
with wings
and eat you, it's all but certain
you'll murmur, "ah, he began with
a classical reference and is ending
with a biblical symbol,
neat but more
than a little predictable."

Letter to a Young Friend

My young comrade:
                    So you aspire to be
yourself and no one else!
                              An aging freak,
for whom there was no choice, wishes you strength
to bear it should you find that which you seek.

Satori

Hey, there's such a place as Ruanda Urundi!
Given the money I could be there
right now with all of my senses working
like Geiger counters
and pinball machines.
                        I could be walking
into a restaurant,
hungry and thirsty,
looking for beer and something
with plenty of meat, well-salted.
                              I could be listening
to the people of Ruanda Urundi talking
at the tables around me, discussing
whatever it is they discuss

in Ruanda Urundi.
                         If I'd said this
yesterday I'd have been lying
because all I knew
was what I'd heard or read.
                         Today
I could bend down, pick something up and say to you,
look, Ruanda Urundi is as real
as this pebble, this flower, this piece of bone.

The Waiter's Smile

The waiter smiles as he announces
he's not permitted to serve me
an ounce and a half of rum because I'm not
wearing a four-in-hand necktie, but an ascot.
It's a rather sweet smile and he bows slightly,
opens his hands as though throwing away a match
with each of them, simultaneously.
All waiters strive to perfect that smile,
that series of gestures. And I bet the privilege
is rated almost as high as a five dollar tip.
He's telling me there are things
my filthy money can't buy. A footman
may have given the last czar that same smile,
that same little bow, may have opened his hands
in much the same manner when he told him
the soldiers had come to take him away.

The Inhabitants

This house is not ours
  and the land on which it sets
    belongs to the ants
who build pharaonic cities
  and consider mankind
    as only another
natural disaster;
  though our cat would argue,
    having established frontiers
which she patrols
  and tries to extend:
    on her own ground
she'll defy anything
  but if caught infiltrating
    the neighbouring territory
will back off from a kitten,
  so strong is her belief
    in property rights
and national sovereignty;
  and the birds
    who probably think
of the earth
  as men think of the sea
    (it belongs to them but they
can never wholly
  belong to it),
    it's possible
to smile at the robins
  who look like
    Dickensian aldermen
as they play tug of war,
  a bird on one side,
    the whole planet on the other
and the worm
  caught in the middle,
    but the nightjars
inhabit a darker

place in the mind
          for nothing kills
more quickly and cleanly:
          it is as if
              a piece of the sky
fell—
          and lately an animal
              has been raiding the garbage
and digging holes
          in the garden,
              a skunk, we think,
though we've never seen him;
          going out after dark,
              I leave on the porchlight;
coming home
          I keep to the path.

The Cloud Dwellers

The other day I talked
with a man of great dignity
who admitted he had once
wanted to leave his seat
in a DC-8 and climb out
on the wing and, what is more,
still wishes
he'd done it.
              The first time I flew
I couldn't get used
to seeing the clouds
from the other side.
It seemed there had to be
people down there
living in tents
indistinguishable from
those great white
dunes tinged with pink.

Their feet would be the
most remarkable thing
about them, in that
they'd be unblemished.
Of course they'd run
when they heard our
engines, run with
their long hair
streaming out
behind them. They would be young
and as they ran they would
laugh, wrap their
laughter around them as
earth children do when
they're pretending
there's nothing of
which they need be
afraid, that it's only a game.

A Little-Travelled Road

A trailer, a sign
reading *Bill's Eats*, somewhere
on the road between
Campbellton and
St. Leonard.
                    Everything except
                    the music stops
                    when I open the
                    screen door:
                    Hank Williams singing,
                    "Your Cheatin' Heart."
The locals,
country boys and their
girls drop everything
and wait. I have the irrational
feeling there's something

I'm expected to do or
say and that I won't
realize what it is
until too late. Then
I have the even more
absurd feeling that
they somehow knew
I was going to
stop here, that they've
been waiting for me.
I can imagine them
saying to each other
on the steps of the
church or at the
filling station
this morning:
Did you know a funny
thing is going to
happen at Bill's
this afternoon?
Better be there.
You wouldn't want to miss it.
One thing I know for certain.
if I'm still here when
the song ends nobody
will play another.
There'll be no sounds then
except the electric
fan humming, vegetable
oil sizzling, the
Niagara roar of
root beer in the
throat of the stranger.

A North American in Europe

I have travelled enough to know
I'll be disappointed
if I go to Waterloo
and don't see the battle.
                              So many places
exist in time
                  rather than in space,
or so my mind tells me.
                              Yet I'm so credulous
I keep expecting
to meet ghosts
and am always surprised
when I find none.

Canadian January Night

Ice storm: the hill
a pyramid of black crystal
down which the cars
slide like phosphorescent beetles
while I, walking backwards in obedience
to the wind, am possessed
of the fearful knowledge
my compatriots share
but almost never utter:
this is a country
where a man can die
                        simply from being
caught outside.

The Hand Puppet's Song

My name is Maximo.
I live in a drawer. I sleep
until the woman invokes me.
"Maximo," she calls.
"Maximo, little clown,
little wise clown, Maximo,
come, speak
to the children, shake
your cap and bells, Maximo, speak."

And the children, when I address them,
shout "Maximo! Maximo! Maximo!
Maximo! We love you!"

Afterwards (I know,
although it happens
while I sleep),
they tell the woman,
my priestess, their teacher,
something of what
I said to them,
having all but forgotten
that she, too, was there.

I am grandfather
and grandson to Osiris,
thunder-voiced Osiris,
whom no less than
three hundred priests
wheeled in a colossal
car through the
streets of Thebes.

The Traveller

It was not the weight
of my feet that tired me,
                        nor the steepness
of the hill,
            but thinking too hard
on how much farther
I had to walk.

            You may have seen me
unstrap from my back
that trunk, half as long as a coffin,
and drop it in the ditch.

It was my destination.

Kyran's Christening

I suppose it's because we're on foot I'm reminded
of a story by De Maupassant, the lot of us walking
toward the church with the baby in its christening gown,
not merely a group of persons together but a small
religious procession, in which nobody feels obliged
to put on a solemn face. We laugh softly
out of kindness toward one another. It's still morning.
The sun is shining
on Kyran. Her eyes aren't in focus yet.
I know that. If I didn't I might think she knew
more than was good for her; she looks so wise,
so pitilessly wise, and powerful for all
her tininess.
            I don't like the priest
who looks bored and reads too fast
and without expression.
                        I don't like
his taking off his vestments

before we leave, tossing them over
the baptismal font.
                    But I suppose he's
at home here: elsewhere it's the most infrequent
guest who is courteous even
to carpets and chairs;
                        and, after all, he's not
performing for me but for his god
whom one presumes will hear him
no matter how bad an actor
he may be.
            Thus Kyran Pittman
renounces the devil and all his works.
"Our baby," one of us calls her, and we laugh
softly, because she isn't,
not really.

The Married Man's Poem

Five years married
and he has never once
wished he dared kill her,
                        which means
they're happy enough.
But it isn't love.

Barbara's Poem

It has been so long, Barbara, since I last wrote a poem for you
and that time, if I remember, I compared your kisses to wine
—I hadn't tasted wine or I'd have known
kisses taste like wine only when one or both have been
        drinking it.
And I may have said your teeth were like pearls
which is a rather horrible thought now that I consider it:

think of watching a girl open her mouth
and finding she has pearl-inlaid dentures.

Now, all these years later, the most beautiful thing I
        recall about you
happened one of those summer days
that had two afternoons, one before and one after supper.

We were lying in the grass — I don't know what was growing there
that day but it was a place for violets
and buttercups, and just beyond the fence
there was wintergreen, and wild strawberries.

My hands were partners with the sun in warming you,
when a field mouse popped out of nowhere
to scuttle across your naked belly
and you were such a child you only laughed.

Meeting

You are as perversely beautiful
as a boy's incestuous wish, the invocation
of an old man at odds with time.
When I look down into your face,
your right eye half-hidden by your hair
as though you peered through rushes,
my desire is so strong,
your response so certain
that even at this party
where the conversation undulates
like the wings of locusts
and only the lights
from our eyes
touch,
your knees
open like a flower.

My grandfather owned a factory
in Yugoslavia, but we were not Slavs.
That was a province that had been taken
from Hungary, but we were not Hungarians.
My father still talks
of how things were done in peacetime.
I tell him, Father, this is peacetime.
Yes, he says, but it is not the same.

If we had gone to bed
together, we might have lain
all night weeping

      for your parents and grandparents,
      for my parents and grandparents,
      for Hungary and Yugoslavia,
      for those who belong nowhere
      and for those who belong to one place
      too much to belong anywhere else.

Perhaps you are not
as I imagine you,
but each of us has only
himself and his
imagination,
so if you say
none of this is true
it won't matter
because I could never love you
enough to make this
your poem and not mine.
Until this moment
I believed you made me kiss you
like a father, no,
it was like a young uncle:
you turned your head
so I could not reach your mouth

and brushed your lips
against my cheek.

    Now it seems
    we kissed
    like lovers
    who have learned
    it is no use
    yet cannot avoid
    some kind of goodbye.

Two Poems to Accompany a Photograph of Sylvia

    I

My young sister, born of
our own love rather
than that of others, and out
of the mind's loneliness instead
of the body's no more terrible
hunger, my Sylvia, my
pleasure in your
loveliness arises
not from the pit of
my stomach as with others
almost as symmetrical
but is almost wholly
contained by
the eyes themselves:
for your sake rather
than my own, I placidly
rejoice that your face
is that of an Egyptian
princess when they
strode naked but for numerous
strands of jewels,

that your breasts are
so proud they'd smile
serenely if they could
at being compared
to anything other
than themselves.
Pomegranates! I would be
unhappy only
for your sake if
this were not so, if
you were ugly. For
I have no wish
to possess you,
am content
that we have chosen,
laughingly,
laughingly to be
sister and brother.

II

My Sylvia you
        are the earlier truer
                Cinderella crying
your cinnamon apples
        to the impervious stars:

Good people all, who will buy from me?

And the lamas come.
        It does not matter
                if this is Baltimore
or the first year
        of the railway.
                        The lamas come.

They appoint you
        bride,

undress you with daggers,
but you, born
    into this tradition
        are not made drunk
by your fear, it lifts you,

fits you for your office, princess.

Your dignity
    would give pause
        had he half a mind

even to death.

Sharon, Sharon

Sharon, you are
one of the reasons
we needn't be
afraid of computers.
I touch the tip
of your nose with
the tip of my finger,
in salute; you
are singular,
a woman whose
loveliness no
micrometer could ever
appraise, it
is so wholly human.

At the Airport

A weekend's absence alters you,
me old bawd, or perhaps it's the oddity
of watching for you from a distance,
of looking through
so many strangers.
                    Whatever the reason
you're different enough
that I greet you
                    somewhat formally
as may befit
            one's beloved come home
safe from a journey.

Playground

Claudine says one of the kids, named Miklos,
wants to kiss and hug all the others,
which frightens them so much they bite him,
the little devils,
                    whereupon he cries
a little while
and then talks to himself in Hungarian.

Anthem
for Charlotte

We forget.
            When I realized last summer
that to me young girls without exception
are beautiful,
            I thought to myself: so
this is what it's like
to be middle-aged.

Yes, we forget.
For I felt the same
                    when I was sixteen;
I remember now.
                    Nothing has changed
except time has given
                    to them a freedom
different from but equivalent
to that it has taken
                    from me;
they wear it so
their legs replace the sun, as candles do;
and I, desirous
                    of them all,
begin to comprehend
why in the great days the oldest and
supposedly wisest
                    men did not think it
beneath them to kneel
as priests to girls
                    as young and
doubtlessly simpler,
                    asking no more
than to offer them
                    oranges
and peacock feathers
                    and flowers.

Poem for George Frederick Clarke

Once again the act as metaphor
                    solidifies,
I feel
      the laying on of hands,
                    reading
the inscription in an old book
given me today by an old man

who has written:

> I have drunk deep from this;
> now it is your turn to drink, and to keep.

There is more
underneath
in Latin.
And it is not
in the least important
that I can't translate it.
For I know what it means.
It was his generation's
way of transforming
an occasion into
a ceremony.
And I wish
I knew some equally grand and simple
response,
certain words or gestures
expressing love with such
dignity, yes
and such reticence.

He Raids the Refrigerator and Reflects on Parenthood

Nowlan, you maudlin boob,
almost blubbering because
two hours ago at the party
your son said, I'll be
fifteen tomorrow, can I
have a whole pint of beer?
Grinning so he could say
it was a joke if you
took it that way; but he
was serious all right:
it's like music sometimes
how serious he can be
about small matters

which you're thereby
reminded were
important.
                And you hesitated,
not because you ever
considered refusing
but because you wanted him
to know that you, too,
value rituals. But
there were only enough
cool ones for the guests.
So you gave him a warm one.
It doesn't matter, he said.
It's okay. But of course it did.
The rite was spoiled
by an imperfection. And now he's
asleep upstairs and you're
holding open the door
of the refrigerator, contemplating
a pint bottle with no more
than two ounces taken from it
and the cap put back so well
you'd need an opener
to take it off again, thinking
of the petty treason
we commit so often
against those we love,
the confidence games
in which parents play
their children for suckers.

Johnnie's Poem

Look! I've written a poem!
Johnnie says
and hands it to me
        and it's about
        his grandfather dying
        last summer, and me
        in the hospital
and I want to cry,
don't you see, because it doesn't matter
if it's not very good:
        what matters is he knows
and it was me, his father, who told him
        you write poems about what
        you feel deepest and hardest.

Cornflowers

I am a saint with a broken wing
        who shakes his fists like the wind.
                          You
are the homecoming
            of the sun,
                an hurrah of grass.
The cornflowers are not yet
        aware they will die soon
            from last night's frost.
They are like the Empress
Elizabeth of Austria
who was stabbed with a blade so thin
she continued to smile
                and did not interrupt
her walk,
        although it had pierced her heart.
Since in this place and season
        they are the only flowers

that do not ask for money
I give you them.
                    Nothing else is beautiful
this hunchbacked October night
except the moon.

Walking toward the Bus Station

The snowflakes are shaped like starfish
and almost as big
as hummingbirds.
                    But I've forgotten
the colour of your coat
although you walk beside me.
Already
            this is part
                        of the past,
imaginary.
                So our mouths say nothing.
There are witnesses
who would swear
they saw us now.
                    In reality
we are each of us elsewhere
and alone.
                I am watching
a bus leaving:
                to board a bus
is to step from this world
                            to another,
a small and private
                        transfiguration.
Or I have prevailed
against the cosmological winds
                            and you did not go:
that same afternoon

we boarded a plane
                    together.
We have grown old in Spain.
And nobody has ever been
so happy except
the most celebrated lovers
                    and they
only in the imaginations
of their most envious admirers.

Doubtless you too are setting out for some place
other than where we both seem to be going.

Song of the Aging Young Man

    I

Persephone's child, I cannot look upon women
except as sphinxes,
                    the most ignorant and stupid
of whom possess knowledge
                    I can never share,
however often
          I attempt the riddle.

    II

Here I am promising to love you
for ever
      when
             I was somebody else
only yesterday
             and don't know who
I'll be tomorrow.

Adam's Song

If we were able to
play this
       game without ceasing,
the time would come
when we were transformed
into pure
      energy,
          a new sun.

I enter your body to forget my name.

Masquerade

You are taking off
your masks, one
after the other
—because it's true
they are all masks,
every shred,
my Domino,
and if climate,
vanity and tabu
vanish tomorrow
we will cover
our wrists with
green ribbons, if
nothing else,
remove them only
with ceremony as
though revealing
at last who we
really are. Or
there will be
anklets of red
synthetic leather

—anything at all
to keep alive
the mystery.

For Marilee

Funny Marilee,
        elsewhere in history
                we, your friends, could abandon
the preliminary
        witticisms, say nothing
                when you enter carrying
the child, your belly
        a clown's bass drum
                under your dress,
say nothing
        but only laugh as though we
                were still little children
and you were about to be
        mother of all the world,
                funny Marilee, holy Marilee.

The Great Rejection

To refuse love harshly
when freely given:
                        perhaps that
                        is the first,
even the only
                sin, and the guilt
                therefrom
a kind of worship,
                as when
red stains appear

on the white petals
                    of the roses laid
around the feet
                    of the miraculous statue.

After Seeing a Watercolour by Jacintha Ferrari, Then 13

Jacintha's Red Indian has skin as white as the dream
of a 17th century duchess
                    when they put arsenic
in cream
            and bathed in it.
                        He kneels beside a pool
that I say is in Japan, there is a bow
beside him,
            but it
                    is chocolate-coated
peppermint. He is waiting
for something beautiful
to happen.
            The daughter of the Shogun
on a white pony with
                    flowers in her hair, that
will be the next picture.
                        And he will see
her reflection
            in the water
                        before he sees
her.
    That is the third picture, and very difficult.

Jealousy

Don't lie,
you hate me,
the jealous
wife accused.

And at first
she couldn't
have been more
mistaken.

But she kept
repeating herself
again and again
and again
until it was true.

A Passing Thought

You taste
        like
                maple honey and
walnuts
        that being the flavour of
my favourite
            ice cream
                  or your flesh is
burgundy in
my mouth:
        I wish
I could say
        that or something
like it
      the kiss evolving
from the bite
          the way it must have done,

my tongue
        licking up
the faintest traces of
sweat
        and rose-scented soap.

Gruel and Plovers' Eggs
    for Al Pittman

The widow's youngest astride
White Mouse, his godmother's stallion,
had better look up:
                there's an ogre sitting
in one of the orange trees,
                    an ogre
who smells like a sack
of decaying lobsters,
                an ogre
whose name is Toe Jam,
                    sitting
on a branch overhanging
the path to the castle
where the magician
has imprisoned the ice princess,
                    an ogre
who'll pop him,
            horse and all, in a pot
to simmer in a sauce
of orange juice, sugar and ginger —
    when I was seven
I outgrew all that,
            now
thirty years later
            I know almost as much
as when I was six.
            Watch out for orange trees:
the ogre Toe Jam is out to eat you.

The Day's First Miracle

If the relationship between
    my window and the sun
    differed,
        if I did not sleep
by day and there were no need
    for both
        blinds and drapes,
            or if either
were another colour,
        if the wind blew
from any other
        direction,
were weaker or stronger,
if this April were not
    unseasonably
        cold, if the window were open
more than a fraction —
        above all
if I were not free
    this morning
    I would not have seen
        a vision
of the absurdly beautiful
    love-making
        of two golden dolphins.

He Talks about His Nightmares

Lately I've lived through nightmares in which
I wrestle with abstractions, often personified
by faceless men sharing
one quality in common. I am asked to name it
and cannot, although it seems I once could.
Or I can't remember
a word. Last night it was the name for

a segment of the body that resembles something
that is neither
a dried fig nor a bit
of preserved ginger,
                          although it possesses
characteristics of both.
                          The answer is always
on the tip of my tongue. I suspect
that's how one feels after
a stroke or a lobotomy.
                          Wondering
what it may portend, I set it down here,
not at all certain
I won't wake up one morning
and hear someone ask, What is the answer?
And I'll almost know.
                          That is what makes it
a nightmare.
                          I'll almost know.
Perhaps this particular
horror can be expressed only
in mathematics.
                          Perhaps there's no place
for it in literature.
                          Do you
begin to understand me?
                          This might be nothing
                          if it were not true

A Dream of Tears and Laughter

Johnnie comes into the room
where I'm sitting alone
in the dark as I am now
asleep in my chair
and he says: Dad,
will you take my picture

when they give me
my death sentence
tomorrow.
                He laughs
and I burst out crying,
wake up with tears
in my eyes, not so much because
they're going to kill him
as because he knows it
so well and doesn't seem to care.

The Dream of the Old Man Who Became a Boy Yet Remained Himself

I am an old man who through magick
has entered the body of a young boy.
Yet not all of me has gone into his body;
part of me remains as it was.
I sit at the head of a long table
in semi-darkness. He does the things
that boys do. Or to put it another way:
he sits at the head of a long table
in semi-darkness, that old man. I
do the things that boys do.
I will be the first man in all of history
to leave two corpses behind him
when he dies.
                I, the boy, have a plan which
I, the old man, oppose,
believing it unspeakably evil.
Come closer, my boy, I say, come closer,
thinking to seize his mind
and take it back,
come closer, and the strain of it
causes me to have a heart attack,
seeing which he laughs
until he finds himself
shrinking smaller and smaller and smaller.

He Is Astonished Upon Opening the Door

Red roses have blossomed
overnight in the snow.
The girl wears blue;
she opens her jacket; you see
the prints of overshoes
on her breasts.

    Batman and Robin
    are racing after
    her, the snow
    flying from their capes,
    fogging their plastic
    goggles.
        Oh, will the flowers explode,
    release a soporific
    gas when they bend
    down with their
    microscopes?

I was a grown man before I knew
it snowed in Arabia.
Englishmen have gone there
to make war and have become
ministers to kings only because
they were permitted to walk
with other men hand-in-hand.

    Ripe olives on black bread,
    flat beer spiced with licorice
    for the men at arms
    in the kitchens
    of the palace.

And you, masked one,
O lordly executioner.

The Dream of the Dangerous Trains

But how will we know one
when we see it, the children
ask me: I've been warning them
about trains.
                    We're standing on
the tracks and there's
a rumbling in the distance.

It will grow, I answer;
in the twinkling of an eye it will change
from a thing so small
you yourselves could
pick it up in your arms
were it a little longer,
into a thing big enough
for you to straddle and
ride like a tricycle.
It will keep growing
until it's as big
as your house, or bigger.
Nothing grows faster
than a train.
                    Remember that,
and this: if you have to
jump, be sure you go
left or right, never
backwards or forwards.

Exile

I am a little child dreaming
                            a dream
in which God
                finds himself
                            in a world
other
        than that
    ·
                    which he remembers
creating. What
                    brought me here?
he asks. Where
                    is the passage
back?
            I am a little child
                            dreaming.

A Dream of Mountains

"Nothing organically wrong,"
the doctor would have said.
                    But the visitor
could not leave
that house in the mountains,
could never get any further
than the back porch
where he stood
watching the horses
                and especially
the charcoal mare
in the corral
                maybe a mile away.
He had never seen
a horse with so long a tail
although it was
beautiful and

　　　　　when she ran
she tossed it
　　　　　up over her rump,
out of the way,
in a manner
that was both
wholly animal
　　　　　and mysteriously
human.
　　　　　There were many
strong horses
in the valley between:
bigger than Clydesdales, yet
shapelier than
Native Dancer, or
the Pacing White Stallion. It
was a country of horses,
as he explained later
to a lady from Idaho,
when she asked him
　　　　　　　　where he had been.

The Encounter, the Recognition

There's a path through the woods, or a corridor
in an empty building. I enter it
at both ends and walk slowly toward myself.
I am wholly drunk.
　　　　　　　I am wholly sober.
We meet midway
　　　　　and recognize one another.
"Hello, Alden," I say.

That's how my best poems are created.

The Dream of Two Voices

I hear two voices talking
about me. One says:
Is he asleep? Are you sure he's asleep?
And the other says:
Yes, yes, if I've told you once
I've told you a hundred
times, he's asleep.
Then we'll have to wait, the first
voice says. We'll have to wait
until he wakes up. Then
he won't know that we're here.

Plea

Knock so I'll know
you're smiling.
Do not climb the stairs
until you hear me laugh.
Friend, it is night
in my soul.
       I hear
a fingernail
scraping glass.

Written While Waiting for Another Chest X-ray

I don't want to die.
That sounds like something said
by one of the more stupid
19th century kings, some Maximilian or Ferdinand
who in his youth admired Byron
and nibbled the ears
of the prettier page boys, in middle age

turned to brandy and took communion
every morning of his life,
grew enormously fat and
in his sixtieth year
summoned a cardinal, said, Your Eminence,
I don't want to die, see that the matter
is taken care of,
                    and with that
went shooting grouse
and killed more than one hundred,
being a most excellent shot.

Night Fears

When the patient sleeps he's not afraid
of dying in a hospital;
it's the closet door
opening
          slowly,
                    what he hears on the stairs.

And he's thirty-six
years old.
          What of Jennifer
crying out in the dark?

Her father
turns on the light,
attempts to persuade her
by dispersing the shadows
that there's nothing there,
although he knows better.

Last Words

You can write of your own death
only as long as there's a part of you left
that doesn't wholly believe in it.
Death, once accepted, stands alone.
It relates to nothing,
can't be transformed or
even decorated. Therefore
is not material for art.

War Games in the Surgical Ward

The child with imaginary arms
and the man, me
in the ever diminishing
hollow core of the only
absolute reality
—I smile on your behalf,
Sir Death, having fashioned
such weapons against
our meeting:
                my own cocked hat,
invisibility,
from right wrist to elbow,
the ceremonial
elastic and cardboard
cutlass that, incredibly,
strengthens my hand,
quiets its trembling.

TermCancClinc

In the euthanasia division
of the Terminal Cancer Clinic, TermCancClinc,
everything is ordinary.
"Do you have an appointment, Sir? May I have your number?"
You search your wallet, find the plastic-coated card,
    hand it over.
"You won't be needing this again, Sir." You exchange
    civil smiles.
"May I have your wrist, Sir?" A nurse attaches
an identification bracelet, takes your elbow
in her hand, not because you need support, but because
    the psychologists have taught her
such gestures are reassuring. "The technician will see you
in an hour. In the meantime take a seat in the waiting room."
"Thank you," you say. Others are waiting.
Two women and a man, all wearing bracelets
similar to yours. They dismiss you
with their eyes. You pick up a copy
of an old issue of *Time*, lay it down, pick up a still
    older issue of *Life*, leaf through it,
        look at the pictures, light a cigarette.
One by one the others are summoned and go out without speaking.
Then it's your turn. The nurse checks the number
on your bracelet. The technician
checks it again. "Would you mind lying down, Sir?"
He rubs alcohol on the spot where he intends
to insert the needle. You smile a little
at the irony of that, but don't mention it
because you've learned
everyone here misunderstands your jokes.
"Take a deep breath," he says. "Breathe out. Breathe in."
His fingers are on your pulse, his eyes on his wrist watch.
Your own eyes seem to be sinking
deeper into your skull, your stomach falling
away from the rest of your body. You think about things
that have nothing to do

with anything. You wonder, for example, if the technician
will wash his hands a few minutes from now
when the doctor pronounces you dead.

The Last Flight

One of the funnier
reasons for my not
wanting to die was
I was curious about
what would happen
afterwards, who would be president
or prime minister,
would any of my friends
ever be rich or famous,
what would my son's
wife be like, would he name
one of his sons for me,
would anyone remember
the Beatles when they
were old men—well,
you get the idea; and
I have a similar
feeling in planes,
wondering what the passengers
think and do when they know
they're about to crash.
Do they all of them
scream with one voice,
do they stop in the midst
of whatever they're doing
so that it's as if
time were suspended, or
do they, as I suspect,
go on with it until
the end, unable

to believe that planes
ever crash except
in newspapers and
on television, unable
to accept the myth or
play any part in it,
even as it swallows them.

The Pilgrim's Tale

Eastwood, Nottinghamshire, birthplace
of D.H. Lawrence—I went there
in somewhat the same spirit as
our ancestors made pilgrimages,
the difference being I felt
I had to laugh at myself.
I should have come here, I said,
eighty-five years ago and inquired
of a shepherd where the babe lay—
making a fool of myself with
such weak jokes because I was persuaded
I was making a bigger fool
of myself by the journey.

                        The curse
on all of us who are too
self-conscious is
we're condemned to
perform vivisection
on ourselves. So I sliced off bits
of tissue from various
parts of my body, examined them
under a microscope, put band-aids on
my wounds and at last decided
to board the train for Nottingham,

remembering
those long ago black nights
I served as night watchman
in a sawmill which
by daylight, half in mockery, half
with braggadocio, I called
Castle Dracula (I never
called it that at night).

              I was seventeen
then and read Lawrence less
because of anything
he had to say than
because he was a workingman's
son — so it said on the backs
of books I bought in
the nearest town, twenty miles
away,

              where we went
every Saturday night in a box
on the back of a half-ton
truck, in the dead
of winter, packed in
like sardines — if there had been fewer
of us we might have
frozen to death, it was that cold but
for the heat of our bodies,

              maybe twenty of us,
boys and girls, intertwined, piled
three and four deep, me with
Lawrence in the pocket of
my green and black checked lumberman's
windbreaker, Sandra Fullerton
on my lap, my hands under
her ski jacket, under her
sweater, under her blouse, there
in the warm sweet

darkness, rocking,
rocking, so long ago it seems that
somehow it was never
the present, but always
the past, that it was past
even while it was happening
so that it was nostalgia
rather than desire I felt
with her breasts in my hands, rocking.

         So I pretended
to admire Lawrence until
I came to admire him, just as I
pretended to be
a writer until I came to be one.

         Be careful
which mask you put on.
It may stick.

         "Ugliness," he said,
"ugliness, ugliness, ugliness."
So I walked the streets
of his village for more than
an hour before I admitted
I found it pretty, all
clean brick and postage stamp
gardens full of flowers.

         But of course he'd never
seen Springhill or Sudbury. The countryside
was as beautiful as he painted it and I'm not
fool enough to describe it, except
I remember thinking
how curious it was, the trees
had so much space around them, as if each
were an entity, and the hayfields
were softer than ours, humanized

—in my country even
where the land was first
broken two hundred
years ago or more, the wilderness
is waiting
to reclaim everything if
we turn our backs, the frost
breaking open the concrete, the wind
broadcasting
seeds in the fissures.

         While in England
everything is
human—if there are animals
that remain wild it is only
because men wish them so.

         Yet in so many
ways his native
village was little
different from mine. Children
screaming "sigh-ite see-ahs! sigh-ite see-ahs!"
Women staring after me
"with that long unwearying
stare of aborigines." A ripple
at window after
window, as though I were a boat
and the curtains
water, opening and closing.

         If you lived in
Eastwood all your life
without ever once
leaving you'd die
thinking oxygen
smelled like coal smoke.
My village smelled of sawdust.

The strangest
thing that happened was
within minutes after
I arrived a car
pulled up beside me and the driver asked
could I tell him
the way to Ripley and without
thinking I told him:
"Go straight ahead; turn
right at the Sun Inn; follow
the Nottingham Road to
Langley Mill Lane, and keep bearing
right." You've read too many
books and remembered
them too well, I said afterwards
to myself, feeling a little
awed, more than a little
amused and for more complicated
reasons, even
a little guilty.

The beer was good
at the Three Tuns where
I got miraculous
as the Scots say
on half and half, thinking
how Lawrence's "black-faced,
sweat-smeared" father got
similarly pixilated before
going home to face that
"superior soul" he'd married.

There are no monuments
to Lawrence in Eastwood and
perhaps that would please him, since
he always professed
to despise museums. At least he'd
pretend to be pleased as he'd have
pretended to deride

me and my pilgrimage. He had a recurrent
nightmare of teaching
school in Canada.

                                There are no monuments but
in the window of
a fish and chips place there
was a sign advertising
a dance with music by
a rock group called
The Sons and Lovers.

Preview of Armageddon

In the last hours of the Cuban missile crisis
we all of us half-believed it was the end of the world.
Nobody talked of anything else.
                            At the office
that afternoon, the rhythm
of work changed: indolence
alternated with a kind of athletic abandon,
which seldom happens
by day, although normal to the night shift.
If one of us had brought out
a bottle everybody might have got drunk.
If somebody had begun praying
aloud everybody else might have done
something equally extraordinary.
                              I'm not sure.
I think that, secretly, we all felt we should be acting
like the characters in science fiction films.
I know I did; if the world blew up
I'd want to be holding
everybody I love in my arms.
                        But there was always a chance
it wouldn't really happen.

For Yukio Mishima

*The novelist, often mentioned as a possible Nobel Prize winner,
stripped to his waist, unbuttoned his trousers and sat down on
the floor of the room. He touched his stomach, gave a piercing yell
and drove his short samurai sword into himself.*
    —*News Item*

You can't hear me, Yukio Mishima. But, then,
a man who addresses the dead is bound to discover,
sooner or later, that he's talking to himself.
The newspapers argue whether
you were certifiably insane
or a buffoon for whom suicide
was the only bit of egocentricity
that remained untasted.
They can't find words for you
as they could so readily have done
if you'd decapitated yourself
while driving a racing car
or in any other equally extravagant
but fashionable manner;
just as they couldn't admit
it was a bull that got Hemingway:
there were hoofprints leading away
from the lodge where his body lay
and a trail of blood
that had dripped from the horns.
That was never published.
But perhaps I understand you better than most, Yukio Mishima,
wanting to restore the sword
to its place beside the chrysanthemums.
The worst way to die
is as a prisoner, at the hands
of a pitiless human enemy.
                        Next to the worst
is death of natural causes.
There are no pacifists
in the cancer ward.

That great war chief
whose people called him *Our Strange Man*
and whom the whites called Crazy Horse,
led his soldiers into battle shouting:
"Come on, Lakota, it's a good day to die!"
My grandfather left
an imitation leather cardboard wallet
containing a Junior G-Man secret pocket,
five greenish pennies, and a will beginning:
"I, Cathal O Nuallain, Prince of Fortara..."
Myself, delirious, coming out from under
the ether and into the Demerol
like a man crawling out of the sea
and into the jungle,
resolved to die like
an Irish prince: an old man's foolishness,
a small boy's games
dignifying the fear, almost
sanctifying the pain.

Detroit Skyline

My eyes believe if
I climbed over the railing
of this Holiday Inn
balcony and dropped
I would bounce lightly
once or twice and then
find myself walking
on the water, and it might be
somewhat like rubber,
it might be almost as though
I were treading on a series
of truck tires. Fortunately, experience
has taught me to distrust
those eyes that also
argue that everything

I've ever heard or read
about Detroit is a lie.
There is no smog, for instance, but a great
pinkish halo; everything else,
sky, water, buildings is
in various shades of
blue-grey, the colour
of silence; it is something beautiful
that men have made,
my eyes tell me. Perhaps nobody lives there;
perhaps the builders of it
dedicated it to their gods
or, more likely, to their goddesses,
and then went away
for ever so that nothing
would disturb it
except the caterpillars
that my mind transforms
into trucks, the ants
that my reason
touches with its
wand so that they become
cars driven by men.
Only the gulls
come near enough
to remain themselves
as I look out from
this window in
a different city,
another country.

Salt Shakers for the Beer

Cool as a cucumber, they say here, and as sure
        as God made little apples
he's three sheets to the wind.
                I don't have to explain,
need only repeat
each word distinctly
to make Franz smile
                Ach!
                Is very good, he says.
As though it were all poetry
and I had written it.

The Three Philosophers

What am I doing here
at a conference of the
Humanities Association?
I am registering the
itch on my left elbow,
the slight congestion
in my left nostril, I
am combing my hair
with my fingers, I am
scratching the back
of my right foot with
the toe of my left,
I am smoking cigarettes,
I am half-listening
to a professor of
philosophy delivering
a paper on the
mathematics of ethics, exemplified by
an imaginary girl
called "Y," and an
imaginary boy

called "X," and an
imaginary fetus
designated as
"X-Plus-Y-Equals-1,"
the question being
should she have
an abortion, "A,"
marry him and allow
the baby to be born, "B,"
or give birth to a
bastard, "C," which reminds me
of seeing a great sword
in the armories of
the Tower of London with
a plaque under it showing
it belonged to The
Bastard of Burgundy,
and thinking then
how splendid it must
have been to be
known far and wide as
"The Bastard of Burgundy,"
to introduce one's self as
"The Bastard of Burgundy,"
to hear the bystanders
murmuring it, "There
he goes, he's The
Bastard of Burgundy."
So that for a few
moments I forget
my elbow, my nostrils,
my hair, my feet, my
cigarette and the
professor of philosophy.
Then I take notice of
the game his
colleagues are playing,
the two of them who sit,
one on either side

of him, waiting
their turn. The one
making notes and
tearing them up,
tapping his palm with
the bowl of his pipe,
shaking his head more
in pity than disgust.
The other chewing
the frames of his
spectacles and out of
professional courtesy
hiding his grins
behind his hand. They
will suggest he
revise his paper before
submitting it to
a learned journal;
they will very gently
correct the slight
error in his third
from the last quotation
from Heidegger, the paragraph
in question having been
revised by its author
in a later volume
thus far available
only in a little known
Bulgarian, Finnish or
Serbo-Croatian translation.
And it may not end there.
He may be lucky.
The Lord may deliver them
into his hands, so
he'll rise to his feet
again and everybody
will know from
his face that he's won
this match, and he'll smile

a smile both merciful and
civilized, and he'll
tell them, oh,
he'll tell them, he'll tell them,
how he met
the great man, Heidegger,
himself; it was during
his last sabbatical,
in Germany, and he took
the liberty of asking
which version best
represented the
great man's most
recent conclusions
—and at this point
almost everybody in
the room will prepare
to emit a little
dry academic chuckle
because they'll know,
just as you and I do,
what it was the
great man answered.

The Night Editor's Poem

A child is lost near a lake
in the woods outside the city;
a man has been found dead
in a hotel and our reporter knows only
that the detectives have sent out
for sandwiches and coffee which
they're now consuming
in the same room with the corpse and a woman
who may be a suspect,
if there has been a murder, although right now
it looks more like suicide,

in which case our photographer
should get out of there as fast as he can
because nobody remembered to arrange for a picture
of the new officers of the Knights of Pythias.
There is flooding
in the Upper St. John River Valley and a cabbie
has been stabbed in Fredericton, and Trudeau
looks like a shoo-in unless
there's a deal which would mean
we'd have to pull the lead editorial and kill
that display of cuts
on page five, and we should do something
on page one about Vietnam, although all there is
so far is the usual round-up
that nobody reads and,

> *Bulletin,*
> *Martin Luther King has been shot*
> *in Memphis, the extent of*
> *his injuries has not yet*
> *been determined.*

I send the kid
for a one column, head and shoulders,
cut, and ask if there've been any deaths
from the floods, because if there haven't been
I can shove that story downpage
and do a two column upper left
display on King unless,

> *Bulletin,*
> *his injuries*
> *are critical,*

and I push everything down
four inches and send the kid
for a one and one-half columns,
head and shoulders, not more than three
inches deep,
          and there's a call from the hotel,
our reporter sounding disappointed
because, sure enough, it was suicide
and that means only three inches

of type on the back page, and
by the time Mac got to the Pythian Castle
they'd gone home but maybe we have a file cut
of the grand chancellor
we can use on provincial; there's a hell of a good
shot of the mother
of the lost child taken when they told her
they'd found the body, one that will stand up
in three columns with everything but her face
cropped out, something good enough
to send out on the wire and,
                    Bulletin,
                    Martin Luther King
                    is dead,
and it's too late
for a wirephoto which means
dig out that shot of him being hit
by a stone in Chicago, I think it was,
and have the engraver mask it so
nothing shows except
his body falling, and we'll set the story
in 12-point boldface, 18 ems, under
an all-caps 72-point Headline Gothic
head and splash it across
the top half of page one,
and it's not until later,
hours later,
eating ham and eggs
at an all-night diner,
shrugging my shoulders
to work some of the ache
out of them,
that I pick up the paper
again and understand
that Martin Luther King
is dead, and that I care.

Professor Algernon Squint Converses with His Fellows

Professor Squint nibbles and sips
the air, as though nothing at all
mattered save his invisible
sherry and cheese. The planet tips.
Men tumble into space; their cries
are smothered by bottomless skies.
Professor Squint nibbles and sips,
or deigns to pass betwixt his lips
that laugh peculiar to a don:
one-quarter cough, three-quarters yawn.

Professor Squint's Valedictory

I was a bad teacher
because I believed
my students
to be my equals. That
is an observation
merely, not a boast
nor even a plea
for clemency.
              We learn best
from those who despise us
a little,
          a very little,
without ever allowing us
to find them out.

Interview

"But the white cow,"
the interviewer insisted,
"the white cow, what
was her part in it, where
did she come in, why
was a white cow running
loose in the corridors
of the Ritz-Carleton
Hotel, what must you have
thought and, perhaps,
most important of all, how
did you manage
to converse with her?"

I've told him at least
a half-dozen times that I don't
know what he's talking about
so this time I say, "There
was no white cow anywhere,
least of all in the corridors
of the Ritz-Carleton and if
there had been I'd not
have spoken to her, nor expected
her to address me. White cows and I
have little or nothing
to say to one another."

The tape being broadcast
with his questions and all
but my final reply
deleted, I find I am now
known as the man who met
a white cow in the hall
outside his hotel room
and when asked what he did with her
was too embarrassed to give
an intelligible answer.

In the Desert

The daughter having confessed, her parents drove her
and her pet dog into the desert where they made her dig
a grave, and then ordered her to kill
the animal, the mother holding it
between her hands, and the father
handing the girl the gun, which she
put to her temple and fired.
                                    That is how it
was reported in *The New York Times.*
                                    But, mercifully,
we know nothing human could be
so simple. It's evident, for instance,
that the girl loved them at least enough
not to turn the gun on them. In the circumstances
even that has a certain terrible beauty.
                                    Carry it a step
farther: they must have done
something sometime to have earned such love.
They were mad, or course. But such imaginative torturers
can't help but feel
a kind of tenderness
for their victim — a fact that offers
not much hope, but a little.
                                    God knows, perhaps,
they loved the dog
almost as much
as she did and were punishing themselves, too,
like persons who burn themselves,
secretly, with lightbulbs
to expiate the murders
they got away with when
they were three years old.
                                    Such omens are not
peculiar to our times.
                                    The same,

saving only the gun, and that
replaced by a dagger,
might have been rendered
into verse by Sophocles.

Canadiana

Footnote for a twenty-first century
history of Canadian literature, if any:
a novelist who dislikes me
and despises my work
writes me a letter
almost every week
so he'll have his carbon
and my answer
to sell to the archives
of a university.
And I almost always
write an immediate reply.

Plot for a Science Fiction Novel

Scientists from another galaxy
capture an earthling
and decide after examining him
that he is a machine designed
for the manufacture
of shit.

Too Much Geography?

Once "Here Be Dragons"
was printed on the sea
that covered this continent.
Now ours is the only
unmapped country.
                    The atlas lies:
we are shaped like Chile
and live on a tightrope
between the ice cap
and the empire.

Religion

The real religion of an age
consists of what men
find it impossible
to disbelieve.
                    Our ancestors
could no more have doubted
the Seignior Cristo, his
parents and paladins,

than I can be wholly serious
when I deny
the principles of physics
and proclaim

the splitting of the atom
is the devil's answer
to certain rites
and incantations,
                    also

that the world is round
only because we've agreed
to call it so.

So Said St. Augustine
for Leo Ferrari

The sons of Light depend on bread
the sons of Darkness harvested

thus God's firstborn son was made
that His youngest might be arrayed

thus the treasurer and the thieves
were transformed on the tree that grieves

and Christ the prodigal divine
eats of the fruit thrown down to swine.

On Events of Varying Importance

When I learned that President Nasser was dead
I happened to be looking
at a man helping a small child fasten its coat.
The man was a little rough, as a parent is
who has changed diapers and knows for certain
children are not made of crystal.
                         The child
kept saying he wanted
to do it all himself; and I thought,
Let him; it's important to him; let him publish
his mastery of buttons and zippers
(as I'll publish this poem);
but quite likely he was happier,
secretly, at being compelled
to be a baby at least
a few minutes longer, and probably
the man, like most fathers,
found it hard to stop
being surrogate for God.
                    President Nasser

was a man and in consequence
died.
       President Nasser
was pharaoh of Egypt.
                       Tonight they're discussing him
on all six television channels and the minister
of external affairs says Canada grieves for him.
In Cairo the crowds are wailing and although
I had no special love for him, I almost weep
with them, tears are so contagious.
                              Long before
you read this there will be another
pharaoh, another minister, and I
may be as dead as President Nasser.
But there will still be
a man helping a child
fasten its coat.
              They'll go on,
the two of them, for ever.

Psalm

adapted from the Romanian of Tudor Arghezi

I search for you through the sounds and the shadows,
and through time itself I hunt for you.
Perhaps you are as much my weapon as my prey.
Shall I kill you at last — or kneel to you?

Believing too much, or believing in nothing,
I follow you constantly without getting closer.
It is as though you were a dream
from which I was afraid to wake up.

I have seen you only as a reflection
in running water. Yes, I caught a glimpse of you
once when I knelt like a wild boar
to drink from a stream full of fish and stars.

In the end we will meet, and fight.
I will destroy you if I can, because I cannot help myself.
Yet I almost wish I could simply
lay my hand on your body and say, "He is."

Folk Song

adapted from the Romanian of Tudor Arghezi

The country is their loom: they weave
threads that entangle and deceive
— so that we're quietly undone
and spare their gentle ears the gun.
Oh, lusty royal spiders nest
in palaces in Bucharest,
where they plot how to trap our flesh
in their cobweb's adhesive mesh.
The biggest bug of all a sun
with silken rays who spins for fun
nets that he tosses here and there,
over and under, far and near,
backwards and forwards, left and right,
striving to tie the nation tight.
My friends, remember you can hatch
infernos from a single match;
seeing cobwebs where'er you turn,
think how beautifully they burn.

Hide and Seek

adapted from the Romanian of Tudor Arghezi

My small and precious ones, I know a strange
game that we'll play some day.
                              I don't know when.
But we will play it.
Some evening, maybe, after the sun goes down.

Old people play it (it's a tricky game)
with boys like you, and girls like you, my sweet.
Poor people play it; rich people play it, too.
Animals play it, and birds, and even flowers.
Everyone plays it well.

We will love one another for ever, you and I,
laughing around the dinner table
under God's roof, the sky;
but one day I will start to walk
more slowly, you will see a difference
in my eyes, my hands will shake and, perhaps, I'll cough.

That's how the game starts, quietly, like the wind.
I'll laugh then and say nothing more.
I'll go and lie down on the ground;
I'll lie there without moving and won't make a sound.
Maybe I'll lie down over there beside that tree.

This game was played in the Bible;
even Our Lord Jesus Christ played it once,
and others: fevers and chills
shook them until they quit.
But they played well.

So don't be sad, my little ones, when they come
and lift me up and carry me away.
They'll put me in what they call a grave,

in soft or hard earth.
You see: the game begins with death.

But remember how Lazarus came awake.
Don't cry. Just wait
as if nothing had happened to me,
as if everything were the same as always.
I'll be meeting new friends and thinking about the game.

Your father has taken good care of you;
he has left you sheep and cattle and barns,
a pasture and a cottage,
enough work for all of you,
and enough for all of you to eat.

Everyone will rise from the dead some day
and come back to where his children wait
and to his wife, still weeping as she spins,
come back to his house without fuss as a man
comes home from his fields at the end of the day.

So grow up to be big and strong, my sons.
Laugh and be happy
as the custom is.
Don't worry if your father goes
away from home for a month or so.

At last, of course, something will delay him,
first one thing and then another.
Your father won't have the strength to come on foot,
for it's a long way
from this world to the other.

You'll be grown up, then,
with your own children around you.
Perhaps you'll know more than your father ever did.
Your mother will have spun her wool, and be knitting it.
And your father won't come home again.

My little monkeys, my beautiful ones,
my priceless possessions,
that is what the game is like.
Two can play it, or three, or as many as you like.

And, oh God, how I hate it.

Scratchings

Every great idea contains the seed of its own destruction.

#

Without God we have no rights, only such privileges as may
be granted us by the state.

#

Definition of a hypocrite: one who is too kind to be wholly
honest and too honest to be wholly kind.

#

The day the child realizes that all adults are imperfect he
becomes an adolescent; the day he forgives them, he becomes
an adult; the day he forgives himself he becomes wise.

#

Nothing is more likely to stunt the intellect than a knowledge
of history unaccompanied by a sense of history.

#

Perhaps the ultimate indignity is loneliness without privacy.

When nothing sexual is regarded as obscene, romantic love
will cease to exist.

#

Men and women are not equal; each is superior to the other.

#

Twentieth-century man is obsessed with sex like the baboons
in a zoo, and for the same reason: it's the only emotional
outlet from his captivity.

That Year on Salisbury Street

I

The worst quarrels between husbands and wives are those
      that take place at night, because if you have to
      leave home at night there's nowhere to go except
      places it's hard to come back from.
In the daylight you can tell the old woman to get her fat
      arse out on the street and hustle her own beer money
      for a change;
you can even stand at the head of the stairs and yell after
      her, as she slams the front door, that you'll ram
      a knife into her stinking guts if she ever so
      much as dares show her stinking face again, the
      stinking bitch,
and, generally, she'll stay away only long enough to
      convince herself that you've begun to think, Jesus,
      maybe this time she really isn't coming back.
Or she can pull out, knowing she can take the kids to the
      playground—not the one at the foot of the
      street where he might come looking for her too

soon but the one three blocks over and six blocks
        south —
or if it's winter she can take them to Simpsons-Sears and
        Eaton's and Kresge's and Zellers, one of them in
        her arms and two of them hanging on to her skirt and,
        when they get tired, stop at the lunch counter in the
        bus terminal for Cokes and hot dogs.
But at night she won't be able to stop the kids from crying
        and she'll need shelter, which she'll have to
        buy either with money, which probably she won't have,
        or with fillets sliced off her soul. She'll have to
knock at the door of a neighbour's apartment. I'm leaving
        the son of a bitch, Helen. I'm leaving him for good
        this time, the lousy bastard. Or she'll have to
take a bus across town to her parents' place, the kids
        bawling all the way and everyone staring at her,
        and there will be her father,
barefoot, pants pulled on over Stanfield's
        unshrinkable underwear, false teeth in a tumbler
        of water upstairs. I told you he was no good, hon.
        You should have listened to me. I told you.
A ceremony will have to be performed. It will no longer be
        possible
simply to drift back. Going back will require
an exercise of the will, an act of surrender. And the longer
        she stays away the harder it will be for him
to perform his own act of surrender: to accept her knowing
        such acceptance will be
a kind of public confession. So when marriages end
        it almost always happens
at night. At least that's how it is on Salisbury Street.

        II

We lived on Salisbury Street that first year. The upper end
        of the street had already become a slum. Naval barracks
        had been thrown up there during the Second World War to
        house the sailors who guarded the waterfront against the

SS commandos that were expected to row ashore some night
   from the U-boats said to be skulking in the bay.
After the war the city bought the barracks for emergency
   housing. They were still occupied twenty years later,
long low wooden buildings surrounded by high military fences
   that nobody had bothered to tear down. They looked like
   pictures of Dachau except the yards were full of dogs,
   most of them spotted brown and white with a rodent look
   about them, toothpick-thin cats whose fur looked as if
   they'd bought it at a rummage sale, and flocks of
   herring gulls, all competing for garbage.
And of course there were cars without wheels sitting on
   wooden blocks, naked dolls sprawling in the mud, brown
   blotches on their body where the pink paint had peeled,
   Heinz and Campbell soup tins,
and many small children with faces like roses that have
   almost imperceptibly begun to wilt.

III

Below the barracks the street was lined with mid-Victorian
   mansions built for the merchant princes — perhaps merchant
   squires would be a more accurate term — who ruled the
   city in the days when a hundred sailing ships lay at
   anchor in its harbour.
Now the houses were mostly owned by Jewish or Lebanese lawyers
   whose grandfathers had pushed handcarts loaded with cheap
   yardgoods along country roads and whose fathers had sold
   blue serge suits from the back steps of horsedrawn
   caravans.
The descendants of the merchant princes were brigadier-generals
   with the United Nations forces in the Congo, Episcopalian
   bishops in California, trade commissioners in Caracas,
   directors of Canada Life or the Bank of Montreal,
or they lived out Dickensian parodies in which Miss Havisham or
   Betsy Trotwood cooked creamed asparagus on toast on an
   electric hotplate in what had been a clothes closet off
   her grandparents' bedroom.

IV

The house in which we lived had been divided into furnished
  bed sitters and one-bedroom flats and almost all the
  tenants were newlyweds who moved out as soon as they
  saved enough money for a down payment on some
  secondhand furniture.
We were young and it was an adventure to be poor. There were
  refrigerators in the halls and sometimes at night kids
  came in off the street and stole frankfurters or ice cream
  or beer. Opposite the house there was a billboard that on
  alternate months advertised Pepsi Cola and Macdonald's
  Menthol Cigarettes.
When you opened the front door the house belched in your face
  —a belch in which the predominant odour was the stale
  dishwater stench of overcooked cabbage and the dirty sock
  stench of turnips. But after the first week you were
  oblivious to the smell by the time you reached your own
  door upstairs.
Because so many of the tenants were young and newly married
  there was an atmosphere of almost communal sensuality.
  The bathrooms as well as the refrigerators were
  shared, one to every two tenants,
so early in the morning or late at night you literally ran
  into half-naked girls and men in the halls. Girls
  in bras and panties tried to open doors while holding
  a carton of milk in one hand and three eggs in the
  other; young men with dripping hair emerged from
  bathrooms wearing only undershorts or a towel.

V

And the walls were thin. There was a girl who made sounds
  almost exactly like the cries of a cat in heat, not
  the cries a cat makes as it mates, but the cries it
  makes when it wants to mate and can't get outdoors.
There was a couple who talked baby talk. Diddums wantum
  kiss kiss. And there was the rhythmic squeaking of

bedsprings and what sounded like bodies coupling in
chairs, against walls, and on the floor.

VI

The landlord had attached a time clock to the hall light
      so that it switched off at ten o'clock and couldn't be
      turned on again until the following night.
I left the radio station around four o'clock in the
      morning, after taping the five, six and seven o'clock
      newscasts, all of which said the same thing in a
      slightly different manner.
For a while I couldn't find my way from the front door
      to the door of our flat without lighting matches, four
      of them, one after the other,
and the first night we spent there I went into the wrong
      house, the house next door, and didn't realize my
      mistake
until I got upstairs and was about to open the door of
      somebody's bedroom.
Later I knew my way in the dark, but it made me nervous,
      and so I bought a flashlight.

VII

Every night except Saturday I climbed those stairs and
      every night as I stopped to take my key from my pocket
      I heard the Fischers quarrelling.
Her voice was shrill; I could distinguish most of the words.
      His was a rumble; I could make out a word only here and
      there.
Sometimes I thought of her as The Fife, and of him as The
      Drum.
You bastard, said The Fife, telling me you were a foreman!
      I found out what kind of a foreman you are!
A roll of drums.
You're not a man! You're an old woman! Are you listening

to me, you son of a bitch?
A roll of drums.
Her voice changed occasionally to a hoarse whisper, presumably
when she remembered that the occupants of the other flats
were probably listening. Sometimes a neighbour pounded
on the wall or yelled through the partition
for them to shut up, for God's sake, don't you know what
time it is? Then there was a brief silence, broken by
the whisper that became louder and louder until she was
almost screaming again.
Perhaps she wants him to beat her, I used to conjecture,
standing there with my key and flashlight. Perhaps she
wants him to beat her but is ashamed to tell him so.
She's furious because he's too stupid to divine what
she wants from him.
Perhaps she even wants him to kill her. Or perhaps she
knows that he wants her to beat him or kill him and
she hates him for it.
But I never found out the answer; although two or three
weeks after they left the police came around asking
questions about them.

Old Town Revisited

I will park on the corner in front
of the furniture store. The day I left
eight years ago, Moses Timmins stood
across the street, on the top step
to the post office. He waved goodbye.
When I went back
for the first time, a year
later, I found he had descended
only one step (there are five)
and was still waving. I'm
telling you the truth. He had moved
less than a foot in twelve months.
This morning, though, he should be

about to put his foot on the sidewalk.
And Henry Ferguson may have finished
closing the door of The Dough Boy Diner
— he was about to touch
the inside handle eight years ago,
and last summer he was almost
outside, but had paused to say
a final word to Mary-Beth MacGuire,
who when I see her next will be washing
the mug she was starting to fill
in 1963 for Standish Morehouse who will
be getting up from his stool to go back
to the office — how many years
I wonder will it take him
to walk that hundred yards? I foresee
myself an old man on his last visit,
leaning on the shoulder of a grown
grandson who may not even be born
twenty years from now, the pair of us
getting out at this same corner. I foresee
Moses, Standish and Henry finally
come near enough to resume
whatever conversations my
first departure interrupted.

They Go Off to Seek Their Fortunes

The three largest immigrant colonies in Toronto consist of the Italians,
the Portuguese and the Maritimers.
— A Torontonian in conversation

They have their pictures taken, peering at maps.
They stop along the road to buy beer, opening
the bottles in ways peculiar to them:
the tough one uses his teeth, the cool one his belt buckle,
the mouth organ player takes a bottle in each hand,
hooks the caps together and pulls
so that only one comes off.

They tell strangers
where they're from and where they're going and how much
their second cousins make in Sudbury. They say,
"I'm from the island," or "I'm from the bay,"
as if there were only one of each in the world.
They wear white socks and copper bracelets.
They light matches on their thumbnails.
                                        They spit.
When they're happy they whoop and when they're sad
they can be dangerous. They're almost never
neutral toward anyone — they either like you
or are prepared quite simply to kick
the living Jesus out of you.
                        They are warriors
for whom it's natural to bid goodbye
with a kind of mock military salute.
                        They greet one another
with a meaningful movement that is part
bow, part shrug, part nod, accompanied
by a slight pursing of the lips,
the barest suggestion of a wink.

Antecedents

Ireland was not
                my people's country, but
their creation myth,
                a dike
against infinity.
            "We are Irish," they always said,
and never the truth, never: "We are a race that existed
in Europe only as a man exists
in the seed
            before it leaves
his father's body."
                Never:
"Our nation is this valley

where we've lived
so long that our young girls may wear
wild roses and lilacs
                    that have sprung
from their same flesh
and our young men suffer dreams
in which they lie crushed under trees and croak
the names of women whom they learn on waking
were their own widowed great-great-grandmothers."

"We are Irish," they said, and never spoke
that which they never needed to hear spoken.

For My Grandchildren, As Yet Unborn

For my grandchildren
who will never know
the beasts of the fields:
my own grandmother
would call from the pasture
gate, "So-Boss! So-Boss!"
It would be dusk, and the cattle
a half-mile away in the trees,
but Old Mother Whitehead,
leader of the cows, would hear her
and come with the others behind her,
not that she cared
whether they followed,
she alone among them
went where she pleased.
Creeters, my grandmother said,
which meant *creatures* which meant *cows*.
And they'd walk not at all
as they'd walked that morning;
they'd come slowly,
slowly, but not stopping;
it was even

a little frightening
the way they came
out of the woods
and down the hill,
so purposeful they seemed,
Old Mother leading them.

Hunger

for Louis Cormier

When I was a little child I dreamt of meat,
half-inch-thick slices of woodsmoked oniony bologna,
dripping ketchup, served with browned potatoes,
peppery baked beans and cold, hard, almost stale
shortening biscuits
                    —and at times I wept
when I awoke, beat the bedding with my fists,
but that was from chagrin, more than from hunger:
I'd not have eaten grass:
                    we were aristocrats,
                        the hungry children
of my country and generation.
                            Later, I kept a picture
of a great platter of ice cream such as might
have been set before a gluttonous Caesar.
                                Cherries,
cherries both green and red, encrusted cherries,
sheeny with sugar crystals, pineapple wedges,
orange sections, sliced pears and peaches, several kinds
of apples sprinkled with spices and syrups
surrounded it, an Alp coated with honey
and decked with nuts, jelly beans, gumdrops and raisins.
I'd take the picture out
in secret, stare at it until
I saw it equally well with my eyes shut.
Better times had come: now we dreamt of food
only when we were awake.

                              I've little right
to talk of hunger, never having died of it,
knowing it only as a civilian
might have known war
in the nineteenth century: safely,
out of range and through a glass, and yet
I believe in starvation as I came to believe
in death only when I was sick abed aged thirty-three.

A Matter of Etiquette

The first time you address the Queen
you say "Your Majesty." Then you call her "Ma'am."
And you mustn't speak to her at all
except in reply to what she chooses to say to you.
There will be an aide-de-camp or a lady-in-waiting
present to remind you of this should you ever
be presented at Court.

But nobody has yet put into words
the etiquette governing the relations
between the men digging
a sewer and their foreman.
                    I'm being quite serious.

For example you must show respect
by the very manner
in which you enunciate his name
but never overdo it
by so much as one-hundredth
of a decibel
or it will be taken
as evidence of subservience
or insubordination.
It may even be necessary for you
to acquaint yourself with

the intricate ritual
of offering to buy him
a beer.
        I know an honours student
in sociology who during an entire summer
was addressed as "Boy,"
because he could not master
the delicate nuances
of this ceremony.

The same young man
was unable to learn
how to talk about
the girls who were
continually passing
and therefore lost
the respect of
his companions

by attempting to be witty
so that he was judged arrogant
and by being so
imaginative that he
came to be almost
ostracized as
some kind of pervert:

he failed to understand
until it was too late

that when it comes to discussing
girls with the men
working beside you
in a ditch you can use only

certain prescribed
sentences and that each
has its own

unique rhythm,
must be accompanied
always by its own
formalized gestures.

Roots

I've seen my great-grandfather only once.
He was pointed out to me
as the fourth man from the left in a photograph
of about thirty men and two teams of horses
posed in front of a logging camp in the 1880s.
You find the same kind of picture
in histories of the west: a posse
come back with the bodies (they used to prop up the dead
with their eyes still open and pretend
to be holding them at gunpoint).
                  And I seem to remember
similar pictures of the Serbian army
during the First World War; my great-grandfather
even wore a sort of Slavic blouse
and the same kind of moustache.
               There are also pictures
of white men after a lynching.
             Nobody is smiling
because these were time exposures
and if you must keep your face still
it's safest and simplest
to shut your mouth, although best
not to clench your teeth because then
you may start to imagine
you're smothering, take a deep breath
and spoil everything;
and their eyes are black slits
because it's impossible
to keep from blinking once you try not to.
Though I don't believe they'd have smiled

even if that had been mechanically feasible.
It was a ritual, then, this picture taking:
the photographer down from Halifax,
a city man in a starched collar and a derby hat,
who put a black hood over his head and sometimes
set off an explosion at the crucial moment.
They knew
this was an instant
that could be held
against them.
So they look very tough and their hands are free
or grip peaveys or axes.
                        I get the feeling
my great-grandfather is trying to convince somebody
he'd use that axe on a man if he had to.
He holds it the way those Serbs held their rifles.
And I have no doubt
he'd have joined a manhunt
or helped with a lynching,
would have thought it unmanly
to have done otherwise.
                        Or maybe it's only
that he's proud of the axe,
maybe he was an axeman like his grandson, my father,
who could make the tallest tree
fall where he wanted it, aim its tip at a spot
no bigger than a fig
of chewing tobacco, and hit it.
I read the histories of countries
and his time seems like yesterday
but because he was human
and my own, he seems so old
as to almost stand
outside of time.
                        It amazes me, thinking:
he must have been at least fifteen years
younger than I am that day the winter sun
lapped up and locked into a small black box
this infinitesimal portion of his soul.

Long Ago and Far Away

The naked children come out of the lake.
It's as though they lived there.
I am one of them. Now the cherry tree
is full of us, like birds feeding.
We rest at last
in the topmost branches. Below us
our shadows
                    dance hand-in-hand
                                        with the wind.

Sister Mary Cecilia

Beware the nuns, they'll eat you;
they shave their heads, my boy,
and spank themselves
with knotted ropes
— not to mention six hundred and sixty-six
other varieties of devilment
that you're too young and Protestant
to hear about.
                    Beware, beware the nuns.

Said Mrs. Grainger and Mrs. Breck
and Mrs. MacPherson and Mrs. Forsythe

to their sons,

to their young sons now gathered on the green
behind the Sisters of Charity convent, cheering

little Sister Mary Cecilia,
yo-yo champion of Saint John, New Brunswick,
which means she's
                    the best in the world.

Little Sister Mary Cecilia,
keep that ecumenical
yo-yo twirling.

Go girl, go!

The Factory Worker's Poem

I am as limp as a puppet
from which the ventriloquist
has withdrawn his hand.
Tonight I don't try
to capture the poems: I'd only break
something or burn myself.
It's enough that they gather
like moths around the matchstick of my mind.

He Takes His Leave

It was as if I'd opened
Grimms' Fairy Tales and lowered myself into
one of the illustrations, become
the stripling taking his leave
of his village, on foot, with a rucksack
containing his other shirt, except I
carried a black cardboard suitcase
and boarded the train, after walking
only two miles: it didn't stop there
unless you raised a flag or,
to be more accurate, fetched from
the waiting room a broomstick
to which a green and grey rag had been
tacked, stood on tiptoe and
shoved it in a rusty iron socket.
The road was muddier

than I had ever seen it
that March day in 1952; I sank
to my ankles, once or twice it
sucked off my shoe.
An old woman emptying slops
called after me, said that she'd pray for me.
Her name was Lilah.
I patted the head
of a half-wild dog.
The wind smelled of sea-salt and sawdust.
I pause at this point to ask
myself if this matters to anyone,
including its author, and decide
at last that it must, if for no other reason
than this: now, nineteen years later,
I sometimes have nightmares in which
it's that same day, but the train
doesn't stop, all the roads are flooded
or blocked with snow, and even
the telephone lines are down,
or, more mysteriously,
the village has been transformed
into an island and there will never be
another boat to the mainland.
When I wake up
the pillow is damp with sweat,
my hands are shaking.

I'm a Stranger Here Myself

Tenth Wedding Anniversary

This is neither to
        take back what was given
                in rage, nor to deny the scars
returned.
        I send you no Valentine card.
                We are human and didn't
live happily ever after.
        We are what our children
                promise they'll never be—
a man and a woman
        who get on each other's
                nerves at times, and have traded
glares of the purest hate.
        This is only to say there has never been
                a moment in ten years
when I ceased to be
        conscious of your presence
                in the universe, never
a thought of mine in all that time
        that wasn't superimposed
                on my constant awareness of
your separate existence.
        If the inhabitants of
                the earth depended
for their survival on my
        keeping them always
                in mind, my world would be
empty—except for you.

At a Distance He Observes an Unknown Girl Picking Flowers

If I think hard enough
of the roses and the girl
breaking them off,
of how the flowers would
smell if I touched them, taste if
I were a child again,
if I remember clearly
how the pain of a thorn differs
from other kinds (it's a little
like learning you've been
the victim of a small
disloyalty), if I convince myself
the girl is somebody
I've known well: Catherine
with whom I used to
bicycle to the Pratt
Farm, the pair of us
in bathing suits; I told her
about alewives, called
gaspereaux there, how we'd shipped them
south, salted, in barrels, more than
a century before, food
for slaves — convinced that
the knowledge made both
the fish and us
more important, a part
of what happened
in books; another time
we were stealing apples and I
mistook her ankle for a branch
of the tree, it was so dark, and
we fell to the ground together, young enough
that the pain of it only
excited us, that and the way
it was replaced slowly, by
the realization that

the entire length of
our bodies touched,
which was like being thrown
into cold water and afterwards
drying off in the sun —
if I think hard enough it will appear
I've drawn something out
of the air, my mind pulling
invisible particles
together, forming a mass,
making.

Out of the Mouths

If only we adults were as wise
as Jennifer who said
she hated me and was going to
hate me for five minutes
and when I told her the time was up
said, okay, then I love you again
— knowing that rage is not
a lifetime commitment, but only
a passage of darkness in the mind,
a cold shiver of the soul.

Like Ray Milland

Like Ray Milland knocked off his feet
In the fog by a lorry bound for Manchester,
I am playing the part of a man who is
suddenly cured of his amnesia
and can now tell his girl friend, played
by Jennifer Jones, his real name
and where he came from. Except that
life is absurd where

a 1940's film is not. (One distinguishes
a documentary by its tangents:
a young soldier mortally
wounded doesn't pray but recites
the lifetime batting averages
of the ten best hitters
in the National League, and
the last words of a priest
I once knew were, "A hobo sandwich
consists of a bum
between two boxcars."
When the husband tells the wife
he is leaving her, she may ask him
does he want green
or yellow beans with his dinner.)
The worst art possesses
a perfection beyond anything
life has to offer, is so rational
it becomes ridiculous.
So here I recall that you, too,
have forgotten who you are,
that we are victims of the same
affliction. I give you your name
as well as my own. We are
Hansel and Gretel, gone
in search of wild berries, escaped
from the child-eating witch, but still
lost in the forest, running—
and it is so dark we could never
hope to find one another
again if even for a moment
I ceased to hold your hand.

In the Night

Best to put off
going back to sleep
until the dark stops
asking questions
—so thinks the man
who has been awakened
by the sound of his own voice
calling out to his wife
who lies within reach
of him:
        Stephanie, Stephanie
—which is not hers
but his sister's name.

Love Poem for a Stranger

I love you because
I am alone and you
have long bare
legs and have smiled
in my direction.
I love you
because men would
envy me, seeing us
together. I love you
because I have given
the little I know
of you to the mythical
woman in my belly. She wears
your hair. I unzipper
you, quickly, push back
your garments to
reach her breasts.
I love you because

I am a man and
it is what is
expected of me.
I love you because
it pleases me to
pretend I love you.
If you don't know
and I don't wholly
admit to myself that
I've no better reasons,
then I can't hurt you,
and so
there's no harm
in it. I love you
and if that's nothing
but a game my mind
plays with itself,
using such bits and pieces
of you as my senses gather,
and if you'd dislike
me, knowing as much, reflect:
at least it makes
me kindlier than
I might otherwise be;
I almost ache
from wishing you well.

In Memory of Sandra, Although Alive

Sandra, when your naked back was
Oceania and each of its small
impermanent blemishes
an island I celebrated
with my literal tongue,
there was no need to tell you,
no need for me
to reach out with words

for what time has taken
where no man's flesh
can ever touch it—
so poems like this one lie.

Seeing and Believing

What is this
that in form
and movement
is like nothing
else?

> A curious but
> by no means unique
> illusion, said
> the engineers
> who built the bridge.

And the man on the
penny-farthing bicycle
swore by
Jesus that it was the ghost of
the Portuguese sailor hanged
for drowning the
harness maker's daughter.

> It is that coming out
> which is within
> water, trees and stones
> as blood is in men
> —so the Abenakis
> might have thought.

I address the question
to my own eyes.
I say to them:

What do you see?

But they have no answer
except that which I give them:

the answer
that the shapers
of my mind
have given me.

At Speaker's Corner, Hyde Park

There are two of them.
They say: Oh, everything.
made by man will be set afire.
St. Michael and Satan
will kick over
the stars like lanterns.
Think,
think of millions of us
calling it thunder at first
and then war and then
saying, no, this is not
what my senses tell me:
rather a blood vessel
has burst, what I ate was
poison, a car struck me,
I am dying in my sleep.
Or
there will be sparks
from the stones —
the slaves having nothing
else to grind into bread,
and there will be nowhere
to run except
with the fire raisers,
assassins for posterity.

They say that afterwards
there will be nothing
that is less
than perfect,
these two priests of
the Phoenix power
that one of them calls God
and the other calls The People.

Night Flight to Montreal

I can see myself
being led from the plane
and into the lights
of the television cameras.

The stewardess who said her name
was Marie-Claude telling the nation,
"Yeah, I talked with the guy. Oh, sure,
I was a little scared of him
at first, the way he kept laughing.
He asked twice for whiskey
and once for chewing gum."

The pilot with that anonymous,
slightly furtive expression
refusing to comment.

And me
        thinking, How odd it is
        that only hours ago I expected
        to spend the night at a hotel
        where I have reservations,
        have a drink with friends,
        fly to Winnipeg tomorrow
—why didn't I take
a magazine from the rack

and go back to my seat
as I intended when
I started up the aisle?
It was a joke on us all.
                    Asking the police what
                    will happen to my luggage.

On Being the Subject of a Documentary

This is the fifth time in quick succession
that I've come out the front door of my house
for the purpose of walking down the sidewalk
past the tallest elm to the red maple,
being careful to keep within eighteen inches
of the curb, as the director instructed me,
and without looking toward the cameras;
and each time there's been a yell
of "Cut!" and it's been explained to me
what I did wrong. The first time I didn't pause briefly
to look about me as men normally do
but lurched out with my head down,
the second time I over-compensated
for my earlier mistake, the third time
I was doing great when a car got in the way,
And the fourth time I shouldn't have
bent down to stroke the cat—that looked too contrived.
So here I go again,
not sure whether I'm helping
to arrange a complicated practical joke
of which I'll later discover
I'm the intended victim,
or whether I'm adding to the number
of lies in a world
in which there are already more
than sufficient
                    and then, slowly, beginning
to understand their trickery is no different

from mine — for instance, this is only
the third time I've come out,
but five seems truer,
and there never was a cat,
although there ought to have been,
and I'm not headed toward the red maple,
although there is one, but in quite another
direction toward an object I couldn't name
without seeming to give it
undue importance.
                    I've nothing to worry about,
being merely one of the instruments
with which the work
is being created,
different from the rest of the apparatus only
in that I'm also a part of the raw material,
like an artist's paint.
                    It is only in films
that the animated tube complains
aloud at the manner
in which the user squeezes it.

First Evening with Peter Pacey

Body English: a pun. Two shy men, each
bearing the other's
weight as well as his own,
until it's only with difficulty
they can lift their arms,
force their fingers
to work like pincers
drawing out the words
that come so hard
the face twists, the eyes
narrow, the teeth
clench,
as though the pain were physical.

Deuces Wild

Dreaming after
an all-night game
the poker player
repeats himself:
a young man, naked
except for a headband
of leather and gold, dancing
before the great bulls
of Crete whose purpose is
to banish motion—he
can outlive them only
by running forward
to meet them, grasping
their horns as though
in greeting, springing
on their backs, and over:
his defence is paradox.

The President dead
for no more reason
than this: the wind that had been travelling
all day at never more than
fourteen and nine-tenths
miles per hour, increased its speed
by one tenth of a mile per hour at
the precise moment when,
for no particular reason,
he turned his head
and met the bullet
that would not have been there
if the assassin had forgotten
to replace a broken
shoelace that morning
or had been kissed
more often or had been killed
by a truck, as he almost was
when he was seven—

it is even conceivable
that you, reader, and I
were unknowingly responsible,
having somehow slowed
of hastened the machinery
of their meeting; although in a truer
sense there is only
one cause for everything:
the reason I am
scratching my earlobe now is
that two stars collided and we live
inside a perpetual
explosion. Chance:
so terrible is our fear of it
that we find it more comfortable
to believe the President was afflicted
with a disease that had driven him mad,
that he organized
a secret legion of five hundred
marksmen, ordered them to kill him,
which they failed to do, only succeeding
in disfiguring him
so hideously
that he has been locked up
in a palace under
the sea or
inside a mountain.

The Social Worker's Poem

"You know them better," said the girl,
whose face glowed with benevolence as from
too much cosmetics, speaking of the poor.
"What can you tell me that might help?"
She planned to do summer social work in a slum.

Do it as a bribe to God, I answered.
Do it because you hate
morons and dirty underwear. Do it because
you are one of those a sense of power causes
to breathe deeply and exhale aloud as if
it were a richer oxygen. Do it to cure
or satisfy some obscure sexual deviation.

But, above all, I said, don't act
from a desire to be loved. Don't ask
so great a payment for your services.
You'll wind up as bitter as the corner grocer
who gave too much credit and went bankrupt.

And remember, Miss, your admonishments
they'll find as irksome as
you're finding these of mine.

Take my word for it. They're human.
Most of them will hate you.

Various Transformations

Said the young African: My family
were great magicians in the old country;
I once saw my grandfather change into
a leopard: this is literally true,
there's not a zoologist on earth could tell
the difference, he played his part so well;
that day he'd come to see me off to school
or, rather, to show me I was a fool
to go—and for a moment what he'd done
tempted me, for no doubt it would be fun
to entertain one's friends and scare one's foes
by turning leopard whenever one chose;
then I came to my senses and I thought:
I could be a magician, but so what?

Even if I improved upon the skill
of all my ancestors so that at will
I became flea or elephant, what good
would it do me or anyone? I would
be better off if I forgot this thing
and took a degree in engineering.

The listener smiled with him, for he thought
it a fine story, factual or not,
especially when compared with his own
experience of brain and blood and bone
straining for years to create something that
projected shadows somewhat like a cat.

We Were Younger Then

The year is 1952: in that drooping decade
before the century got its second wind,
when being young seemed such a waste of time
that we who were young then will always feel
we deserve a refund.
                    John Diefenbaker and I
sit on two cardboard boxes that once contained
White Swan toilet tissues and are now
filled to the top with stereotype engravings
of Santa Claus, reindeer and Christmas trees,
in a basement where the cobwebs do to the windows
what cataracts must do to the eyes, and the dust
rises and falls in accordance with our breath,
searching through back issues of *The Clarion*
for the one in which we reprinted the full text
of his Bill of Rights for Canada.
                    He talks about
Sir Winston and Sir John.
                    Our laughter raises
miniature dust storms.
                    Here is Lincoln born

in Ontario, Andrew Jackson come
from Saskatchewan. He will free us
from them, too, and all such
most admirable oppressors.
                        The year is 1952 and already
there are those who see in him the man who will
redeem the pledge (it is as though we had
left our country with the pawnbroker).
                        When at last we find
what we've been looking for he continues
to sit there on the box until he's read
every word that he wrote,
giving at frequent intervals
a little half-grunt of satisfaction,
while I, nineteen years old, congratulate myself
on being within arm's reach of greatness.
That was so long, oh so very long ago.

Dear Leo

Old friend, there are so many
of you, so many of me,
and more of each of us
showing up all the time
that I think if we make
old bones our relationship
will be a variation on
that old story about
putting one grain of wheat
on the first square
of a chessboard
and twice as many
on the second, and so on,
doubling the number
each time and realizing
long before you come to
the sixty-fourth square

that there's not that much
wheat in the world.

If I were honest
I'd hesitate
when asked if I know you,
meaning do I know the one
you usually let
represent you in public,

hesitate and grope
through the past

before answering:

it has been so long
since I last talked with
the person
of whom they speak.

The Old Gentleman

If you want to ask
a question, the chairman said,
begin by giving us
your name and address.

So the old gentleman
seated near the back
of the auditorium,
when it came his turn, said
he was Louis St. Laurent
and came from Quebec;

and we all of us laughed:
because that's who he was
and it was the kind of little joke

one expected of an elderly
former prime minister;

but the next time
he said the same thing

and the time after that,
said it quite simply

and it became obvious
it wasn't meant to be funny,

wasn't meant to be anything
other than courteous,

like his holding open the door
for whoever happened to reach it
at the same time he did

and never lighting a cigarette
without offering the pack to
the person in front and the person behind
and the persons seated
on either side of him.

Among Life's Pleasures

Having found that,
unknown to each other,
the two of us when
we were much younger
lived on neighbouring streets,
this stranger and I,
drinking gin and tonic
forty thousand feet
above the North Atlantic,
become partners

in creating a golden age,
a mythical city
where everybody we knew
was either good or funny.

The Little Flower Girl

It is always the same
little girl that is chosen
to present the flowers to
the wife of the visiting
dignitary.
   Look closely
    the next time.

Her original home was
in Transylvania and she was first
photographed handing roses
to the Archduchess Otto,
niece-in-law of the Emperor
Franz Josef.
    That was in 1891
and in that picture
she appeared to be
about eight.
    She looked no older
almost eighty years later
when the television cameras
caught her doing the same
thing for Pat Nixon
in Bucharest.
    I'd be scared
to meet her eyes.
     But, of course, the wives
of archdukes, kings,
regents, presidents,
prime ministers and commissars

never look at her.
They're too busy smiling.

I've been one of a crowd
that was addressed with so much
affection I almost forgot
the speaker didn't know me
until afterwards when
the audience broke up
and there was an instant
on his way out of the hall
when he singled me out
with a glance, became almost aware
of my existence, then
dismissed me as
nobody—dismissed me as a lover
of walking upon beaches
might flick a single
grain of sand from his sleeve.

Answer to a Small Child's Question

What would I do?
What would I do?

What would I do, you ask, if I suddenly knew
the world was about to blow up?

I would shut my eyes
and cover my ears

the same as you.

Vertigo

Fearful of high places
I can hardly resist
the urge to drop to my knees
when I stand in the street
and look up
at the top of almost any
high building—
I can see myself there.

And that is so much
like the remembrance
of how often the boy
that I once was
came near to taking
the one step
over the edge
and falling off
this world
into another.

It is late at night. I am fifteen
     and hide in an alley
with Paul Templeton whose dark eyes
     continually
dart about like dogs who have scented
     fear,
dogs so conditioned to subservience
that they cringe even while attacking.

But the victim
is delayed

—there is time to pretend
we've been playing a game
and I've become bored with it,
time for me to withdraw myself
gradually so that he'll not be

entirely sure that he's right
when he calls me a coward.

But what if he'd been able to say:
Listen, can't you hear? He's coming.

Then I couldn't have run.
We'd have had to go through with it.

Acceptance and Rejection

For a few moments the busload
of teachers and students from Ontario
disembarking with their luggage
in front of the hostel in Fredericton
mistook me for a member
of a similar tour that had passed through
earlier that day.
          For those few moments
we were all of us
fellow adventurers:
I could tell from their eyes that they saw me
—which may be as much as we have a right to ask
of strangers, not that they love us
but that they see us.
          I'd have liked to stand there
sharing with them the mild hysteria
of arriving somewhere tired and together,
the mild delirium of belonging,
of knowing everybody else to be equally
road-weary, hungry, thirsty and dirty.

Four O'Clock in the Morning

The cat is massaging her head
against the legs of the young man weeping
into his hands,
hands with which he both muffles
and masks his despair.
                        The cat is purring
on the rug
                and at long intervals
a car passes;
                and as always the nightjars
are chirping amidst the cedars
and chokecherry bushes between
this house and its neighbour.
                                The cat lies down
beside the young man's boots.
And I sit in my pajamas
still befogged by the strangeness
of being awakened by a knocking
If first heard in a dream
                        in which
I descended a spiral
staircase to the great doors
of a castle.
                The young man is struggling to
collect himself.
                It is not inconceivable
one of us will speak
of the weather
which has been the hottest
in forty years, the papers say;
as it turns out I offer him
coffee
and if he says he wants it
I suppose I'll ask him
about cream and sugar.
                        The cat toys
                        with his bootlaces.

I ache with love for him
having myself been slapped
across the face by the universal
disorder of things, and despise my helplessness
almost as much as this
preoccupation with my own
place in the affair.
                    Still, perhaps, it is better
to be numbed
than inspired
by another's grief.
                    The terrible paradox
is that such loneliness as his
is as old as the world, and yet
nobody but him has ever
experienced it. My history and such
as I know of mankind's,
everything I have learned
in thirty-nine years
                        —all that is nothing
to him who might be falling
through space ten million light years
away from the earth.
                    The cat rolls over
on her back, and the young man
smiles absent-mindedly and bends to stroke her.
Another car passes
with someone like us
at the wheel.
                    The nightjars chirrup.

Siege

My mind besieged in
its crumbling castle:
by day the enemy
snipes from his great
wheeled towers,
undermines the walls;
I hold the stairs
to the bells
whose laughter
reinforces me;
by night he infiltrates
but, being inhuman, is
not fully aware how
powerless I am:
animal and angel
alike are wary of
us because we are men,
hybrids, never wholly
predictable. He whispers.
And I dream
I am neither
alive nor dead,
my nose and jaw
sawn away, so that it
is worse, far worse
than that earlier
time when I shut
my eyes while I hid
the mirror behind
a door or switched
off the lights and sat
in the dark,
never saw myself except
as reflected in
the eyes of others
who weren't quick
enough in turning away

—that and the
remembered reality
of being fed through
one tube, drained
through another, the
urine burning
as it seeped from me,
drop by drop.
Believe me, I would gladly
spare you this
if I could.

Sicknesses Impervious to Words

Our distrust of one another,
our disbelief in ourselves: sicknesses
impervious to words.
He wants me to know he admires
something I've done, so he apologizes
for being such a fool as to mention it,
adds at once that he despises
praise, desires nothing
from me in return and
(this last again and again)
no, no, no, he isn't lying.
And I want to embrace him,
not so much from gratitude,
although that's part of it,
as out of sadness
for both of us,
                yes and another
darker part of my mind wills me
to choke him into listening;
but unless I'm drunk
all I do is think
these things to myself

and stand there
for ever and ever
red-faced and stupid.

He Continues to Try to Avoid Being Caught

A memo to myself: Don't tell
anyone that a fiend from hell
bent over you last night and grinned.
Ask why you whimpered, blame the wind.

Unfinished Poem

Bring me black slippers.
The corpse would dance.

Marriage

After seven years
I've almost succeeded
in freeing my wife
from her ludicrous fear
of electrical storms.

Tonight she parted
the curtains to watch
the lightning burst open
like an enormous golden
flower, consume itself, die
to the accompaniment
of the sound the sky might
make if it were

solid and could be
cracked open from
horizon to zenith.

And I flinched.

After seven years.

That much of her
implanted in me.

It Begins Quietly

Her madness is apparent
in acts that no one
except he finds
extraordinary. He wonders
if that is how it always
begins. Not with murder
but with the intermittent
reversal of old habits,
done half-mischievously,
so that if he betrays
surprise or
uneasiness, she is free
to laugh it off,
her eyes
needling,
while the others
try without success
to understand
him.

Postscript

The poet having quarrelled
violently with his lover
and having written it all down
is conscience-stricken
when he overhears her
vomiting in the next room.
His words came
as painfully
but were elegant
—which it is clear now
they had no right to be.

Parlour Game

We were sitting there
hating one another when
some friends dropped in
who've always said
we're the most loving
couple they know

and of course the two of us
went into the act
as usual, each afraid
of the other's equally
strong inclination
to give the game away,

both sneering inwardly
for the first five or ten
minutes and then
both trying not to burst,
without knowing whether
the laughter that came
would be savage or joyous

—and within half an hour
we caught ourselves exchanging
silly and affectionate
smiles even when
nobody else was watching:

for the millionth time,
starting over again.

Cold Comfort

Well, at least
I won't always
be young, he says.
At least that's
something.
            Reminding me
of how I, too, once
mistook for
symptoms
of youth those
afflictions
that come from
being human.

Nostalgia

I look at a picture of my wife, my son and me
taken eight years ago, when nothing was as good
for us as it has been since:
I, for one, have seldom been happier
than I am now;
                and yet I'm moved
almost to tears, not because I'd like
to bring back the past,

but because I know so well
that I couldn't, even if I wanted to.

He Addresses Himself to One of the Young Men
He Once Was

If you had not said you loved her —
                              but that
was the only way you knew,
                              being so young and such
a clown:
              made to be a man too early and consequently kept
a child too long,
                    you were speechless, yet unaware
there was no need to speak.
And because you were pitiful
                              she was pitiless
— that is the word,
                    pitiless,
                              taken to mean
no more than the absence
of pity — and did not even permit you
to be present while she hurt you,
                              worse: may have borne no more
malice toward you than toward the worms
she skewered on her trout-hooks
that afternoon you fished;
                              (she'd not have believed
                              her ears if you'd told her
                              each of them seemed to you
                              a miniature, black
magical caduceus).
                    It was yourself you wanted,
                              after all, and not this
woman.
          Whatever pleasure
                    came from her body was

in the rehearsal or
the re-enactment of
what may never have been,
                              what you had no way of knowing
is often little more than
                         a wholehearted
                                      sneeze.
Forgive me.
              A comedian volunteers to buy
affection at the price
of self-abasement.
                  A fool unwillingly
                              pays more for less.
You were a fool and I am
                         too often tempted to
play the comedian.
                  I give you only
a home for your ghost,
                     and one
                              fraternal voice
joined in the general laughter.

Endings

There is nothing left but
a silence so wilful it becomes
a third presence, that
and the shared memories
that turned on them, the habit
of doing this and leaving that to be done
by the other and, most conclusive of all,
a studied reluctance
to hurt: in the good times the bumps came
when least expected, now
they know the way so well
they can pass one another in
pitch darkness and never touch.

Each of them is alone in
a house haunted by the other's ghost
so that he hears her footsteps
and doesn't speak,
knowing she'd misunderstand.
        If only there were some
sacrament for the occasion,
a ritual of
few words prescribed by
tradition and accompanied by
appropriate gestures.
        It would be best if it made
the participants smile —
say if there were a shrine
near the centre of every city
where there were whatever flowers
were in season, wild birds and
little animals (but not in cages),
and a permanent
Punch and Judy show,
the whole presided over
by a minstrel, a juggler
and a dispenser of
free wine and hashish,
        and lovers could go there
        or friends
        and walk out
simply as strangers.

Prison Riot

The prisoners, having taken control
of one wing of the penitentiary
and suddenly finding themselves as free
as most of us, at first broke every rule
within their power: They ran in and out
of one another's cells, made lots of noise,

set fires here and there, knocked things about,
until, exhausted, they regained their poise
—whereupon they set up a government
and courts to judge the criminal element,
beating to death two known informers, an
incestuous father and another man
locked up for burglary whose mortal sin
nobody afterwards could quite determine.

He Perceives That His Son Is Becoming a Man

Love is nothing I will
but what is done with me.
I would have you stop
like a plucked flower:
                  Take care
when I reach out my hand,
                          be cruel if you must,
as I would be if I could.

Nor was it malice
moved the queen
to represent
herself as an apple.

The gift was as it came
from the tree,
it was the giving
proved venomous.

If there are times,
as there have been
and will be,
when love withdraws
for its own reasons,
make such use of them

as you can. Move quickly.
They will not come often.

While I work harder
at my part:
the brain once again
learning to do
what the heart cannot.

Argument

I'll be as sentimental
as I want and if you don't like it
then to hell with you,
was what the father told
the poet who had
sat down to write
about their mutual son
coming home after
five months in Europe.

Not in my book you won't, the poet said.

The Process of Progressive Revelation

There's so much you
don't know about
being older until
you are:
        secrets
that everybody older
shares and is tempted to
equate with their cost
and thereby over-value.

That's as true of turning
one age as another, although
later even the commonest
expressions mean something
different than before,
most of all the conventional
reply to "How are you?"

The Fish with a Coin in Its Mouth

A picture pops into my head.
A picture I don't recall ever
having seen before.
                    A ship,
huge coils of rope
rougher than a cat's tongue,
great sweet-smelling piles
of lumber, masts reaching for the sky,
a pit of darkness that must be
an open hatch.
                    Many people are there
who feel that in coming
they've done something
important.
                    I am among them,
a small boy in shorts
and a blue beret.
                    Perhaps there is a band
and perhaps the people
are cheering
or perhaps that is only how it feels.

Oh that! My father says when
I tell him. Your uncle and I
we took you down to Hantsport
to see the *Bluenose*,
the fastest fishing schooner

there ever was. You were about
three years old.
I'd have thought you'd
have forgotten that.

And so I had
—until one night
after thirty-seven years,
for no apparent reason,
it all came back.

Poem for Barbara and Lindsay's Wedding

If, three-quarters of a century from here,
a certain woman looking for something else
among old, dusty, half-remembered things,
should happen upon the photograph of you taken
tonight, she might show it to her daughter
and say to her:
                    Look at your great-grandparents
the day they were married; what funny old cameras
they had and what funny old tables and chairs,
and how funny the young men looked
with those big moustaches and their hair
down to their shoulders!
                    And they might laugh
a little at you and by implication at the rest
of us minor historical figures
who went about in clownish costumes
uttering quaint expressions.
                    But then
if there should be enough of you,
Barbara, in that woman, she would add:
Child, although you'll not believe this,
there was a time
when they were as real as you;
I seem to recall they lived

then in a small town beside a river
where there were trees and almost every house
had a little plot of grass
around it, sometimes with flowers;
I suppose they drove
to church in the kind of funny old car
you've seen in museums;
and they were young—this was so long ago
that all of the old people were young then;
your great-grandmother
can't have been more than twenty;
the family legend is
she was so lovely, smiling through her tears,
an onlooker compared her to a rainbow.

On Names and Misnomers

One name is not enough
for anyone. It was not me
you heard reading these poems
before an audience.
The posters should have said:
Gilbert Cuthbertson will present
poems by Alden Nowlan.
                          And the man
drinking wine in your kitchen
after the reading:
he ought to have been
introduced as Tom Solomon, a friend
of Gilbert Cuthbertson's and
an acquaintance of
Alden Nowlan's.
                          It's the same with you.
Why should you be expected
to answer to the name of

                          (insert your signature
                          in the blank space opposite)

at times when you're really
someone quite different?
It would be better
for everyone concerned if
you could say, I'm sorry, but
today you're talking to
Janey Lamont or
Marilyn Trenholm or
Sammie Jefferson or
Francis Vivian Dangerfield.
Because that's how it is.
Each of us contains multitudes,
every one of whose
personalities is split.

The Enormous Radio

There would come the sound
of footsteps. Nothing more. The sound
of slow, heavy footsteps growing
constantly louder. That was enough.
More than enough. The mind began
to shape the thing, began but never
completed it. So there was no end
to the horror: the imagination driven
almost mad, it was so near to being
alone and absolutely free.

Small Compensation

I might have been more
comfortable with women
if I'd been born
Polynesian.
            On the other hand

I could never
have derived so much
harmless enjoyment
from the dentist's little
yellow-haired receptionist
bending over to open
the lowest drawer of
a filing cabinet, her
vermilion skirt
rising far enough
to uncover her
underpants: white
and trimmed
extensively
with lace.

The Chianti Drinker's Poem

Sitting on somebody's bed
in a room crammed with students
drinking Chianti from Dixie cups
I hear myself say: "That was
twenty years ago,"
in the casual tone
I'd have used in speaking
of something that happened
yesterday.
       I don't remember
ever having done that
before; even as recently
as when I was thirty-five
I'd have said, "That was
when I was fifteen," or
"That was in 1948,"
almost in the same way
the fifteen-year-old
that I used to be

would have said, "That was
before I was born," or
"Herbert Hoover was
elected in 1928,"
and could have been
elected in 1876, for all
it meant to me —
even my personal history
did not involve me
directly: it was as if
a child actor had played the part
of me in the earlier scenes
of a film based on
my life and times.
      But tonight I hear
myself reporting
from the past
as an eyewitness
      and I reflect that
twenty years ago I was
much the same man
as now — oh, I was prettier
and had not seen
one-hundredth as much,
but the core was the same.
      And I recall other
men saying to me
when I was the age
of these students
or younger, "That was
twenty years ago,"
referring to
Lindbergh's flight
or the shooting of
John Dillinger or the birth
of the Dionne Quintuplets
or the abdication of
Edward VIII or an incident
in their own lives

that took place
while Bennett was
prime minister,
       and for the first time
I understand how real
all that
must have been
to them.

A Night for Hot Punch

Everybody's standing on one foot
to put on an overshoe
or turning on the headlights
or helping somebody into a coat
or kissing
or shaking hands,

when I hear her laughing and telling the others:

Did you hear that?
He says
he's going to
pray for me!

And I wonder if she's laughing
because I'm drunk or is it
that she knows
I sometimes profess
to be an agnostic
or can't she think
of anything else to do—

anyway I feel like a fool
I do
and wish I hadn't said it

but what I meant was
I felt good,
I liked her,
I wanted her
to feel good too.

The Road to the Border

Each of us has no choice
but to suffer
for the others.
                The sacrifice
consists in no more
than bearing one's share
of the pain.
                I am hitchhiking.
A car stops
fifty yards ahead.
                        I run up to it.
The driver asks me,
"Are you headed for the border?"
And when I tell him, "Yes,"
he says, "So am I," and drives off,
leaving me, revenging himself
on his wife, his kids,
his employer, the government
and God.
                But if there had been time
and I had been able to
laugh back at him and shout,
"Good luck," instead of
"You bastard," we both might have been
happier now.
                I know that I would.

On Being Temporarily Blind

If I had been born blind
and were not waiting
for these bandages
to be removed,
I would think that men
other than myself were
spherical,
          for that is how I picture
the source of
the voices.

No, of course I'd have touched
somebody at some time
and learned different:

although how strange it feels to be
one blind man shaking
the hand of another!

I had always heard
the blind learned more
from touch than others.
That is not true of this
amateur: the hand in mine
is no particular
object
         but simply
                  a solid,

another part of
the absolute
hardness that I know to be
divided
         into walls, chairs
         and tables
but no longer
think of as such.

I am surrounded by
some one substance
that I cannot
                penetrate

and I wish I could shake off
this body of mine and become
lighter than air,
                one of the beach balls
and balloons
with whom I converse
as they float around me.

In the Shopping Centre

Bricks that would melt and drip
if touched by heat, a grate of the same
material, and flames
that burn nothing—a plastic fireplace
seems the perfect symbol
for this shopping centre
where almost everything reminds me
of an island touched once,
briefly, long ago
by civilization:
we remember how things looked
but never clearly understood
their purposes, and know nothing
about principles,
so that everything we make
is like the planes the Papuan highlanders
are said to have built
out of wire and cardboard boxes
after the air force left.

Incident Observed While Picking Up the Mail

The elements have had their way
with this man as with any other
natural object. The rain has left its mark
on him as on the stone.
He looks down into the face
of a boy about eight years old,
a face so open to the world it reminds me
of a cat whose claws have been clipped
—it is that vulnerable.
They wear bib overalls and rubber boots
standing at a counter
in this small-town post office
and out of the corner of my eye I watch
the boy sign the man's name
to an unemployment insurance cheque.
He writes very slowly and with great care.
I am tempted to follow them
across the street and into the bank
so that I can see them smile
at one another, lovingly,
as the cashier examines
the signature and finds it good.
Father and son—it would be impossible
to decide which of them is prouder.

In the Newsroom

Phone the woman
whose husband and kids
were killed, we need
more information, the
editor says.

And each time you expect
they'll hang up

after cursing you
for the ghoul
you know yourself to be.

But that almost never happens.
Almost always they sound
very formal but pleased
the newspaper has called.
Often they'll insist
you hold the line while they check
a date or a spelling.

Not having had time
as yet to remember
that death is permanent.

Body and Soul

If the intern were out to persuade me
that I have no existence apart from
my body, he couldn't have found
a more convincing argument
than the calcium he's
injecting into me.
                    The trembling
has almost stopped
where seconds ago
my fingers and toes
were each of them
a marionette
being worked by a child
made hysterical
by his own ineptitude.
                    My jaws
have ceased
to rattle like spoons
in the hands of

an Acadian dancer.
                        I'm no longer
frightened by quick movements
glimpsed from the corners
of my eyes.
                    The cripple's malice
gives way to a benevolence
akin to the lassitude
that follows love-making.
My saliva tastes of cinnamon.
I glow.
I've stopped being suspicious of my wife.

A Pinch or Two of Dust

*—The dust being from Culloden, Scotland, where, in a battle
fought in 1746, the last of the great Celtic societies was extinguished.*

A friend has given me
a pinch or two of dust,
an ounce at most of soil
from a field where our ancestors,
his and mine, were ploughed into
the compost bed of history, a people
who had outlived their gods,
the last of the old barbarians
destroyed by the first of the new,
magnificent fools who threw
stones and handfuls of earth
at the gunners until they themselves
became part of that earth and thereby
made it theirs for ever,
their blood indistinguishable now
from it, their blood contained
in this pinch or two of dust
as in my body and the body
of the friend who gave it
—this soil not only between

but within
my fingers, a part of
the very cells that shape this poem.

Vancouver Poem
for Elizabeth Brewster

"Vancouver is an un-Canadian city,"
Betty had said, although probably
thinking about something quite different,
and I, thinking about something different,
had agreed—a conversation of no
importance except that afterwards
it came to us that it must have been the reason
the cabbie who'd driven us in from the airport
practically spat in our faces when we paid him:
he was an East Indian, and people
who looked vaguely like us
must have hurt him so badly that
he could mistake himself for
a mountain range or the Pacific Ocean.

Their First Meeting
for Charlie Clarke

The Great Dane sees the two
young bulls at the same
moment as they
catch sight of him, and
they all three freeze
there in the pasture,
                    the dog
staring at the bulls,
                    the bulls
staring back—

                    the question is
who will run?
                    Somebody must.
They are taking
so long to decide
that it may be they
know as I do
                    they'll never again
be given a choice:
                    he that runs today
                    must run for ever.

In the Officers' Mess
for Gladys and Ian Fraser

The cellophane-wrapped
young technocrats, most of them
graduates in engineering,
have had one beer each,
have applauded the old general
with the fingertips of one hand
patting the palm of the other,
have smiled and said goodbye
in the tone of voice used
by barbers and dentists when
working on small children and
by almost everybody when
addressing a drunk.

The romantics too have gone
in their scarves and berets
and with six or eight ounces
of good Scotch in their veins,
but they'll be back after
they've jogged their four miles.

The general has shaken hands
with all of us, a man possessed of
that humility that sometimes
truly beautifies near-senility.

So right now this place belongs
to the third component
of the Canadian officers' corps:
the roaring boys from places
like Burnt Coat, Economy,
Widower's Mountain, Virgin's Cove,
Sally's Tickle and Desolation Creek,
who express love by emptying
their tankards over
one another's heads,
do parachute rolls off the tables,
dance on broken glass and do
imitations of Harry Hibbs
singing Newfoundland songs
about Belfast.

Later the romantics
will come back, wearing sweatsuits,
to down three or four more
doubles and refight with bottles,
tumblers, matchboxes,
cigarette lighters and swizzle sticks
the battles named on
the regimental flag

—and those of us who haven't
flaked out will watch and listen
to them with that rapt
expression that comes to
the faces of drunken men
in the presence of something
they can't fully grasp but know
to be of vast importance.

The Rites of Manhood

It's snowing hard enough that the taxis aren't running.
I'm walking home, my night's work finished,
long after midnight, with the whole city to myself,
when across the street I see a very young American sailor
standing over a girl who's kneeling on the sidewalk
and refuses to get up although he's yelling at her
to tell him where she lives so he can take her there
before they both freeze. The pair of them are drunk
and my guess is he picked her up in a bar
and later they got separated from his buddies
and at first it was great fun to play at being
an old salt at liberty in a port full of women with
hinges on their heels, but by now he wants only to
find a solution to the infinitely complex
problem of what to do about her before he falls into
the hands of the police or the shore patrol
—and what keeps this from being squalid is
what's happening to him inside:
if there were other sailors here
it would be possible for him
to abandon her where she is and joke about it
later, but he's alone and the guilt can't be
divided into small forgettable pieces;
he's finding out what it means
to be a man and how different it is
from the way that only hours ago he imagined it.

A Note on the Public Transportation System

It's not hard to begin
a conversation with the person
who happens to be seated
nearest you, especially when she's been
reading with apparent interest
a book that's one of your

favourites and can't find
her matches.
                    The difficulty is
once you've spoken you can never
go back to being comfortable
with silence,
                    even if you learn
you've nothing to say
and would rather not
listen.
          You can stop talking
but you can't forget
the broken wires
dangling there between you.
                              You'll smile
almost guiltily
when your glances
accidentally bump
against each other.
                    It may get so bad
that one of you will have to
pretend to fall asleep.

An Unanswered Letter

An aunt writes me that the better families
in Lockhartville, Hastings Mills and Frenchman's Cross
are disgusted with me for fattening my purse
by selling lies about my relatives,
not excepting my poor old grandmother who took me in
when I was eight years old and homeless.
It's a good thing for you that you can write, she says.
You could never make a living doing anything else;
you never did an honest day's work in your life.
She adds that unless I stop printing stories
like that last one she's going to do
some writing of her own, beginning with

an account of how my mother, her sister-in-law,
abandoned me the way no bitch would.
That should contain some spicy titbits, she says.
And I wish I could write back and ask her
for the details of that old scandal,
but she'd be certain
to misunderstand. I think of her trying
all her life to be thought genteel,
her life's ambition to entertain
the Women's Institute without anything
happening to spoil it, sending away for
fancy cookie cutters so she could serve
little sandwiches shaped like hearts and diamonds
topped with Cheez Whiz and an olive,
and listening all the while for the car to stop
(there was usually a hole in the muffler),
listening for the slamming of its doors,
the drunken laughter
of her high-booted, bellowing bog Irish menfolk
once again come home too soon. I think of her
wanting so little so desperately
and obtaining so much less,
ending up with nothing.
And for an instant I wish,
for her sake I could be two
persons, one of whom would write
Grace Livingstone Hill–type novels she could leave
where they'd be sure to be seen.
"He's my nephew," she'd explain. No,
although she's ashamed
of the local dialect she's never been
able to rid herself of it.
"He's my brother's boy," is how she'd put it.

The Terrible Choice

"Kill me," begs my wife or my grown son
        or my dearest friend
writhing in anguish on the roadside
        or in a hospital bed,
as those about to be burnt alive
        used to plead
to be strangled first, a mercy
the executioner generally granted them
        as long
as he could do it without getting
        his hands burned.

"Kill me, please," and I hope I could
        do it
—but without expecting pardon, without
        denying my guilt.
I hope I could do it, knowing it to be
        evil; that
is a quality lacking in this age:
the willingness
to act out of love or pity while
        confessing
that not everything they demand of
        us is good.

A True Story

"I could mow lawns," the poet said. "In the spring
I could transplant flowers. I might even like that
Or I could wash windows—
no, I'm serious," he added because the professor had begun
to chuckle at this young man whom he'd described
in a long essay in *Canadian Literature*
as a writer of rare gifts and great promise.
"I need a room where I can hang my pictures

and have my books around me for a while.
I thought you might find me a job here
at the university as a maintenance man or groundskeeper."
The professor answered, "But we can't insult you
like that, my dear fellow. You'll have to wait
until something suitable becomes available.
Can't you imagine what it would be like
for those of us who teach your poems?
We'd look ridiculous. Anyhow, I know you must be joking.
That humour that so cleverly balances
English understatement and American exaggeration
is among the aspects of your art
that I find most admirable, and distinctively Canadian."

A Good Thing Happened Today

"You're the poet," says the cabbie,
looking me up and down with neither
suspicion nor deference, real or
affected. "What's it like
being a poet?" He wants to know
purely for the sake of knowing.
His ignorance does not frighten him,
nor is he proud
of his knowledge, although aware
he possesses it. Everyone is better
and worse than he in one way or another,
in consequence his equal. I perceive this much
in his face and voice and answer him
the best I can. "I thought that might be
how it was," he says. "But I wasn't sure."
He is satisfied, not greatly impressed
but certainly not contemptuous. He accepts me
into his world. We drive on,
the two of us, together.

The Great Electronic Window

The people in that world
have only two
senses. They see and hear.
Although it appears they must
formerly have been able
to taste and smell—
one deduces that
from certain of
their gestures
and obsessions:
it is as if they had reason
to live in fear of
the atavistic as
represented by
armpits and onions.
And while by their nature
they can never touch,
it would seem
they can conceive of
the sensation and
derive satisfaction
from making believe.
Once perhaps they were as we are,
as we become more
and more like them
—and soon nobody anywhere
will want to be
anything
but only to play
at being something.

After Reading the Correspondence in *Penthouse* Magazine

There'll be nothing more
on television tonight.

Switching off the set
is like acknowledging
the loss of a friend.

You make yourself a sandwich,
pour a glass of milk.

It's time to sit down
with pencil and paper
to write about lapping
anchovy butter from
the navel of your wife's
nymphomaniac
adolescent sister,

although you never had a wife,
long ago gave up hope
of ever having anybody

except such wraiths
as you can conjure
from your letter box,
Mister Name Withheld.

Murderers

I have known eight murderers, five of them well.
Oliver, who blew off his father's head and liked
to drink root beer while chewing licorice.
Gabriel, nicknamed Angel, who stabbed his girl
and who found it impossible to eat
chicken and a salad containing eggs

at the same meal, although he liked both.
"It makes me think of embryos," he explained.
Big Angus, who locked his neighbour in his own barn
and then set fire to it, burning him alive,
and whom I loved for his awkward gentleness.
Joel Crabtree, who was never arrested
for shooting his wife although the entire village knew
approximately where he'd buried her.
And Philip Beaver. A clear case
of diabolic possession, it was said
by the Protestant missionary
to the Indians, who spent most
of his time in English-speaking churches
where he talked to the Sunday School children
while wearing a war bonnet and moccasins
and taught them the Maliseet and Micmac words
to *Jesus Loves Me.*
Not so, said the Catholic chaplain, who refused
to sign the petition for commutation, arguing
that a murderer is more likely to be convinced
of his need for salvation if he knows
that he's about to die.
Buck, one of the guards, who in
his spare time sold something called
the Lifetime Family Bible Reading Plan,
said he was worried
about the books with pictures on their covers
of naked girls.
                "And you don't fool me either,"
said Philip. "What's it to you if they hang me?
I know your angle. Your name in the papers.
Yesterday I heard you on the radio."
                                Sneeringly:
"'Ladies and gentlemen, save Philip Beaver!'
Who do you think you're kidding with that stuff?"
His father had said to me, "Whatever happens
to my boy, his blood won't be on your hands."
That had made me proud; perhaps my pride was greater
than my compassion. Somebody had asked

what I hoped to accomplish and I'd answered,
proudly again, "I'll show the government
there's someone who doesn't want this man to hang."
So, thank you, Philip.
I thanked you then and now I thank you again.
Your gratitude might have tempted me too much.
While not as bad as you thought me, I had sinned.

The Jelly Bean Man

"He carries jelly beans," a neighbour told us
when we first came here. "You're lucky you don't
have any small children."
                          He's the Jelly Bean Man
and the first words he ever said to me
were, "Kiss it and make it well,"
he having observed my wife
bump her forehead against the door
of our car while getting into it
with her arms full of groceries.
"It's nothing to grin about," he said.

So I kissed her above
and between the eyes, and he said,
"Love her; she is the daughter of
Cronos and Rhea, the sister and wife
of Zeus. Here I have a gift for her.
She will share it with you."

And he insisted that she take
two cinnamon rolls
which she and I later ate
at home, very slowly,
with dairy butter
—each bite was like hearing
a little ripple of simple music.

Later we learned it was true
he carried jelly beans and distributed them,
but only as an uncle might or a grandfather
—and, oh, it's so easy to teach
your small daughters and sons
to accept nothing
from strangers, to keep well back always,
to stay out of arm's reach,
to be prepared to run,
so easy to tell them
about evil,
so hard to tell them
about innocence,

so impossible to say:
be good to the Jelly Bean Man
who gives candy to children
from no other motive than love.

Hands

Watching another's hands
do something they do well
and therefore with grace,

something done without
reference to the mind

—a good carpenter
hammering nails,
a country woman
peeling vegetables,

gives me such pleasure,
makes me feel so secure

that I drift child-like
into sensuous drowsiness.

Scratchings

1.
Reflect
before doing unto
your neighbour what
you would have him
do unto you.

He may have different tastes.

2.
A drunkard
likes to be drunk.

An alcoholic
can't stand to be sober.

3.
No one is more
pitifully foolish
than the person
who attempts to prove
by argument
that the world is round.

4.
The trouble with being God
is that you have to do all the work.

5.
The perfect parliament
would include
delegates from
the living,
the unborn
and the dead.

6.
The best thing about
writing fiction is
your characters
can't hit you back.

Act Two

She thinks that
which she fears is
behind her, and so
she runs
toward it.
        Worse
it can be dispelled
only by another
and equivalent
act
of the will.
        Next
she will break
through the glass
of the mirror,
screaming.

Fire!

The Fire Chief tells me
it often happens that
somebody doesn't want to
leave a burning building.
Usually, it's an old
person, he says.
        He's seen many
of them sitting

in their favourite
chairs, while the walls
around them turned
into honeycombs.
                    Few things are more
beautiful, he says, than wood
at the moment it ceases
to be wood and becomes
solidified flame and would be
transparent if the eyes could bear it.

I myself covered
fires for a newspaper.
                    You'd be
astonished how seldom
I saw an unhappy
face, although everyone
kept saying how terrible
it was.
            Especially at night
there was exultation
in the eyes and voices
of the spectators waiting
for the roof to collapse,
a cheerful purposefulness
in the gestures of
the firemen, and the
victims, such of them
as survived, seemed exhilarated,
standing barefoot
on the sidewalk, some
wearing nothing
more than a blanket, all of them
aware that tonight
almost anything
they said or did
would be forgiven them.

Aftermath to a Plane Crash

"Excuse me, sir," says
the man with the microphone.
"We're conducting a poll
on public attitudes
toward cannibalism."

Well, the theologians
seem to have decided
that God is a committee.

But our ancestors knew
there are times when
decency consists
of keeping silent.

The Broadcaster's Poem

I used to broadcast at night
alone in a radio station
but I was never good at it,
partly because my voice wasn't right
but mostly because my peculiar
metaphysical stupidity
made it impossible
for me to keep believing
there was somebody listening
when it seemed I was talking
only to myself in a room no bigger
than an ordinary bathroom.
I could believe it for a while
and then I'd get somewhat
the same feeling as when you
start to suspect you're the victim
of a practical joke.
                    So one part of me

was afraid another part
might blurt out something
about myself so terrible
that even I had never until
that moment suspected it.
                    This was like the fear
of bridges and other
high places: Will I take off my glasses
and throw them
into the water, although I'm
half-blind without them?
Will I sneak up behind
myself and push?
                    Another thing:
as a reporter
I covered an accident in which a train
ran into a car, killing
three young men, one of whom
was beheaded. The bodies looked
boneless, as such bodies do.
More like mounds of rags.
And inside the wreckage
where nobody could get at it
the car radio
was still playing.
                    I thought about places
the disc jockey's voice goes
and the things that happen there
and of how impossible it would be for him
to continue if he really knew.

Witness to Murder

The cameraman must be running backwards
in front of the soldiers and their prisoner
who wears black shorts and a sportshirt
imprinted with sunflowers
and has sandals on his feet
and does not look as if he understands
that he is about to die — although we know
he would not be there on the screen
unless something horrible
were in store for him.
                      I hear myself talking
to his picture:
               Make a run for it! I shout.
There's a chance you'll make it.
Grab for a gun, maybe you'll take
one of them with you.
                    But he can't hear me.
He keeps on walking.

The Middle-Aged Man in the Supermarket

I'm pretending to test the avocados for ripeness
while gaping obliquely at the bare brown legs
of the girl in the orange skirt selecting mushrooms
when she says, "Hi, there, let's make love."
At first I think that she must have caught me
and is being sarcastic and then I decide
she's joking with someone she knows, perhaps the boy
    weighing green beans
or the young man with the watercress, so I try to act
as if I hadn't heard her, walk away at what I hope
is the right speed, without looking back,
and don't stop until I come to
the frozen-food bins, where I'm still standing,
gazing down at things I almost never buy, when

I become aware
she's near me again, although I see only
a few square inches of brown thigh, a bit of
        orange cloth
and two symmetrical bare feet. I wish I could know
her body so well I could ever afterwards identify her
by taste alone. I rattle a carton
of frozen peas, read both French and English directions
on a package of frozen bread dough. She still
        stands there.
I wait for her to say to me:
"I fell in love the moment I saw you.
I want us to spend our first week together
in bed. We'll have our meals sent up. I'm even prettier
when I'm bare and I promise I'll keep my eyes shut
while you're naked, so that you'll never worry
that I might be comparing your body with that
of a previous lover, none of whom was older
than twenty, although the truth is I like
fat hips and big bellies — it's a kink
        that I have:
my nipples harden when I envision
those mountainous moons of flesh above me."

The Fire Is Not Quenched

The triangular fingernails
of March penetrate the skin.
Something from the first
age of the world — here
at the city dump,
in the dusk, encircling the fire,
a ring of stray cats, each of them
lying on its belly
in the warm ashes, with its head
resting on its paws, and its eyes
narrowed to slits.

You are right,
little fellow creatures,
it is good,
very good
            to be alive.

Hey!

The window!
            I've never in my life
laid eyes on a dawg
            that ran as fast
                    as that big gray bugger
over there
            to the right of the trees
                    in the parking lot—
must be a race hound!
            On
            second
            thought,
don't bother:
            it was the light,
                    the way it falls
this time of year
            and a couple of sparrows.

The Magic Man

I'd like you to meet
a friend of mine,
Bruce Armstrong.
                    He's a magician.

Bruce tells me
I embarrass him
by always adding that.
                    It's childish.

I'm sorry, I say to him.
I promise
I won't do it again.

He shakes his head and laughs.
You're hopeless, he says.
Hopeless.

            Then he makes a fist
            and out of his hand
            there flashes
            a great flaming sword!

It's all done
with props, he
explains — the liar.

By Crate from the Moon

The human brain is not an organ of thinking but an
organ of survival.
  —*Albert Szent-Gyorgyi*

The others were about to take off from the surface
        of the moon
in a box about the size and shape of a railway car,
which must have been mounted on a platform to which
        there was neither
stairs nor ladder: because I found I would have to
        lift myself
by the strength of my arms alone through a doorway
about five feet from the ground. I wasn't strong
        enough
and for a long time nobody would help me.
Then at last two passengers
whom I didn't recognize got up from their seats
and came to the back of the box, where the doorway was,
and one of them took me by the right arm and the other
        by the left
and they dragged me up and on to the floor
where I lay panting as the great yellow disc fell
        away from under us,
the brightness of it almost blinding me.

That was the only noteworthy thing that happened to me
today and no less circumstantial
than any other event in my life. Yet I'm required to
        register it
as a kind of cerebral nocturnal emission, the
        alternative being
martyrdom—if not by men then by one of the many
        thousands
of Objects moving toward me, of Things that stand
        in my way.

Question Period
— While attending a conference on the teaching of poetry in high schools

I am the victim of cancer called upon to address
an assembly of surgeons. I am the man who built his own house
and did it so well that the architects
drove out from Halifax and questioned him.
"My hands did it," he told them, "and hands don't talk."
I am the farmer who when he was asked why
he had married one woman rather than another said:
"We'd had a good summer followed by a bad winter;
there was a shortage of potatoes in Cuba;
all during January the snow was so deep
I couldn't get to the wood lot;
and she was there."
        I am the man who knows The Answerer's
other name is Captain Death.
        Blue flowers have appeared
along the edge of the lawn in front of my house,
blue flowers of which I know only
that they are beautiful and don't grow wild
in northeastern North America, and were never planted
by me.
        What are they? Where did they come from?
Their secretiveness is like that
of children planning a surprise
for someone they love.
        So much whispering.
I will do my best not to hear.

In Praise of the Great Bull Walrus

I wouldn't like to be one
of the walrus people
for the rest of my life
but I wish I could spend
one sunny afternoon

lying on the rocks with them.
I suspect it would be similar
to drinking beer in a tavern
that caters to longshoremen
and won't admit women.
We'd exchange no
cosmic secrets. I'd merely say,
"How yuh doin' you big old walrus?"
and the nearest of
the walrus people
would answer,
"Me? I'm doin' great.
How yuh doin' yourself?
you big old human being, you?"
How good it is to share
the earth with such creatures
and how unthinkable it would have been
to have missed all this
by not being born:
a happy thought, that,
for not being born is
the only tragedy
that we can imagine
but need never fear.

The Night of the Party

Never have I seen women
wiser or more beautiful.

Never have I known men
so witty, so sensitive.

Here in my living room
are the twenty most remarkable
persons in all the world.

And me, the one fool,
who must dance
although too heavy
on his feet, sing
although his vocal cords
are out of tune.

But that is the price
I pay for such
companionship.

My friends,
I do not get drunk for myself,
I get drunk for you.

Smoked Glass

A Very Common Prescription

I store a tube of tears in my refrigerator.
Many people must do the same.
It has been an excessively dry summer
and you use your eyes more than is good
for them, the doctor said.
At the drug store I was embarrassed
to see what it was
that he had prescribed for me.
Tears! Why, good God, I mean
I cry almost every day of my life.
If I've no better reason
I've only to relax my grip
to have my eyes moisten
at the memory of certain
scenes in old movies:
say, Gregory Peck's funeral
in *The Gunfighter*. Surely,
that ought to be enough.
I was tempted to say this
to the clerk when she handed over
the medication. Lady, it's not
what you think, my heart isn't
made of flint; believe me,
I hurt too. But that wasn't as bad
as reading the fine print
when I got home. Keep tightly
sealed and refrigerate
after use, it said.
If we have house guests I'll hide
the tube at the bottom of
the vegetable crisper.
And to think there are factories!
I picture them as being
windowless, lit by pale blue bulbs,
and containing row upon row
of workers in smocks and hairnets
who sit on long benches, bend

over long tables,
weeping into sterile tissues
for forty hours a week,
men and women who when they're asked
their occupation have to answer:
tear-maker.

On Being Detested by a Friend

I know of only one person I like
who detests me. There could be others.

I like him better
each time I learn
that he's tried again
to injure me.

He does it so clumsily
it's obvious he's never
done it to anyone before

and afterwards he
despises himself;
his grin is ghastly
with guilt when we

come face to face
and must talk.
This happens
once or twice a month:
ours is a small city.

I don't think he knows
that I know he detests me
but I'm almost sure
he knows I like him

and is miserable
because of this.

I wonder if there's
anyone I detest
who likes me?
I think I would like him.

Cousin Wilfrid's DT Blues

It is not elephants. I would not laugh at them
as I climbed the fire ladder to the moored balloon
and the rungs turned into broom straw and I fell
towards their tusks and the crocodiles. But I would forget
as soon as it was over and I home, here in my bed.
It is not elephants, nor are there snakes and spiders.
Nothing like that. The setting is always
one with which I'm familiar or, rather, it combines
people I've known and places I've been
in curious ways. A house will have been moved
hundreds of miles and contain rooms from another
house or apartment; and people I knew
when I was a child and never saw again
will be in partnership with others
I've met only this year. A professor of English
and a physician will be running a shoe factory
where I used to work but in a different town.
The past will have been altered
in ways that matter greatly only to me:
the woman to whom I'm married is not
the woman I married but another I might have
married, and I know this. And something is required of me
—now we've come to it—something is required of me,
something in my line of work, or there's some test
I must pass, there's always something I have to
do, something I must do if life is to continue
to be worth living, something I've done before

or very much like something
I've done before. And I can't. Oh, I can almost
do it, that's the worst of it, I have it almost
within my grasp. But I can't. And it takes a long time
to wake up, it takes a very long time to wake up,
because I'm not asleep, you see, this is different
from being asleep. No, it is not elephants.

Knowledge and Power

The world is gone mad
at (what time is it?)
4 a.m.
        Huh, what kind of man
believing he hears
something monstrous
happening just outside
turns first to his watch?
        A schizophrenic
reporter, me,
yanked away by the screams
of two small children
fighting in the dark,
babies
who've crawled here
from God knows where
to fight and are
screaming horribly.

They're cats, of course.
But I've got to stop it
—not the fight.
but the sound of it.
Got to.
        I hiss
from my bedroom
window and they

scatter, one
through the tall grass, one
into the bushes.
                    Afterwards
I go down and let Hodge in.
She looks like
a particular kind
of human being,
a respectable person
who has done something
crazy in public
for the first time
and knows he'll do it again.

Old cat, you make me
uncomfortable
in this strange,
dead of the night kitchen.
You could kill me easily,
couldn't you, although I'm so big
and you're so small, attack me in my sleep.

And when I tell this
at breakfast, with sunflowers
on the table and fresh
strawberries,
                    Claudine says
she's thought, once or twice,
no more than that,
about the two-year-olds
with whom she works,
of how much violence
there is in them,
of how the eighteen,
if they came at her
all at once, could
beat and bite her
to death in minutes,
if only they knew it.

In the Garden

"When I die
I'll grow wings
And fly.

        Don't grin,"

said the caterpillar,
crawling by.

Full Circle

In my youth, no one spoke of love
where I lived, except I spoke of it,
and then only in the dark. The word was known
like the name of a city on another continent.
No one called anyone his friend,
although they had friends. Perhaps they were afraid
to commit so much of themselves,
to demand so much of others; for if they'd said,
"We're friends," as they never did,
it would have been a contract.
As it was, they could quarrel,
even hit one another if they were drunk,
and remain friends, never having said it.
Where nothing was sworn there could be no betrayal.
Nor did they touch
casually; their persons seemed to occupy
more space than their bodies did.
Seeing an adult run we'd have looked first for the reason
in the direction from which he came. We never met trains;
my people were like that.
                    It was not enough for me.
"I love you," I said.
Whispered it, painfully, and was laughed at;
hid until the wounds healed and said it again,

muttered it.
Wanting to be loved, "I love you," was what I said.
And I learned to touch, as a legless man
learns to walk again.
                    Came to live among people
who called anyone a friend
who was not an enemy, to whom there were no strangers:
because there were so many, they were invisible.
Now, like everyone else, I send
postcards to acquaintances, With Love —
Love meaning, I suppose, that I remember the recipients
kindly and wish them well. But I say it
less often and will not be surprised
at myself if the time comes when I do not say it,
when I do not touch, except desperately, when I ask
nothing more of others, but greet them with a wink,
as my grandfather might have done, looking up
for an instant from his carpenter's bench.

There Was a Time When Children Died

We knew there'd been a time when children died.
Every old person in our settlement
possessed a brother or a sister who
would never age. Those small Victorians,
the boys in stockings and the girls in frocks
that bent the grass, had chased their barrel hoops
and spun their tops the day before; their names
were those we answered to; they ran beside us,
not knowing what we knew. Diphtheria
or typhoid, one of those plagues (cholera
being another) which sound so much like
a witch's synonyms for Satan, had
their throats between its thumbs and soon the lamp
would rise and float above the table, whirl
until the house was whirling, too, and then
go out and leave such darkness that they'd try

to find their hands and couldn't. Aubrey, Clare,
Amantha, little ones who might have been
my great aunts and great uncles but instead
were almost playmates of that bare-kneed boy
who lives on only as a ghost in me.

The Visitor

Last summer we found a sleeping bag
in our back yard, under the cedars
where we don't mow the grass.
Someone had slept there.

A friend had arrived late
the previous night, we decided,
and hadn't wanted to wake us.
He'd got up early and gone
to see someone else.

We stayed home all day and waited for him.

But nobody came. And the sleeping bag
was still there next morning
although it hadn't been slept in:
you can tell a bed that's been used
recently from one that hasn't
been—the disorder of
the former is in sharper focus.

Should we have brought it inside?
Should we have called the police
on the second day or the third
or the fourth? Perhaps. As it was
we forgot about it

until this spring
when we crammed it into a garbage can.

I think it was its rottenness, the sick
feel of it in my hands
that made me believe something
horrible could have happened
to whoever it was
that lay down that night
on the ground within fifty feet
of our house, just outside the light
from the bulb above the back door
or, if nothing harmed him,
that he ran away,
that young man with terrible eyes,
because he wasn't sure he could resist
temptation a second night:
for he must have watched us,
moving about the kitchen,
sitting down to dinner,
getting ready for bed,

he could have attacked us while we slept,
and how can we be sure he won't come back?

On the Barrens

"Once when we were hunting cattle
        on the barrens,"
so began many of the stories they told,
gathered in the kitchen, a fire still
        the focus of life then,
the teapot on the stove as long as
        anyone was awake,
mittens and socks left to thaw on
        the open oven door,
chunks of pine and birch piled
        halfway to the ceiling,
and always a faint smell of smoke
        like spice in the air,

the lamps making their peace with
    the darkness,
the world not entirely answerable
    to man.

They took turns talking, the listeners
    puffed their pipes,
he whose turn it was to speak used his
    as an instrument,
took his leather pouch from a pocket
    of his overalls,
gracefully, rubbed tobacco between
    his rough palms
as he set the mood, tamped it into
    the bowl
at a moment carefully chosen, scratched
    a match when it was necessary
to prolong the suspense. If his pipe
    went out it was no accident,
if he spat in the stove it was done
    for a purpose.
When he finished he might lean back
    in his chair so that it stood
on two legs; there'd be a short silence.

The barrens were flat clay fields,
    twenty miles from the sea
and separated from it by dense woods
    and farmlands.
They smelled of salt and the wind
    blew there
constantly as it does on the shore
    of the North Atlantic.
There had been a time, the older men
    said, when someone had owned
the barrens but something had happened
long ago and now anyone who wanted to
    could pasture there.
The cattle ran wild all summer,

sinewy little beasts, ginger-coloured
    with off-white patches,
grazed there on the windswept barrens
    and never saw a human
until fall when the men came to round
    them up,
sinewy men in rubber boots and tweed caps
    with their dogs beside them.

Some of the cattle would by now have
    forgotten
there'd been a time before they'd
    lived on the barrens.
They'd be truly wild, dangerous, the
    men would loose the dogs on them,
mongrel collies, barn dogs with the
    dispositions of convicts
who are set over their fellows,
    the dogs would go for the nose,
sink their teeth in the tender flesh,
    toss the cow on its side,
bleating, hooves flying, but shortly
    tractable.
There were a few escaped,
    it was said, and in a little while
they were like no other cattle —
    the dogs feared them,
they roared at night and the men
    lying by their camp-fires
heard them and moaned in their sleep,
    the next day tracking them
found where they'd pawed the moss,
    where their horns had scraped
bark from the trees — all the stories
    agreed
in this: now there was nothing to do
    but kill them.

Land and Sea

Old men repeat themselves.
In other words: speak songs.

Can't let the sea be,
the land can't.
                    Won't ever
leave her in peace.
                    Has to keep
troubling the waters,
the land does.

            This from
Captain Thorburn Greenough
of Hall's Harbour who, in his prime,
could have sailed a bucket
through hell with his handkerchief,
they say.

The land won't let the sea be.

You'd of sailed under
canvas, you'd of knowed that.
Wouldn't of needed me
to tell you.
            The shore!
We never felt safe
till we was out of her reach.

The Red Wool Shirt

I was hanging out my wash,
says the woman in North Sydney.
It was a rope line I was using
and they were wooden pins,
the real old-fashioned kind
that didn't have a spring.

It was good drying weather.

I could see the weir fishermen
at work.
      I had a red wool shirt
in my hands and had just
noticed that one of the buttons
was missing.

Then I looked up and saw
Charlie Sullivan coming
towards me.
He'd always had a funny walk.
It was as if he was walking
sideways.
      That walk of his
always made me smile except
for some reason
I didn't smile
that day.
      He had on a hat
with salmon flies
that he'd tied himself
in the brim.

Poor old Charlie.

It's bad, Mary, he said.

I finished
hanging up the red wool
shirt
        and then I said,
Charlie, it's not
both of them, and he said,
Mary, I'm afraid it is.

And that was that.

Campobello Island Cemetery

I guess he just happened
to be driving past
and when he caught sight
of me kneeling on the grave
must have thought
I was praying or something.

The truth is
I was parting the
white and red wild roses,
irises and raspberry
bushes the better to read
the quaint verse on
the stone above the
two young brothers,
fishermen, who drowned
together, twenty years ago.
Such things interest me.

Now he's asking which one
of the Babcocks am I,
would I be Ernest's boy
or George's eldest?

He grew up with them,
he tells me, and there are
tears in his voice
as he recalls how
he helped lift
their bodies from the Bay.

But they weren't
my father and uncle.
I don't belong here.
I'm nobody.

He takes my hand
in both of his
and waits for me
to say something.

And I wish I were
wearing a mask
or could run away.

The Glace Bay Cabbies

Each of the cabbies in Glace Bay, Cape Breton,
    has a friend
who rides beside him, all through the night.

They carry on long, intimate, restful
    conversations,
laugh drowsily together, stop
at take-out stands to buy coffee and fish and
    chips
for themselves while the passenger sits
alone in the back seat, under a street-light
    besieged by moths.
They have known each other all their short
    lives,

each driver and his companion, started
    kindergarten
the same day, took jobs in the mines,
were laid off together,
have been driving a taxi ever since,
although only one of them is listed
on the company payroll. They say the same
    things,
more or less, tell each other the same
    stories
every night, he whose turn it is to listen
doing so as attentively as he did the first
    time,
even reminding the other where he was, if
    they've been interrupted:
you were saying such and such, he'll say, and
    the dialogue
will resume at precisely the point where
    it left off.

However, the driver alone addresses the fare
    and this only
when it can't possibly be avoided and in a
    different voice.

The Unhappy People

Professor, may I introduce you
to two of the Unhappy People, whom you've
    described
as inhabiting a cultural vacuum
somewhere between the swamps of Frustration
and the salt sea of Despair.
May I present my wife's cousins, Corey
    and Brent.
You will note immediately that their teeth
    are translucent,

the colour of reconstituted powdered milk,
which can be attributed to hereditary
      malnutrition,
as their lack of ear-lobes can be ascribed
      to inbreeding.
You are free to make notes, if you wish.
At worst, they'll merely laugh at you.

Professor, I must ask you to forgive
the mandolin, the five-string banjo, the
      guitar, the fiddle
and the jew's-harp. I must ask you to
      bear with
Brent when he dances—he prefers it to
      walking to
the refrigerator for another beer—and
      Corey when he scratches
his groin in symbolic tribute to the girl
      in the yellow bathing suit
playing with a frisbee on the grass across
      the street.
I know it's distracting when, for no
      apparent reason,
they break into song. I can understand
      your not laughing
with them when they talk about driving
four-year-old cars at one hundred and ten
miles per hour down dirt roads with the
      police behind them,
of overturning and wondering drunkenly how
      to shut off
the headlights, until logic triumphed and
      they kicked them out.
I beg you not to be disturbed when they
      whoop
at the tops of their voices—it's in
      their blood, .
I'm afraid, their way of declaring an
      instantaneous holiday

and, besides, Brent got out of jail
      this morning
or, as he puts it, got back from his
      annual vacation,
having been locked up this time because
      he didn't
know his own strength, he says, and when
      he was refused service
at the liquor store, being drunk, forgot
      he was carrying
nothing under his left arm to offset
      the force of his right
pushing open the door on his way out
      and so, purely by accident,
drove his fist through the glass:
it could have happened to anybody, Your
      Honour.
he told the Court.
      You must excuse Corey, Professor,
like every member of his family he walks
      in and out
of rooms without thinking it necessary to
      offer
any explanation. When they arrive at my
      house
or any other, they open the door, come in,
      sit down
and, perhaps, switch on the radio. They'd
      expect you to do the same.
If you go to the window, Professor, you'll
      see
that he's talking with the girl in the
      yellow bathing suit
and already has her laughing. "Once you
      got them laughing,
you're as good as in bed with them,"
      Brent says. In celebration
he jumps up again and dances. They've
      brought venison

and wild rice and a half-dozen jars of
        their mother's
homemade preserves and pickles, fresh loaves
        of her bread,
two double cases of beer and a forty-ounce
        bottle
of dark rum, having shut down the cannery
where Corey works in honour of Brent's
        homecoming.
"I said to hell with 'er, let's tie
        'er up,"
and with unanimous approval of his
        fellows,
conveyed without a word, he tied
        her up well
by making certain delicate adjustments
        to the machinery
when the bosses weren't watching. His
        laughter and his brother's
laughter and the laughter of the girl
        in the yellow bathing suit
mingle and rise like water from a
        garden hose, spraying the windows
from inside and out. The passersby turn
and smile, a neighbour's dog runs to see
        what's happening,
a host of starlings take wing, the
        tiger lilies are in flower
at the edge of the parking lot next
        to this house.
Professor, I don't suppose that you'd
        care to arm-wrestle?

From the Memoirs of Tom Long

Both times I went Out West
I worked for the same Dutchman.
Drove a team, a horse and a mule.

Other fellows, they liked to
poke fun at me and my mule,
his big ears and all.

But I'll tell you something,
Mister Man:
a mule's got more brains
than a horse. A mule won't eat itself
to death and a horse will.

Never drove much after that.
Father was the teamster,
drove horses all his life.
It was him that told me a horse's eyes
is different than a man's eyes.

Horse thinks a man is fifteen feet tall.
Wasn't for that, horse would take over
        the world.

He'd Lived There All His Life

Luther, the only blind man
in town — which made him a character
in the unfolding chapter
of everybody's private
serialized novel.

Newcomers often went
out of their way to be
kind to him.

The theatre manager,
for instance, picked him up
in his car whenever there was
a change of show and
drove him home afterwards.
(This was before television.)

Other newcomers read him
the papers or listened
very patiently while
he told them the same
boring story for the tenth,
fifteenth or twentieth
time, depending upon
how long it had been
since they'd moved here.

Poor old man! they said
and remarked how little
the locals ever did for him:
some who'd been his neighbours
all their lives
spoke of him with loathing
or told coarse jokes.

In a small town you can
come to know somebody so well
that his eyes can be put out
without this becoming
the central fact
in your relationship.

Peace of Mind

My wife works beside a woman
who says she's never troubled.
They're packing Easter baskets,
one hundred and forty yesterday,
one hundred and sixty today,
each containing several
hollow chocolate-coconut eggs
and a hollow chocolate-coconut rabbit.

"This place will drive you nuts
if you let it get to you,"
says the woman who is never troubled.
"Me, I don't bother. Two nights a week
I play bingo, eighteen cards
all at the same time.
Try that and see if it don't
sweep everything else
out of your mind.
It's a lot safer than
running around with men
and a lot cheaper
than getting drunk."

The Kookaburra's Song

Mickey, our cat, lay under the woodstove.
I'd stretch out on the floor,
legs on cool linoleum, arms on warm tin,
and study her face, knowing if I kept my eyes
        on her
I couldn't help but laugh. It was the
        solemnity
of her expression that tickled me
in the ribs like an uncle's fingers on
        pay-day,

that, and something about the shape of a cat's
        head:
a child will laugh at triangles,
they're such funny circles.

And what laughter! I'd roll over on my back,
kick myself free of the floor and walk on
        the ceiling.
(But only when there were no adults present:
they'd have grabbed me by the shoulders and
        pulled me down.
Don't do that, nobody can walk on the
        ceiling, they'd have said.)
I'd walk around the crystal mushroom that
        had been a lamp,
then I'd either walk down the wall
or turn a half-somersault, laughing all
        this time,
change into a horse as easily
as throwing on a coat and gallop out the
        kitchen door.

Nowadays I laugh best at the looking-glass
and it laughs with me, noiselessly. We should
        carry,
each of us, a hand-mirror and when introduced
hold it up, face outwards, laugh with the
        funny fellow
who has lain awake all night and thought
        how terrible
it was that he, of all people, had to die,
who has sat on the side of his bed and almost
        whimpered
not so much because today will end as because
there'll be an end to tomorrows,

not so much for what he'll lose as for what
he can never possess: in other words,
for those uncounted centuries that will

be held without him,
and who, at last, still seated on his bed,
        has burst out laughing
because what else was there for him to do,
        thinking
how ridiculous it would be if anyone else
felt this way and, then, how ludicrous it was
        that everyone did.

There was a time in between when I never
        laughed,
when nobody does. Adolescents blow
        invisible instruments,
turn their tongues into small hammers
and their teeth into xylophones, run
        barefoot
up and down the keys of an immense
        piano.
But they don't laugh. It's not the same.
Watch closely, listen carefully
and you'll perceive the difference.
It's not something they do when they're
        alone.

If I could turn and meet myself as
        I was then,
gaze into that solemn face, those
        unblinking eyes,
I suppose I'd laugh until I cried,
        then laugh again.

The Plymouth Valiant Song

I'm not a good man.
Cars don't trust me
and rightly so;
the fool teaches his
apprentices to fear
making fools of
themselves and
it works for him.

An icy patch ahead
and a snow-bank behind,
me behind the wheel,
cursing like a carpenter
with his thumb in his mouth,
and four nameless men
pushing. Oh, my God,
what if I run over them?
I've never learned
the language in which
they yell instructions.
A car would speak it.

They remind me of
the teamsters of Lunenburg
who used to bellow
at their oxen in
the tongue of their
ancestors or an off-shoot
therefrom, without knowing
it was German,
taking it to be only
the style in which God
had intended men to
address draught cattle.

If I ever spoke to
an automobile it

would hiccough once
and stall
halfway through
an intersection.
I'm not a good man.

Should the car kill one
of them it will be laid to me.
They'd never blame her.
Her! They call the machine
Baby and me nothing.
Come on, Baby, they say.

Oh, and they arch
their backs until
they look scarcely human.
They rock her, they
thrust and thrust again.

I tell them they've
already done more
than enough for me,
remind them they'll
arrive late somewhere,
say to them — and I half
mean this — that, in fact,
it would be rather fun
to stay here the rest
of the night.

I don't matter.
They keep pushing.

They push until
she screeches,
shudders and is freed,

then all but pat her
steaming radiator,

all but whack each other
on the butt like hockey players.

Leaving,
they wave away my thanks.
And so they should.

Big Alex

He was one of those big men
who always look as if their collars
are too tight and their shoes pinch.
This comes from having been
big since birth, I suppose,
from having never fitted in.

I was fifteen, with peach-fuzz
on my upper lip and the legs
of a newborn colt,
as wide-eyed as a kitten,
though I'd not have recognized
myself on the street:
why bother memorizing
a face you'll soon discard?
The very young never know what they
      look like.

Kid that I was, I'd greet him
fondly with a fist in the belly.
Other than that we never touched
nor thought of touching or ever
resolved for any reason not to touch.

We weren't friends. I doubt if a man
      can be
a friend to a boy when in every
      department

where he's not the boy's superior
he's his inferior.

We never once talked of anything
        important.
I laughed in his face, not thinking.
He was Big Alex, who would put up with this
from me, Big Alex my bodyguard
who had nicknamed me Robin.

I gave him nothing
except what he saw in me.
What there was between us
was at once strong and incorporeal
like the scent of lilacs.

He would stare at me sometimes
the way a monk might
stare at the boy Christ.

The Drover

Last week a farmer I knew by sight
was killed by a bull. Today I'm standing
in a field with thirty of them,
at least fifteen of which are watching me.
They graze for a time, then lift up their heads
and stare as cattle do, with that sorry innocence:
it's as if their species had been
lobotomized and they almost remembered.
Country-bred, I'd have walked among them once
without fear, only respecting their prejudices.
Now I wish there were a fence between us,
mainly because I don't wish to look foolish
and no longer know how cattlemen define prudence.
I'm uncomfortable, and if I were here
for a different purpose I'd be a little afraid.

At work as a journalist, I take on another
identity, become The Man from *Maclean's*
or *Weekend* or the *Telegraph-Journal*.
Headwaiters give me better tables
not because they know who I am but because
I know who I am, don't you see,
and bulls are less apt to gore me.
But to get back to the farmer
who was killed, I'm accompanied by a drover
who's telling me that bulls
are just big kids. They bellow and tussle
but there's no malice in them,
he says, when they drive their horns through
a man or trample him, it's because they don't
realize we're so soft. It's all in fun. He knuckles
one of the yearlings behind the ear.
Nice baby, he says, nice baby. This lad weighs
twelve hundred pounds. Imagine him jumping
into your lap. Nice baby. Playful as a kitten.
Of course, once they start they finish you,
the drover says. Can't blame them for that;
it's the smell of blood that does it.

Change of Address

Our first night here
and I can't sleep
because of the footsteps.
Every house, every
apartment that I've lived
in has made sounds
peculiar to itself
and I've stopped
hearing them after
·a week or so, except
when I've been alone
for too long.

The old place on
Parks Street whimpered,
for example. What's that?
guests would ask, some
of them frightened, though
they always laughed.
The ghost of a carpenter
who believed in
cutting corners,
I'd answer.
I'm not sure what
we heard on Britain Street.
It kept me awake I know,
so it couldn't have been
footsteps. In an apartment
they're nothing. It's different
in a house where you know
everybody's walk and besides
everybody else is asleep.
I suppose the lumber
wasn't properly dried
or the basement leaks.
It won't bother me
much after a night or two.
The old house where I grew up
howled. It would start
in the cellar and before
it reached the attic
the building would be
shaking—I almost said
shaking from head to foot.
I never got used to that.

The Second Show
for Ian and Bev Cameron

A river of faces
rushing out of
a movie theatre
as we go in:

the faces of
initiates!

Their colour higher
than ours,
they look better-fed and
have permission to smoke.

A hundred of us
know-nothings
shuffle towards
the ticket-takers
while our betters
on the other side
of the long rope
laugh and play with
their car-keys.

They've seen and heard
things we've not.
They know the punch-lines.
They've been given the passwords.

Doubling Back

"That old man scares me,"
says an old woman.
It's clear she means me.
I was only fourteen then.

This often happens, the mind
broken loose and floating
in a lake of time.
Somebody should have told me
it wasn't my fault.
But nobody did.

The boy walks with his head down,
kicking pebbles.
This is Visiting Day
with wheelchairs on the lawn,
sunlight on cellophane-
wrapped baskets of soft fruit,
carnations everywhere because
they take so long to die.

When I was in Grade 3
I longed to have an arm
broken so I could wear a sling
or better, much better,
but probably too much
even to hope for,
to be half-blind:
it was the patch I wanted.

Something horrible is
holding on to the boy now:
a skeleton in one of those
flowered frocks
that old women wear.
If I were an old woman
I'd dress like an old man.

I'd refuse to be mocked
with bright colours,
refuse to go out
with my legs and arms
so hideously exposed.

You expected human
bones to be white,
not yellow. This one has claws.
"Take me with you, Daddy," it says.

He wrenches free and walks faster
toward the parking lot
and his father's car.
They'll never drag him here again.

"How can you stand this place?
I can't wait to get home."

The gate man is not unkind.
"I'm afraid you're already there,
old boy," he answers.

Autobiographical Note

The poet says, you'll never guess
what happened to me last night.
I made love to the most beautiful
woman in the world.

And the eunuch answers, yeah,
but what good did it do you?
You didn't get paid for it.

The Carpenter's Misfortunes

A found poem, taken from the December 9, 1876, issue of the Carleton Sentinel, *published at Woodstock, N.B.*

Herman Ott could not get
a living as a carpenter
and consequently became
a grave-digger. This
employment made him
melancholy and he says
he was unable to
repel the idea that
he ought to bury
himself.
      So he dug a grave,
shot himself
at the brink of it
and fell in.
      He had arranged
several bushels
of dirt to fall on him
when his body knocked out
a prop, but
the contrivance did not
work nor did the
bullet kill him.

His physician advises
a change of employment.

RCMP Raid Cape Breton Cockfight

—a recent newspaper headline

Come ye humanitarians
and raise a rousing cheer!
Thanks to the horsemen there'll be no
cockfight at Whitney Pier.

The fancy had laid down their bets,
all set for hellish sport,
when men in spurs kicked in the door
and dragged them off to court.

Some thirty of our feathered friends
were rescued from the pit.
St. Francis of Assisi must
smile when he thinks of it.

There were no crowing champions
that day, no bleeding wrecks.
The civilized and kindly cops
wrung all the roosters' necks.

Our Exalted Brother

A used car salesman may be king and priest
to the dark gods, may wear a sacred chain
and rule that portion of the mystic East
encompassed by the hall on Fifth and Main.

Enthroned, he bids his deacons kiss their swords
and swear that they will give their lives, and more,
to keep the Order's secret grips and words
from infidels beyond this temple's door.

Then, barefoot, led by spearmen and a drum,
the novices, each in a hanged man's hood,

kneel at a torchlit altar and become
for ever brothers of the brotherhood.

He puts aside his chain and occult tome.
They play a little poker and go home.

Telephone Poem

There's much to be said for taking out
        the telephone.
I tore ours off the wall once and felt
        like a fool
until the event passed into family
        legend.
Since then I've never thought about
        that night
without feeling expansive. The memory
        is enough
to make me invite friends to dinner.
Anyone who has ever torn a telephone
        out by the roots
will know what I mean. It enlarges
        the soul.

But a man who called the company
        and formally requested
that the instrument be removed
        scientifically,
that experts in green uniforms,
        wearing their tool-belts
low on their hips, be sent to
        extract it:
there would be the guest who
        expects to be asked to carve.

Here Lies

Here lies
Timothy Foley,
born September 26, 1850
at Boston, Massachusetts,

Fenian,
soldier of a
half-imaginary Ireland,

he came to help kidnap
Canada
and was shot to death
near this spot

by an unknown member
of the Victoria County
Militia,

thus becoming
the only casualty of
the Battle of Schofield's Farm.

Damn the guide
for grinning when he
tells the tourists this.

A Certain Kind of Holy Man

Not every wino is a Holy Man.
Oh, but some of them are.
I love those who've learned
          to sit comfortably
for long periods with their hams
          pressed against their calves,

outdoors,
with a wall for a back-rest,
contentedly saying nothing.

These move about only when
        necessary,
on foot, and almost always
        in pairs.
I think of them as oblates.
Christ's blood is in their veins
or they thirst for it.
They have looked into the eyes
        of God,
unprotected by smoked glass.

Mr. DeLacey and His Guest

The old blind man has welcomed
Baron Frankenstein's hideous creation
into his house.
                The monster chops wood
while DeLacey teaches him Latin.

But since the cottage consists
of only one small room and a loft
and this is real life
the arrangement can't last

— not with the host playing
his guitar before breakfast
and the guest asking endless
questions about ontogenetics.

What Colour Is Manitoba?

My son, in Grade III or IV
and assigned to make a map,
asked us, what colour is
Manitoba? and refused to believe
it didn't matter, provided
it wasn't the same
as Saskatchewan and Ontario.
I remember his face.
I've seldom observed
such constrained rage
except in small children
and university professors.

But it's a common failing,
this excessive faith
in one method of denoting
boundaries. In his atlas
at school, Manitoba was
purple-brown. Similarly,
the road maps indicate
that I live less than
five hundred miles
from my birthplace.

There are truer charts.

I'd never once used
a telephone
in the nineteen years
before I left there,
had never eaten a hamburger;
I could milk a cow by hand
or yoke an ox, knew a man who
once as a passenger
in a heavily-loaded
stage coach inching up
one side of a very steep

hill in California
had got off to walk
and as a result of this
— the downward slope
being equally precipitous,
the horses being compelled
by the weight behind them
to gallop and he having to
run to catch up—
was mistaken by the driver
for a highwayman, and shot:
the scar was still there
after fifty years.
Little else had changed
in our village since
the mid-eighteenth century
when Coulon de Villiers
passed through with his troops,
seven years before
he defeated young George
Washington at Fort Necessity.
Scraps of grape-shot worked
their way to the surface
of the earth the way bits
of shrapnel are said to
emerge at last through the skin
of an old soldier.

Add to all this
that it wasn't the same
for everybody, even there.
My family was poor.
Not disadvantaged — curse
that word of the sniffling
middle classes, suggesting
as it does that there's
nothing worse than
not being like them.
We were poor — curse that word, too,
as a stroke victim

half-maddened by his inability
to utter a certain phrase
will say "shit" instead
and be understood.

A sociologist,
belonging by definition to
one of the lesser
of the ruling sub-castes,
comes from Columbia University
to study a community
in Nova Scotia not very different
from where I was born.
A Tutsi witch doctor among Hutus.
He finds, according to
the *New York Times*, that
almost everyone he meets is crazy.

It's as if a chemist
had analyzed a river
and declared that its water
was an inferior form of fire.

There are secrets I share
with the very old. I know why
we fought in the Boer War
and how in the lumber camps
we cracked the lice between
our thumbnails and it made
a homely sound, was a restful
occupation of an evening:
cracking lice, we were
like women knitting.

Altogether apart
from that, I bear tribal
marks, ritual mutilations.
My brothers and sisters
fill the slums of every
city in North America.

(God knows this is no boast.)
The poor, whom the Russians
used to call the Dark People,
as if it were in the blood.
I know their footsteps.
We meet each other's eyes.

Midnight Caller

Don't leave your boots
out there. They'd freeze.
Bring them in where it's warm.

Everyone else is
in the other room
talking with the dead.

I wouldn't joke about
anything like that.

Come see
for yourself.

That's why it took me
so long to answer
your knock.

At first I thought
you were one of them

rapping "yes" or "no,"
which seems to be all
these spirits ever
have to say for themselves.

They're not very clever,
the dead that come to seances.

A Royal Visit

A boy who's perhaps ten years old
strolls past the Mounties, past the City
      Police,
past the soldiers, past the man from
      Scotland Yard.
What if he were a midget with a gun in
      his pocket?
He hands the Queen something and she
      takes it.
Neither of them smiles. He walks back
      in the crowd.
Nobody else seems to notice this.

The Queen moves on, surrounded by people
who, in a sense, cannot see her
any more than they could see the boy.
What they see is a life-sized,
      three-dimensional,
self-propelled portrait with audio
of a Queen,
           not this woman
who keeps looking down at the object
      in her hand
as if it pleased her but she wasn't sure
what she was expected to do about it.

I suspect that she's asking herself:
Was the boy taking part in a ceremony
with which she's not familiar?
Was there something she failed to do
because her aides forgot to warn her?

She is still carrying the child's gift
      when she gets back in
the Prime Minister's car. Recognizing it
      now, I think to myself
how sad it would have been

for the boy if she had let it drop or
        had passed it
to the man in uniform to whom she passes
        most things
and he had thrown it away at once, as he
        almost certainly would have done,
foolishly thinking a four-leaf clover to be
        of no importance.

Fanfare

I've never before heard a fanfare of
        trumpets
except on television or radio or in
        the movies,
which means that until tonight I've believed
        that
I'd heard a fanfare of trumpets but
        now I know different,
hearing the real thing from the gallery
above me and to my left, with the trumpeters
not bare-legged actors welcoming Moses,
as played by Charlton Heston, home to
        Pharaoh's palace
after conquering Ethiopia,
but members of the Royal Canadian Regiment
        Band
in Boer War scarlet tunics and sun helmets
signalling the arrival of Her Majesty
Elizabeth II, Queen by the Grace of God, and
        all of a sudden,
by God, she is a Queen—which is to say,
        I've been watching
the woman all week and it keeps happening,
this transfiguration: it's as if once
        upon a time

there was this little middle-aged lady
        who'd been sea-sick
all the way from New York and was kept
        awake all night by the fog-horns,
had a backache, an aide said, and whose face
        had that disconnected
look that comes with numb exhaustion,
but this little middle-aged lady had the
        power
to rise several inches into the air and
        float
as she's doing now, and to glow
as if there were a light inside her.

The Magician and His Wife

At first he treated her
as his equal,
the woman he loved,
but this made her weep.

So out of pity he changed her
into a doll
that he works with strings.

Now she sings all day
and smiles at him in her sleep.

One Night Stand

A woman who's not supposed
to be there has climbed
on the stage.
                The singer

doesn't know what to do
with her and he's
not what she thought.

They're talking
but we can't hear what
they're saying.
The audience hates this.

Three thousand people
would hurt her if they could.

Until she came along
each of us was alone
with him.

Living in a Mad House

Living in a mad house
is not very different
from living anywhere

although there's a barber's chair
in the bathroom
and no handles on the water-taps

which makes a bent teaspoon
a status symbol: when a man
reaches in his pocket and
takes out his water-key,
purchasable for ten Librium
capsules or fifty books
of matches, it's as if
he'd flipped up the tails
of his tail-coat
and sat down;

no surgeon could be prouder
of washing his hands.

Living in a mad house
is not very different
from living anywhere

although it's good manners
to play bridge after breakfast
and only those who've earned
ground parole are offered
a choice between porridge
and cornflakes:
choosing porridge
would be like refusing
a raise, the attendants would
more than likely report it

to the doctors, whose visits
to the wards are reminiscent
of Old Russia, the Inspector-General
in a white coat with an intern
in a white coat on either side
of him and white-coated orderlies
bringing up the rear,
met by ward attendants
in blue-gray tunics who
would have to move
their heels and elbows
no more than an eighth
of an inch to be
standing at attention.

Living in a mad house
is not very different
from living anywhere.

On Saturdays, the kids
on insulin, go to

the movies downtown,
six or eight of them,
escorted by an attendant
named MacPhee, one of
those unfortunates,
so full of goodwill
that they flutter
like a bird too
well-fed to fly,
whose mere appearance
in a crowd of children
is enough to create
near-anarchy.

It's less than half a mile
from the gate to the theatre
and so they walk there and back,

spreading out, mingling
with the other pedestrians
like a brook joining a river,

having fun with MacPhee
until they stand in the lobby
where, all of a sudden,
they become Those People
from the Asylum.
The word spreads like
a breeze ruffling the grass.

Their revenge is to act
much younger than they are,
to scuffle and giggle
as they file into
the back row seats
reserved for lunatics
and the lights go down.

The Rules of the Game

Supposedly spoken not by God but by man, specifically
western man in the last quarter of the twentieth century.

Thou shalt not throw a Molotov cocktail
into a public house nor shalt thou lie in wait
for thine enemy at a bus stop, lest
thou meet him face to face.

Thou shalt not go forth alone
against thine enemy, nay, nor in pairs;
in small numbers thou shalt not go forth
    against him.
Thou shalt go forth in armies, thou shalt
    fly
high above his cities and drop eggs of death
on a thousand public houses; thou shalt sit
in an air-conditioned room and thou shalt
    lay thy finger
on a certain button and thereby slay
    thousands
and tens of thousands, nay, millions
    on another continent.

Thou shalt not hold up a train,
instead thou shalt obliterate it, and all
who ride in it, thou shalt shell it from
    the sea;
nor shalt thou take possession
of a school, instead thou shalt send bombers
to rain fire bombs and jellied gasoline
upon many schools. Thou shalt not be a
    terrorist,
in other words,
        thou shalt be a warrior,
for the one is hateful in mine eyes and
    the other glorious.

Election Song

Down the street they came with torches
like a roaring human sea,
chanting, "Up with Sir Mackenzie Bowell!
Statesman! Man of Destiny!"

Mackenzie Bowell, Mackenzie Bowell,
may thoughts of your vanished fame
help us keep things in perspective
as we vote for what's-his-name.

The Commonwealth Games Open

You're standing in a crowd
of 35,000 people and
they start to sing
a song you've never heard before,
"God Defend New Zealand."

Everybody but you
knows it so well
that no one else
bothers to listen.

I'd call that lonesome.

He Is Entertained by the Chairman of the Department

It's not the same here, the chairman
of the department cautions me.
We're close enough to drive
to Toronto and back
in an evening. Did you know
that in Toronto you can have

the Sunday edition of
the *New York Times* delivered
to your door the day it comes out?
Life here moves at a faster tempo
than where you are, Down East.
One must adjust to the rhythm
of a different century, one
might almost say.
But you understand that,
I'm sure. Have you been following
this thing in Ethiopia?
A sad business.
I was there
three years ago,
one of a delegation.
We had tea with the Crown Prince,
as he then was.
            A charming fellow
although, obviously, not
the man his father was.
Are you often in Boston?
You'd have no trouble, then,
learning to live with us
in Kitchener.

Ex-Sergeant Whalen Tells This Story

The Burgermeister,
                that's what the Dutch
call their Mayors,
                Burgermeisters,
the Burgermeister of Nijmegen,
he gave us a big spiel.
                In English.
I still know some of it
     by heart,
although this was thirty years ago.

The Germans came;
               we got fed up with them.
The British came
               and showed us what to do.
The Americans came
               and told us how great they were.

Then the Canadians came

and so long as they had
      a bottle on the hip
            and a girl on the arm
they didn't give a damn
               who
ran the country.

Well!
naturally we gave
            the Burgermeister
three
cheers
and a tiger.

        But the joke of it was
the Brits and Yanks —
they thought he'd paid
them
    a compliment!

Poor silly buggers,
they cheered too.

The Departure

Watching him walk toward
the plane I wish it wasn't so easy
to get used to his being here.

It's only when he's leaving
that I remember
this wasn't a homecoming.
He wasn't returning
from a visit, but visiting us.

So that after the first day
or even the first few hours
we didn't say or do
anything special,

when we ought to have
sat up most of the night,
drinking Jamieson's whiskey
out of pewter mugs,
singing Irish songs,
talking,

and got up early
the next morning
to go snowshoeing
in the woods and fry steaks
over a bonfire,

or something like that,
Johnnie, my son,
but I always forget
that you're a guest.

The Apology

Forgive me, friend,
for I've wounded you.
Look!
     I'll kneel
at your feet,
        like so,
            and beg.

But you must be quick.
You mustn't hesitate.
You must lift me up
          now
and not a second later,

or the magic will turn

and I'll despise you
instead of myself.

Doctor Johnson's Unfounded Fear

Doctor Johnson argued
for an hereditary
aristocracy
on the sensible grounds
that your average Lord
has an average mind.

He believed average minds
deserved to share in
governing the state.

Doctor Johnson feared
that a free electorate
would confer power
only on men of genius.

The End, Plus Twenty-Four Hours

About twenty-five hours
after you left me, bang,
the door popped open and
this little old woman
in a turquoise dress
slammed herself down in that
big chair by the window
just long enough to say
—this isn't the dressmaker's!

You should have heard her:
it was as if it were my fault.

A trifle, this,
and nothing to cry for.

But I would have told you
when you came home

if you were coming home

and we would have laughed.

Not Fingers or Wool

Now that my hearing
has twice failed me
I understand that
deafness is not
fingers or wool,
although that may be
how it starts.

Strangers
stand at the door

and do not ring,
friends walk in
through the walls,
my wife appears
from out of nowhere.

I am expected
to behave as if this were
commonplace.

And there are times
when others play games:
let's have some
fun with him, they
say to one another, let's
move our mouths and not
make a sound, let's
babble senselessly
in his presence,
let's play
baiting the deaf man.

There are times when
deafness is
believing this.

In the Blood

Oh! says my aunt, not
to me but to my all but
stone-deaf uncle,

neither of them
having seen me
since I was a child
and it so awesome
to be together now:

the three of us have
aged thirty years
this afternoon and
they're far from
convinced I'm who
they've been told;
I only half-believe
they're who they say.

Oh! says my aunt, you're
losing your hearing, are
you, that runs in our
family, we all go
deaf as a post,
sooner or later,
didn't anybody
ever tell you?

Nobody ever did.

What's this, says my
uncle, what's this you
say?
  Deaf!
shouts my aunt,
pointing at me.

Did you say deaf, says
my uncle. I nod. My aunt
nods. It has been
established that we bear
the same mark
in our flesh.

We smile, almost
lovingly, at one another.

The Boil

Am I alone
        I wonder
in finding pleasure
in this,
      the thumb
and forefinger
rolling tight
          a corner of
the handkerchief,
           then
forcing the spear
of twisted cloth
         under
the ripe core
of the boil
in my own flesh,
           prying it
free,
     burning
the wound clean
with alcohol —
         now
at last
      master
rather than
         servant
of the pain.

Under Surveillance

The tall, thin man
in the beige topcoat,

who looks to be between
thirty-five and forty
and walks with a slight limp,

is coming out of
a hardware store
where he passed two hundred
dollars in counterfeit
bills: Canadian 20s.

He's visited five
places in ninety
minutes, bought watches,
rings, a sports jacket,
cigarettes and
fishing gear.

A woman and a child
are waiting for him
back at the car

according to the
police radio here
in the newsroom.

Maybe he's whistling.
He doesn't know
that both ends
of the street
are blocked.

Curious Encounters

That man coming down
while I go up
the airport escalator
—I know him,

open my mouth to speak
before I realize
it's Johnny Carson.

But what's most
surprising is
his facial expression
is the same as mine was:

the eyes seeming to
stare both
outwards and inwards
as the mind stretches
in both directions,
tries to lift an object
out of the past
into the present and
vice versa—this
in the time it takes
to blink.

The moral being:
nobody gets used to
being known by strangers.

Oh, it's not hard
to get used to crowds,
that's another matter,

but meet the eye
of anybody

with recognition
and for that instant
he'll recognize you.

Junkets[1]

You magnificent
redhaired runt!

I wish I could
telephone you
right now
and ask you over.

I've got a new
second-hand pinball
machine.

There's gin.

And we could
send out for
Chinese food,
if you liked.

I don't suppose
you've ever tasted it.

But you're so
far away.
I could never
reach you.

---

1 *Junkets was a nickname of John Keats, given him by Leigh Hunt, an incorrigible maker of puns.*

And even if
you were here
in town
I'd be afraid
of intruding:
I'm like that.

Worst of all,
it would never
work,
Junkets:

I'd keep thinking,
dear God,

I'm talking
with John Keats.

Back to Earth

Three hundred people,
everyone of them loving me,
that night I read verses.
I don't apologize for this.
I wanted to hug everybody.

Boarding the flight for home,
I smiled at customs officers,
tried to joke with policemen,
inquired after the health
of the stewardesses,

nodded at anyone
who looked me in the eye,
winked at rude children;

if I'd met a snake in the aisle
I'd have stooped to pat it.

Saw my luggage searched
a second and a third time,
was required to show
some identification
other than my ticket,
and was viewed with
universal suspicion:
one child hid his face
in his mother's dress
and blubbered, another
stuck out his tongue at me.

The steward said
I'd have to stop
being so friendly.
The other passengers
were complaining.

That part about
the steward is a lie.
But if I hadn't run out of
love, shortly after take-off,
it might have come to that.

In Less Time Than It Takes to Tell It

If I live to be a very old man
(and one of my ancestors lived in three
        centuries,
from 1798 to 1902),
I'll probably confuse, terrify or move to
        pity
an adolescent girl, somebody like you,
Elizabeth, by giving her presents she

finds neither
useful nor enviable nor pretty, things
that would have pleased such a girl
when I was a boy, if I can find them,
a charm bracelet, for instance, though I'd
    rather clothe her
in a skirt that winked mischievously, and
    panties.

You make me think about old age, Elizabeth,
you and the sun that is bright enough
    that we see
through your blouse and slacks, as we
    ought to.
I think of the aged and ailing King David,
to whose bed, as medicine, the elders brought
    someone like you.
The clods snicker, but what took place then
may have been both sad and wonderful.

Gandhi, too, they say, slept with the young,
only slept with them and, I suppose, woke
    often
as I do who am middle-aged (as we grow older
nothing happens while we're asleep for
    what happens wakes us),
woke often but left her to sleep away the
    night:
it was enough for him that she was there.

This was a form of worship. Oh, Elizabeth,
Elizabeth, Elizabeth, if I were an ancient monarch,
if I were a Hindu sage,
if this were a distant time, another continent,
if we were refugees, if there were no other survivors,
if a ship had sunk and no one else
had reached a life-boat, if you had escaped alone
from a burning cottage and come to me
or, single-handed, had rescued me from an avalanche...

Until Then It Had Been Such an Ordinary Day

Until then it had been such an
    ordinary day,
poached eggs on toast, a morning
    newspaper
that contained no surprises
    (and it's
the unexpected that disturbs us
    most
when we read the papers,
not the merely tragic or horrible),

until then it had been such an
    ordinary day
that, looking back, it seemed to
    him
that he had felt faintly uneasy,
    as though
there was something he was leaving
    out.

A day like any other: you stirred
    the simmering
water to create a whirlpool into
    which you dropped
the eggs, lifted them out with a
    spatula,
dried them carefully over the
    sink; there was war in Africa
and Dagwood Bumstead was hitting
    his neighbour, Herb,
over the head with a baseball bat.

Then it happened — no, then it began to
happen, no, that's not true either, except
in retrospect, for there's no law that says
we have to answer the door or admit whoever
is waiting there (it was like that);

and there were many times in the next
hour when it could have ended
quietly and been forgotten or, in
	the hour following that,
if you'd kept your head you might at
	least have spared
yourself the police, flashbulbs and floodlights,
those gray humanoids filling the pavement
who've come in packs to see.

Upon This Rock

Probably, he will be a quiet man on weekdays,
employed at one of those jobs where a large number
work more or less alone and there is little
	conversation.
I can picture him sorting letters with a machine
or weighing baggage at an airport;
he gives his superiors no cause to complain;
there is no special reason for anyone to notice him
in the locker room or the cafeteria.

He rides home on the subway or on whatever
	will have replaced it
two or three hundred years from now. (This is
	set in the future.)
Occasionally, his name appears in the news
but never prominently. Still, he is the Pope,
	recognized
as Vicar of Christ and successor of St. Peter
by the few thousand Christians that are left.
His Holiness Innocent XIII, and after him
there will come another and another.

Tower Green

Would it be in good taste
to take a picture of Tower Green?

often ask myself such questions.

The night before
Catherine Howard
was executed
she had them bring
the block to her,
that she might rehearse
dying gracefully.

The act of a Queen, I called it once
—a misjudgment natural to youth.
A true Queen would as lief have winked
at the headsman. Rather, the gesture
of a pert girl (she was twenty-two).

I love you, little Catherine,
and you won't mind my camera.
But it appears that one of the Beefeaters
is furious that I've dared
to desecrate this spot.

He waves both arms,
seems to mouth curses!

I shrink a foot
in height; it's a wonder I don't
slink away on all fours.

Then I understand:
he believes I was swindling him
out of a tip.
                Life still goes on

in the Tower of London.
I'd forgotten that.

Here is a spiritual descendant
of the warder who carried
the block to the Queen's cell
on the night of February 12th,
fifteen forty-two,

another poor man
with a thankless job to do.

If I Could Be Certain, God

If I could be certain, God, that
        you were watching us,
it would be enough. I'd ask less
        of you than an actor
asks of an audience: merely that
        you be there.

You needn't suspend the laws of
        the universe for me.
I'd be embarrassed. And the prospect
        of living for ever
would frighten me almost as much as
        death does.

But if only I could be certain that
        you were watching us
as we, at our best, watch one
        another,
with undemanding affection (now
        I find myself
asking more of you than any actor
        has a right to expect),
but if only I could be certain that

when the worst happens,
as it will, I won't be alone,
        you'll be there,
you or someone like you, not to
        hold my hand,
not to touch me, not to whisper
        in my ear,
but merely to look on — how splendidly
        I might perform for you !

The Green Avenger

If I go mad or, rather, say to hell
        with this
and let the crazy man out,
sick and tired of playing Atlas
        to the door
of his closet, of holding it shut
        against him,
I hope he learns how to sew
and can make himself a costume,
preferably of green and gold,
with a mask and a hooded cape.

It would be marvellous if he could
        master
the use of some forgiving weapon,
such as the lasso. I wish he could
        drive
a very fast car or a motorcycle,
painted green and gold. But if I
        go mad
I want this to be real. The car
        and the motorcycle
and, probably, the lasso also
are far more than I dare hope for.

He could laugh differently than
      anyone else
and lose his fear of falling. If
      God is good,
he won't be caught changing his
      clothes
in an alley; there'll be many nights
when he's seen bounding
across the roof-tops, leaping from
one tall building to another,
his cape outspread — the Green Avenger!
And people won't make fun of him,
except nervously, not if God is good.
When his madness kills him,
let it be with a degree of dignity.
Let the onlookers believe
as he does, if only for an instant.

It's Good to Be Here

I'm in trouble, she said
to him. That was the first
time in history that anyone
had ever spoken of me.

It was 1932 when she
was just fourteen years old
and men like him
worked all day for
one stinking dollar.

There's quinine, she said.
That's bullshit, he told her.

Then she cried and then
for a long time neither of them
said anything at all and then

their voices kept rising until
they were screaming at each other
and then there was another long silence and then
they began to talk very quietly and at last he said,
well, I guess we'll just have to make the best of it.

While I lay curled up,
my heart beating,
in the darkness inside her.

I Might Not Tell Everybody This

At the Head Table

Returning the same way as I went,
passing effortlessly and unnoticed
through the walls, I slip quietly back
inside my body, which is where I left it,
sitting on a chair in a large room, one among hundreds
of such bodies similarly seated
at long white tables that bear the remnants
of a meal, every face adjusted
so as to appear interested, but few wholly succeeding,
possibly because the owner is unskillful
or has drunk too much wine, or perhaps
because the equipment itself is faulty.

I check my watch; five minutes to go
before I start my speech. Here at the head table,
the Premier stirs and straightens;
he too has come back, it seems. The Bishop
is still far, far away, as are the Mayor,
the President of the University, and the two
members of Parliament. But they are all of them so adroit
at setting the controls on their bodies
for occasions such as this, that their neck and facial
muscles respond flawlessly; at intervals, each head
bobs as if in agreement, or cocks itself slightly
to one side, as if in polite dissent;
their lips open and close on cue, as if smiling,
while the toastmaster rattles on, quoting Churchill.

I ask myself, as every public speaker must,
should I stay here while being formally introduced,
or re-adjust my own face and risk another flight
out through the roof, across continents and centuries—

My Beard, Once Lionheart Red

My beard, once Lionheart red, is now yellowish-gray
like a rainy sunset; a child, having seen the statue
in the Victoria and Albert Museum, of Silenus, the satyr
and foster father of Bacchus, and then noticing me
in the crowd, embarrassed her parents by pointing out
the resemblance; and yet, strange to say, I am happier
than when I was a boy and might have passed for the messenger
from Apollo to Helen, had I worn my hair long, and been
      naked, and had I known.

Happier, I suppose because I have all but abandoned
      hope of ever reaching
the lost island of answers, of ever catching up
      with the tribe
that left me behind as a baby, of meeting my real parents,
the King and Queen, of being adopted officially by God.

Happier, I suppose because I expect less and less
of everybody; where once I wanted all of creation to
      love me,
I am now almost content to have my presence acknowledged
with a semblance of kindness and a measure of grace.
I rarely make a nuisance of myself, as I so often used to do,
by passing out love, left and right, as if giving away kittens.

Happier, I suppose because I have tasted enough of fame
to know that it is not flavoured with sugar, as I
      had thought
when I studied it hungrily in pictures, but with salt;
and, also, that the potion does not transform the one
      who drinks it,
but instead creates for him an illusionary twin, in
      whose activities
his part, whether of proud or bemused brother,
is never more than peripheral; people seem to sense this,
for they treat him as if he were not altogether real,
will say to him, casually and with no apparent wish to

be other than polite,
how amazing it is to find him so fat when he is known
    to be dying, slowly, of cancer.

Happier, I suppose because I was bound hand and foot,
    sewn in a blanket, thrown
into the pool of the man-eating crab, and broke free,
bearing wounds that will tug at me always, like the claws
of beggars, so that I cannot forget how wonderful it is
to get out of bed, stand up and walk, pick up a glass,
fill it with water, lift it to my mouth, and drink, with
    only enough pain
involved in each phase of the process to remind me that
    I am fortune's child, and richly blessed.

What Happened When He Went to the Store for Bread
for Michael Brian Oliver

Because I went to the store for bread
one afternoon when I was eighteen
and arrived there just in time to meet
and be introduced to a man who had stopped
for a bottle of Coca-Cola (I've forgotten his name),
and because this man invited me to visit
a place where I met another man who gave me
the address of yet another man,
this one in another province,
and because I wrote a letter and got an answer
which took me away from the place where I was born,
I am who I am instead of being somebody else.

What would I have been if I hadn't left there
when I did? I would have almost certainly
gone mad; I think I might have killed somebody.
But even if something else had saved me
from madness, I would not be the same person.
I'd have spent thirty years in a different world

and come to look at things in such a different way
that even my memories of childhood and youth
would be different; it might even seem to me now
that there was never anything to escape from.

And then too, there are those who are other
than they would have been, because of some small act
of mine; I played a certain record once
because I liked it, and because he liked it too, a stranger
became my friend and, as such, met the woman
he married, and now they have two children
who would not have been born except for my taste in music.

Carrying the thought farther still, there must be
people in cities that I've never visited
whose lives have changed, perhaps not because of what
I've written but because I wrote: it might be
they didn't like my play and so left early
and because they left early something happened
that would not have happened if they'd stayed—
I put it that way so as not to sound immodest.
God knows, there's not a lot to boast about
when so much seems to depend upon the time of day
a boy goes out to buy a loaf of bread.

Word from the Losers

Wandering through books as though on a beach
with eyes downcast for wreckage from a battle
at sea, I've collected such messages
as have come floating in from the lost ships
of history's losers.
                    For instance, the tea
was dumped into Boston harbour to protect
the liberty of Boston's tea merchants
to go on making profits of one thousand
per cent,

and those old French aristocrats
were mostly farmers in patched breeches, lucky
if, besides their patents of nobility,
they owned a cow, a pig and half an acre
of cabbages,
                    and those still older Romans
would, ordinarily, kill a Christian only
if the Christian insisted — furthermore,
the lions usually were so afraid
the would-be martyrs had to torment them
much as the matador torments the bull,
which, come to think of it, could be
how all that business with the capes got started.

If Lucifer had done to God what God did
to Lucifer when there was war in Heaven,
destroy his army, imprison him in a pit,
then, of course, the Devil would have dictated
the Bible, beginning with how he rescued
Adam and Eve from the jungle where they
had been kept naked, hungry and ignorant.

Small Craft Warnings

"A storm is coming," my wife said
yesterday when she came home from
the day-care centre where she works
in a small room with 18 two-year-olds.
That afternoon, they had refused to sleep.

"Sunny throughout the weekend," said the weather forecast.
This morning the sky was clear.
It was still clear when night fell.
"It will be a bad one," my wife insisted:
"the children were wild today. By five o'clock
they were clawing at one another, screaming."

This has happened before.
So I'm not surprised when
a thunderbolt with a sense of irony
knocks out the electric power.

Now they're moving furniture
in Heaven; and a crazy-drunk ogre
keeps tripping over this house.
There is rain enough for Noah.

I wonder, do the little ones sense
atmospheric changes too faint to be
detected by our electronic gadgetry,

or does the wind blow and the thunder roll
because they danced and cried out
to Yama, the Weather God, and he willed it.

Chopping Onion

for John Jones

Chopping onion—doing something, anything,
reminds you of someone and you smile
although nobody's there; with me now, it is
        chopping onion
that does it and the friend is one I haven't seen
since Mitchell Street and the nightshift. He brings it all
back: Haymarket Square at rush hour, when it seemed
that everybody else was driving home as I
        drove to work,
and then ten or twelve hours later, heading
        home myself,
the fog off Courtenay Bay so thick that I'd
        stop
every few hundred feet and get out to take
        my bearings
(by now there was nobody on Crown Street

except cops and cabs).
It's as if it were yesterday, instead of 1963.
Hey, John, do you remember
the Great Antonio who would burst into the
     newsroom bellowing,
"Me strong man! Pull bus with hair!" And do
     you remember
how you used to hide a pint of rum in a filing cabinet
marked "New Brunswick Liquor Control Board"?
There's so much, none of which has anything
     to do with
chopping onion, except that we ate our lunches
     at our desks
and it was you who introduced me to
chopped onion and sliced pepperoni on a hotdog roll,
to which you in turn had been introduced by a friend
     at work
who had been introduced to it by his wife, who was Italian —
so that sitting down to eat, I join hands briefly
not only with you but with a long line of people
stretching all the way to the Two Sicilies in King
     Bomba's time;
and, what is more, it is good to be reminded of
all of the gifts that we've been given — a long,
     long time ago
a boy named Owen taught me how to tie a bow-knot
     in my shoe-laces;
that took all one afternoon, I think — and I've
     learned so much else,
big things and little things, but it is mostly
     the little things
that connect with some one person and some one place.
Chopping onion, then — I quietly rejoice in yet
     another form
of Holy Communion and the Laying on of Hands.

The Gospel According to St. Thomas

We are in Nazareth and the first boy we see
    is the young Lord Jesus.
He is perhaps ten years old. Then we see
    another boy.
This one is running.

They collide and the Lord Jesus falls.
    We might smile at this.
Except the other boy dies. The Lord
    Jesus kills him.

We hear about the schoolmaster. He is not
    dead.
But he will never again use his right hand.
Nor will he ever forget the Lord Jesus. Nor
    will Hanani
ever forget the Lord Jesus. His son fell
    dead
like the boy we saw in the street. His
    mistake was
to destroy the fish-pools the Lord Jesus
    had made.
And the parents of Zeinunus still insist
it was the Lord Jesus who threw him down
from the house-top. Sensible children
treat the Lord Jesus like a King, spread
    their garments
on the ground for him to sit upon.

Joseph plucked him by the ear once and
    might have taken a stick to him,
as the schoolmaster did. The Lord Jesus
    scowled
and muttered something to the old man:
    he never tried that again.

It is all there in the Apocryphal Gospels
which the Fathers of the Church kept out
        of the Canon.
I used to think how right the Fathers were:
the Lord Jesus would never act like that, I said.

Oh, but he would, he would. That is precisely how
a ten-year-old would behave if he were God.
Just as a child-God might bestow the power of speech
on a mute girl who kissed him, heal the
        midwife who delivered him
and the son of the chief priest who touched
        his swaddling clothes
that were hung on a post to dry, yes, and
        restore the dyer's cloth
that he himself, the Lord Jesus, had
        thrown in the fire,
bring back to life the son of Zeinunus, whom he had
        pushed from the house-top.

These things too are recorded in the Gospel
        of St. Thomas, which also says
that no miracles of either kind are known
        to have occurred
between the twelfth birthday of the Lord
        Jesus and the end
of his thirtieth year. Having amazed the elders
        in the Temple,
it seems that he went home, and for eighteen years
studiously restrained himself from being God.

"Why So Sad, My Dear?" Said Queen Anne

"Why so sad, my dear?" said Queen Anne
to George of Denmark, her lover,
the Kingdom green under her feet,
the windy blue sky above her.

"I'm not sad," he lied, and he took
her hand in both of his, squeezing
so hard that she winced. That was all.
He let go. They were young. A pair
much given to playful teasing.

So, hoisting her skirts off the lawn,
she ran in a swirl of laughter;
and he, lost to her flying hair,
breathed deep and went running after.

You ask why he had looked so sad.
Why, because the grass was growing,
only the sky is for ever,
and he, who was alive like us,
knew which way the wind was blowing.

We Found Him Kneeling

We found him kneeling under the front porch,
frozen to death. (Until now, he'd been hidden
by the deep snow.) He must have fallen asleep there
that night last winter when he left for Victoria.
(Once before he'd decided to bed down outdoors
on a winter's night; his mother had awakened me
at some godawful hour and said, "You'll have to
do something, do you hear me, he'll die."
That time she had happened to look out.) This time she cried
a little and then together we carried him
into the living-room and laid him down on the sofa.
He was wearing his uncle's tunic, designed
for the Maine State Troopers and worn
by the police in several little Canadian towns
along the border. There wasn't an ounce of flesh
on his bones and his skull was as thin as paper.
Then we remembered the telephone calls.
There was one only last night from Whitehorse.

Did that mean there was two of him,
one here and one there, and if so
would the other one die too when these
bones finally crumbled? I put his mother's
Hudson's Bay coat over him—and just in time:
his friends were outside, five or six of them
whom we hadn't seen in months, Ralph and the others,
standing in the fresh white snow,
as if keeping an appointment.

His Day in Court
for Mark Paul-Elias

The other prisoners, who would be happier if
        forcibly stripped naked
than if made to dress differently, wear blue
        jeans and stare quizzically
at the old dude in flannel; I wear my one good suit
and feel almost as ancient as I must seem
to these children, all of whom have the stray dog look
of the full-time loser. To them I am nothing more
than a slight change in a familiar atmosphere.

The cops are the good-natured kind who treat their charges
like imbeciles; it's curious how the police
come to resemble their conception of
a criminal: our Sergeant actually drools,
although he hides it well with his handkerchief.

My lawyer and the Crown Prosecutor discuss my case
as if I were somewhere else: my defence against this
is to study their socks, shirts and neckties,
        which perfectly match
their suits, but do it subtly—Browning was right
when he said that at times the soul is strengthened more
by the appropriate clothes than by religion.

"My lawyer," I said; but the truth is
he is not mine, I am his; it is I who must
ask where to go and nothing ever is where
I thought, but always up or down a staircase
or at the other end of a twisting corridor.

The courtroom is ingeniously designed to make the Judge
appear to be at least a head and shoulders taller
than anyone else here. So great is his authority
that the very temperature is whatever pleases him.

I feel great remorse, my lawyer murmurs,
bending as if under the weight of my repentance,
his voice so sorrowful that, for an instant,
I feel ashamed of having made him surrogate
for my sins, and love him as a little boy would.

Through all this, a foolish thought keeps
        coming back to me:
this was bound to happen some time, how much better
it would have been if it had happened sooner;
say, when I was eighteen and carried a knife under my shirt,
selling booze at country dances; then today my friends
would tell new mutual acquaintances, "He used to be
a street punk," and since I'm every bit as silly
as anybody else, the pleasure that they'd take in this
would please me too.
                    A time comes when the game
of *this is what I was when I was younger*
offers the same kind of satisfaction
as once came from playing, *this is what I'll be
when I'm grown up.*
                    Mercifully, we don't
linger long in the present: it can be rough there.

A Pair of Pruning Shears

The trees around this house are killing one
another. This summer, the maple and the fir
sucked the life from the spruce, having first
shut it off from the rain and then walled in its roots
with theirs, so that at last it died in a desert
five feet in diameter. The maple still
bears wounds from that struggle, a withered limb
for instance, and now the fir has turned against
its old ally and bars it from the sun,
while, a little distance away, the young birches
gnaw away at the beech and will bring her down
unless she succeeds in smothering them first;
and, afterwards, the winners will go at it—
"You ought to have pruned them," a neighbour says,
who knows about such matters. "It's the same
with everything," he tells me. "Even rhubarb.
Look at that fine patch you inherited from
the former tenants, gone to weed because
you didn't take a knife to it. It needed
to be cut back almost to the roots last season.
Now it's too late." So I start with the rose-bushes
that were so elegant when we moved here but now
have sprouted hideous tentacles, each of them
black and bare except for a few red flowers
at the tip where, if this were a different kind
of horror story, there would be a mouth.
I take a knife, a saw, a pair of shears,
waiting until it's almost dark because,
being awkward at such tasks, I'd rather not
be watched, and drinking a quick double gin
because I'm loath to destroy anything,
never knowing where it might lead or end;
I take a knife, a saw, a pair of shears,
and soon I'm breathing hard and there is sweat
in my eyes and my heart is saying no, no, no,
reminding me that this body of mine is
a rickety Empire, in no shape for war,

Byzantium in 1450, Turkey
in 1914; I saw off the tentacles,
and scissor at the live, green undergrowth,
the thorns making me think of Gulliver
and the Lilliputian archers; there is blood
on my hands and forearms when I stop; the walk
is buried in debris, with a few spots
of red on the black and green; they're the flowers
that ought to have been mouths; because of them,
it is as if the bushes had bled too.

I'm still sitting there when the stars appear,
another drink beside me on the steps,
my rested heart now saying yes, no, yes,
but in a little while I'll go inside
to wait for spring. How good it would be then
to come out and look down at the black stumps
of the rose-bushes, stumps like rotten molars,
and see there in the grass a different shade
of green, one touched with gold, new growth,
the fresh stalks as supple as the partner in
a boy's lascivious dream, and glorious,
glorious and absurd, in the way of all
such living things that reach up to the sun
to touch it, though they've risen only scant
inches above the earth—an argument,
perhaps, although admittedly a weak one,
against the rumours, widespread and persuasive,
of Death's total, unconditional victory.

The Seasick Sailor, and Others

The awkward young sailor who is always seasick
is the one who will write about ships.
The young man whose soldiering consists in the delivery
of candy and cigarettes to the front
is the one who will write about war.

The man who will never learn to drive a car
and keeps going home to his mother
is the one who will write about the road.

Stranger still, hardly anyone else will write so well
about the sea or war or the road. And then there
        is the woman
who has scarcely spoken to a man except her brother
and who works in a room no larger than a closet,
she will write as well as anyone who ever lived
about vast, open spaces and the desires of the flesh;
and that other woman who will live with her sister
and rarely leave her village, she will excel
in portraying men and women in society;
and that woman, in some ways the most wonderful
        of them all,
who is afraid to go outdoors, who hides when
        someone knocks,
she will write great poems about the universe
        inside her.

And Now the Good News

Thank God for McCord, Hunt and Liddy
who gave us cause for hope
that human freedom shall endure
so long as abject stupidity
does not perish from the earth.

Here's a toast to all bunglers,
blunderers, blockheads,
numbskulls and dolts.

Three cheers
for bird-brains,
hare-brains
and lame-brains.

May they be fruitful
and multiply
and continue to
replenish the ranks
of the CIA, the NKVD
and all other
regiments of spooks.

Ghost Stories

So many of my friends live in haunted houses
that I have all but decided to install a ghost,
a benign one, of course, and no blood relation
to my wife or me: I don't believe we'd be comfortable
with either her ancestors or mine around the place,
they would almost certainly feel obliged to interfere
in the traditional way, knocking objects about or
        smashing them
to remind us of certain events in family history
which were about to repeat themselves.
Perhaps old Mrs. Winthrop would be suitable,
a former tenant who kept insisting she'd come back here
as they carried her off to the Home
where, thirty-odd years ago, she died. Did I say "benign"?
I wonder if the dead ever take kindly
to those who have displaced them; Granny Winthrop
could have been half-mad at the end, hating those who
        had ousted her
from this house that her husband built with his own hands
before sailing away to be killed in the war.
Imagine waking up with her face, dead except for the
        eyes and mouth,
only inches from yours. On second thought,
I don't want her as a house-guest—as much as I'd like
to have someone of my own to talk about with our friends
when they bring the dinner table conversation around
to the red-coated soldier, said to have been shot

for desertion, whom they've often seen
peering in a window, or the white-faced young woman
		in hoop-skirts
who opens the door of the master bedroom, stands there
just for an instant and then disappears,
or the unaccountable chill, accompanied by a
		scratching sound
that seems to come from somewhere inside
the freshly restored 18th-century cupboard.
Our friends' ghosts seem to fit very nicely
into their domestic arrangements, judging from the tone
in which they discuss them over coffee or while
		nibbling cheese,
whereas I'm more than a little uneasy
just thinking about old Mrs. Winthrop and half-afraid
that she might decide that there is no need for
any further invitation than the one I've extended
in this poem in which, knowing nothing
about the history of the house I live in
and thinking I wanted a ghost, I made her up.

A Night in 1938, and the Night After

The first time I saw electric
light, the Queen of Heaven
appeared. This was not light
to see by, this was
light to marvel at. All
evening we sat, adults
as well as children, in that
light and did nothing
else. Next day we waited
for Uncle, as head of the
family, to decide the time
had come to switch it on
again. I held my breath
as he pulled the chain, but

the Queen of Heaven did not
return. In a little while,
the adults picked up
the playing cards. Oh!
how I despised them
for that. Then I saw
that the shadows were
gone, the places where
I could roll myself into
a ball or kneel or stand very
still, and not be seen.
I used to do that
and listen. Sometimes, I would
slip out of the shadows when
nobody was looking and
switch cards on them. It was hard
to keep from laughing then.
Now, no matter how
small, quick or quiet
I was, I would never
again have that power.
I could never again
make myself invisible.

Why are you crying?
Uncle asked me.

The Practice of Mercy

Beginning the practice of mercy,
study first to forgive
those who have wronged you.

Having done that,
you will be ready
for the sterner discipline:

learning to forgive those
you have betrayed and cheated.

Sister Williamina in the Valley of the Nashwaak

"Always carry out when you're sober the promises
you made when you were drunk," Hemingway said. He
        would have been pleased
with John and me for taking Sister Williamina
        for a drive
through the Valley of the Nashwaak, farm country.
        At every spring
we stopped for water, he and I, to keep from
        bursting into flames
from spontaneous combustion; and there are many
        springs in the valley,
each of them with a pipe installed, for drainage
        and to water the cattle —
God, we were thirsty.
But her quiet joy in everything proved to be as
        contagious
as laughter (and there was laughter too); we saw
through her eyes, and it was as if this were our
        first visit
to this valley — this province — this country even.
        Each rockpile in a hillside pasture
became an altar set in acres of lupins and daisies,
each zig-zagging pole fence became a monument
to man's ingenuity and strength; the groundhog in
        the road seemed aware
that his presence pleased us; we saw the original
Crow of Sadness and Two Crows of Joy, about which
        the rhyme was made;
each wild apple tree that had once called to mind
        the bones of mastodons
dead for ten thousand years was now in full blossom
        like a young girl's longings.

And Sister Williamina—for lack of a better word,
      I'll say that she danced,
as she danced and danced that night long ago before
      she left for the first time ever
the Newfoundland outport where she was born. She
      told us this,
I'll bet you've never heard of a Paul Jones. That
was the dance we danced. This was almost forty years ago.
I danced with a boy and kept stringing him on—do
      girls still say that?—
about the great things I was going to do in St. John's.
Of course, in our eyes there was no bigger city on earth.
Oh, my! He was impressed. Somehow I couldn't bring myself
to tell him the truth: that I was going to enter a convent.
Her laughter now was that of a parent; we each of us
      become father or mother
to the child we once were. And we laughed with her, sadly.
But sad for that girl, not this woman, for whom a
      drive in the country
was a greater adventure than a year in China would be
to many of us, children of surfeit. She took the
      flask of spring water—
it was one of those touristy things encased in leather
      with a picture of a Mountie—
and remarked how funny it would be if a Mountie stopped us.
What would he think of two men and a nun passing back
      and forth
a bottle meant for whiskey? Then she drank joyously,
      as if thirst were another
of God's gifts; and in her company I was almost
      persuaded that it is.

The King of the Wood

To become priest-king
of the Sacred Grove
of Diana at Nemi,
you had to kill
the priest-king that was.

It's like that in politics.
Except that now
when it's all over
you're left to bleed
not beside a lake
but in the carrion smoke
of an hotel room,
surrounded by the stale crusts
of forsaken sandwiches,
and nothing but scum remaining
in the ice-buckets.

The Premier on the telephone
to his wife. "It's a bad one," he says.
Across from him, the television screen
almost overflows, so large has become
the presence of his successor.

An old man, alone.
A young man—just such a young man
as that old man used to be—
lifted to a throne of shoulders,
exalted with lights.

He

He has five senses,
plus desire.

He is separate
and alone.

He knows about time
and takes up space.

One day he will die.

He answers to my name.

There Is a Horrible Wing to the Hotel

There is a horrible wing to the hotel.
Unspeakable things happen there.

The toilets are plugged.
There is excrement on the floors
and urine in the bathtubs.

In one room I saw a dog
eating a kitten.

And people live there.
Like that young man with muscular arms
who mistook me for a thief
and would have beaten me with a club
except that I refused to fight back,
knowing that he was so much stronger
that it would be no use.

We became friends, he and I,
and there was a boy who stole

two small triangular pieces
of copper or bronze
from the young man's room
and gave them to me—
I think they may once have been
attached to a trophy.

I hid them when the young man came looking
for them, because I was afraid
of being beaten, and watched him beat the boy.

But one night on the roof we released balloons
in the shape of little animals;
there was a bear, for instance, and a giraffe
which was bright red, and a blue rhinoceros.

They flew very high, those balloons,
and I am afraid of heights, yet I watched them
like everybody else, until they vanished
into that enormous, spinning funnel of blackness.

They flew very high and fast,
and I have never seen anything that looked so free.

He Visits the Shrine of a Saint

Whenever I see the indentations left in granite
by the knees of generation after generation
of human beings, not all of them worshippers,
some of them, doubtless, only carrying out
what was then a social obligation, others not very
different from the poker player who gets up
when his luck is bad and, by way of incantation,
walks around the table, still others whose purpose
was to please somebody, perhaps a parent out of kindness,
perhaps a superior out of fear or ambition
in an age when Mother Church could make an Emperor

or cause a King to submit to the lash,
whenever I look at such marks in a slab of stone
and reflect that most of those who helped to make them
have left no further trace of their passage,
it hardly matters to me whether faith or folly
moved them (when addressing mysteries for which
there are no words in any language, it seems only sensible
to give proper names to the more benign ones,
such as hope fulfilled, and to call them saints);
what does matter is that they came here, to this place,
and here performed a supremely human gesture;
I'm reminded of how Xerxes felt when he looked out
        at that vast army,
and it came to him that not one of them would be alive
in another hundred years; that was 2,500 years ago,
and he wept; but this is not so sad as that: when I envisage
all of those ardent pilgrims in the dust
and think of how they each made their minute imprint
and then vanished, thousands upon thousands
of them, none much wiser, none a bigger fool
than I have been, none guilty of a crime
I could not have committed, none much better
(not even the saint himself) than I might have been,
then I am almost at peace with the knowledge
of how quickly time will close the little space
        between us,
and my breath become one with theirs and the wind;
and so, laughing at myself as at any other
child doing something quaint, I say a prayer,
and might kneel down, if I could do it
without feeling fraudulent or being seen,
and if I could be certain that I had the right.

Vampires

A vampire will give you
his bed and sleep on the floor.
They're hospitable folk.

Not only that,
they make superior guests,
the kind that get up at six,
go to the farmers' market
for fresh eggs and mushrooms,
then make omelettes for
everybody else's breakfast.

It stands to reason:
their survival depends upon
their invitations being accepted,
the old legends are very explicit
on that score: you enter
of your own free will
or not at all;
moreover, a vampire can't
simply walk in:
he has to be asked.

So, they talk well
and listen better
than almost anybody else.

You can't make them angry
and if one of them angers you
it is like this:
                   You wake up.
He is bending over you.
There is blood on his lips.
You fight back.
                   The other
picnickers say:
"Don't you remember?

You must remember.
There was a snake
and you might have died
except he sucked out the poison."

There is blood on his lips.
You fought back.
It is you they blame.

Star Light, Star Bright

46 years old — and I still wish
on the evening star.

If I'm alone I even recite the rhyme
under my breath
as I did when I was five.

I've never told this before.
I'm telling you because
you're like me: silly
and afraid of the dark.

Bend closer.
I know a far greater secret:
everyone else is too.

He Runs Into an Old Acquaintance

"It's so good to talk with somebody
from the old neighbourhood," she says.
It has been twenty years since we last met.

And now we exchange bits and pieces of the past,
whose tangible equivalent might be

the odds and ends I carry in my wallet,
a St. Jude's medal, old photographs taken
by a machine at a fair, membership cards,
and what-not; as happy with each other
as anybody would be who has found
a witness who can swear that he was where
he claims to have been. Then, too casually,
she says, "I missed you terribly at first."

To think she even noticed that I was gone!
Dear God, and to think I never once dreamt of asking
her to go walking with me by the river
or share in any of the other rites
performed by boys and girls when we were young.
She was so beautiful, is still, and I
stuttered when suddenly addressed by strangers,
couldn't carry a tune or dance or drive a car,
bumped my head constantly—a creature
part ape, part owl.
                        How could I know she saw
something in me I'd never seen in a mirror?

I ache with wishing I had touched her then.
What happened next wouldn't much matter now;
it would be all the same if we had only
looked at the water, hand-in-hand, just that
and nothing more, of if we had made love until
we had emptied ourselves in each other.

But it still matters that she'd not have laughed,
that she would have smiled and said, "Yes,"
if I had asked; and I didn't know.

The War Lost

The war lost, the city reduced
to rubble, the long siege
in its final days—
history tells us
that the workers go on
with their work,
as best they can,
clocks are punched,
milk and newspapers
continue to be delivered
within blocks of the enemy's
flamethrowers, husbands and wives
bicker or make love,
children are taken
to the zoo, the theatres
remain open, the amazing
machinery of ordinariness
keeps turning, turning.

Moonscape

On the night of September 30th, 1978,
I drove from Fredericton to Hartland, New Brunswick.
As always, the distance was 70 miles; but this time
        the countryside
was peopled by a strange tribe: worm-white dwarfs
who slashed at the passersby with razors and
        buggered them with dildos.
I wasn't badly cut and none of them succeeded
in sodomizing me. Upon reflection, the strangest thing
is that it seemed it was like this every day
when I drove home from work
in a wagon drawn by a centaur. We discussed the weather.

Later that same night, I met Elvis Presley
who was in his late, corpulent incarnation but
astonishingly energetic, especially when we played
with his only slightly smaller than life-sized
toy trains, riding the locomotive roofs like surfboards.

He nicknamed me "Noth-lin," pronounced as in Memphis,
from "Nowlan" and "northland." We were friends for
        a while.
Then, "Better get lost," said one of his sleazy
        hangers-on.
"Do you want me to get lost?" I asked Elvis
        Presley.
"It won't hurt my feelings if you say, 'yes'."

"And it won't hurt my feelings if you get lost,"
        he replied.
I could tell from his tone that he meant
I could stay if I liked and we'd continue as before.
But I left out of pride, and afterwards regretted it.

Later still, it must have been
almost daylight by this time, I was a young poet
who, before he went on tour,
always bandaged his wrists,
knowing what pleases an audience.

Friends and Lovers

She says, "I love you, but
I cannot comprehend
how such a reprobate
can be your dearest friend."

Neither one knows as yet
that Joe or Bill or Jim
is just a name for what
she most dislikes in him.

The Secretive Fishermen

It is dusk now, and the secretive fishermen
are trolling for boys on the highways
north and south of here: a tradition.
It is what you do when you work in a bank,
for instance, or for the government,
and share your neighbour's hunger but not his tastes.
You drive back and forth, back and forth,
in the twilight, and it can be dangerous;
men have been killed for it, and not one
of their murderers has ever been convicted.
Yet they are peaceable men, even timorous
about most things, men of moderate views
and modest ambitions, whose daytime dress
is always quietly correct; for the most part,
they have always lived here, and their fathers
worked for the bank or the government before them.
If they were married, it would be to women
much like their mothers, who belonged to
the usual organizations, cooked the usual meals,
and thought the usual thoughts. Instead,
out of necessity, the meek and mild accountant
rides out in search of adventure like
the Red Shadow, and Sir Percy Blakeney
risks death as the Scarlet Pimpernel,
except that this time the road is real,
just as the boys are not made of glossy paper
and therefore cannot be undressed
with a flick of the fingers turning over a page
nor be made to disappear in the same way:
they are co-authors and may change the script,
out of fear or disgust or because it amuses them,
so that it ends badly, with the Pimpernel
beaten bloody, the Red Shadow turned into
a monstrous parody of a baby-fat two-year-old,
blubbering, and naked except for an undershirt.
Still, it rarely comes to that; there must even be times

when it is almost perfect, in its way: two strangers,
each of them a tourist exploring the Mexico
that is the other's body. It can't always be
as sad as dusk for those lonesome travellers.

Hospital Parking Lot

Too bad the architect
hadn't been 70 years old
or afflicted with emphysema.
Then the parking lot
wouldn't have been built
downhill from the hospital.

It's a long climb for
the old married couples.
(Nobody comes here
alone if he can help it.)

Soon, they're so weary
they can think of nothing
except lifting one iron boot
and then the other.

They go blind
like marathon runners.

The space between them
widens with every step
as though in accordance
with a law of physics.

The stronger, younger
or more desperate of the two
plunges ahead.
The other one falls farther
and farther behind,

until everyone is alone
on Mount Heartbreak.

They're not reunited
until, at last,
one of them reaches
the door and pauses —
that pause says it all,
there's no need for prayer.

A White Book Lies Open

A white book lies open
on the Pope's coffin.

A page rises,
stands upright
for a moment,
falls
and is still.

As if the corpse
had stood up
in its white burial
garments
to draw just one
more breath.

Seeing this,
our ancestors
would have dropped
to their knees.

We call it the wind.

Déjà Rêvé

I know what comes next.
I've lived through this before.
I'm not sure how or when.
There it is!
The phrase and gesture
that ought to explain
everything:
surely it follows
that a process so strange
should be to some great purpose.

But it never is.
Not with me.
Oh, I read the future;
somebody says and does
something I knew
somebody would
say and do.
But I'm never ahead
by more than a second
or two, and nothing
extraordinary
ever comes of it

except this:
the heart skips a beat
and, in the mind's eye,
there's a partial
eclipse of the sun.

Only When My Heart Freezes

Only when my heart freezes
do I covet the power
to hurt an enemy
as you and I can hurt
each other, my son:
with a thoughtless word,
a careless glance,
an unexpected departure.

You crush your tears
in your fists.
Every door in the house
bangs shut.

And I too am afflicted
like the refugee orphan
who leaves a full table
with breadcrusts
to hide in her pillow.

We understand why
Johnson gave
that terrible shout
when Boswell left him,
without a word,
and galloped ahead
to search out an inn.

"If you had not come back,
I had never spoken to you again,"
the old man said.

The pair of them,
half-mad,
like you and me,
and night falling
in a strange, wild country.

Legacy

adapted from the Romanian of Tudor Arghezi

All that I'll leave you when I die is a name
    in a book
which they'll say is mine. Take it in the
    long evening
which stretches all the way from my farthest
    ancestors to you,
across the ravines and ditches which they
    bridged or climbed,
and you too, so young, are expected to conquer.
The book is only a single step, yet it is your
    solemn charter,
won by slaves and serfs who strained beneath
    their loads:
sacks filled with their own bones, handed down
    to me.

So that I could change a spade into a pen,
our ancestors suffered together with their oxen,
and gathered the sweat of a hundred years to
    give me ink.
I kneaded the words that they spoke to their cattle
until they were transformed into visions and icons.
Out of their rags, I made wreaths; and from old
    poisons
I made honey. From their hearths I took
the ashes of the dead and made them live again
in a god of stone and paper who holds the world
in his lap and watches over you.
All the pain and sorrow of our people
I put into a single violin
and as the master heard it played
he danced like a he-goat in the spring.

We withstood the whip, and now the lash turns into
    words
and becomes a live growth that spreads in the air,

bearing at its tip, like a grape, the fruit
of ancient and endless sorrow.

However soft her bed may be when she reads it,
the Princess will suffer in my book;
for words of fire and steel are mingled with
        the soft whisper
in the book that a slave wrote and the lord
        reads without knowing
that in its depths there lies all the rage
        of my forefathers.

The Comedians

How our remote ancestors must have giggled
when one among them first dared to suggest
that babies weren't begotten by the sun
as everyone believed, but started growing
because a man had wrestled with a woman.

Surely, they hooted down that simpleton,
just as in later times the greatest surgeons
were understandably amused to hear
someone assert that fewer of their patients
would die if only they would wash their hands.

Today, we laugh at them because they laughed;
but, of course, we'd laugh too if told the best
method of contraception is to cross
one's fingers, or that physicians cause cancer
by leaving their groins unshaven; and tomorrow,
a hundred or a thousand years from now,
they'll laugh at you and me because we laughed
at something equally preposterous.

When a Man Loves His Son's Bride

When a man loves his son's bride
he is apt to praise her
but not sensibly and with decorum,
as a father should.

It is not inconceivable
that he will give a Christian name
to each of her pretty toes,
so that one of them becomes
Rosebud, for instance.

Oh! Let us blush for him!

Should she belch at table
he will say that she coughed,
and worry.

"Silly old fool," you say.
But playing the ninny
may be his proper part
in the ritual.

Perhaps he should put on
long ears and bray.

When a man loves his son's bride
it would be dangerous
for him to praise her
as artfully as he could.

I'm Simply Walking

I'm simply walking,
I think.
Or standing there.
I'm not afraid,
which means the
homicidal maniac
must be dead.

I can't tell where I am,
but that is only because
there has been no reason
for me to ask myself:
what place is this?

Nothing horrible
has happened.

I'm simply walking,
except
this time I'm not a man;
I'm a woman.

The most extraordinary
thing about this
is that it is
of no importance.

Perhaps that's because
there's nobody else here.

I put one foot in front
of the other
and think no more
about being a woman
than a woman would.

If I'm wearing a dress,
well, what of it,
I must be accustomed to
wearing dresses.

It's nothing at all like
putting on your sister's
panties and frock
when you were twelve
and wanting to be seen
like that,
but please God never
recognized.

Watch me, Sir
Looking Glass!
You said then,
and twirled
like a top

until you thought
how awful it must be
to bleed like that.

A Momentary Glimpse

Sitting all alone
in the centre of the city
of Trinidad, in Cuba,
surrounded by people,
donkeys, 30-year-old
automobiles, every one
of them painted
the same colour,
reddish-orange,
and all the 17th century
Spanish Colonial

architecture,
I grin and make
friendly faces
at a little boy,
about two years old;
and his mother,
who is very young
and beautiful,
makes him take
his thumb out
of his mouth —
maybe the Gringo
will want a picture —
in response to which,
he kicks her,
hard, in the ankle,
and, oh!
the expression
on her face
as she dances
on one foot.
It is not at all
what you'd expect,
what it says is, Aie!
isn't he the funny
fellow, this
little rooster
of mine, of mine;
look at how high
he carries his wings;
see how the bright red comb
on his head stands
erect,
and how he shakes
his spurs; Aie!
see how he struts,
this funny fellow
of mine, of mine,
my little gamecock.

Heard the Voices Again Last Night

Heard the voices again last night.
All over the house. A man's voice
and a woman's.
               Months ago, when it began,
just the sound was enough
to frighten me, knowing I was alone,
that there was nobody else here.

I'd switch on the bed-lamp and read,
preferably *Time* magazine,
it makes everything seem
so blissfully banal.
When *Time* asked, "Is God dead?"
even that question ceased
to matter very much.

Now, when they wake me,
his baritone, her soprano,
I'm not really afraid;
I've convinced myself it's only
chemistry and a minor riot
in the brain, part of the price I pay
for my twenty-year affair
with Nancy Whiskey.

But I'm careful not to
know what they're saying.
I don't put my hands
over my ears. That wouldn't do
any good, anyway. They're already
inside my head. But I keep
pushing them back, pretending
they're house-guests
conversing quietly, their host gone to bed.

Sometimes I think
it's getting harder

to shut out the words.
I'm not sure. But last night
it seemed they were louder;
I know they laughed more;
and once it was as if they were
listening at the door
of my bedroom. I keep expecting
one of them to speak my name.
God help me, I think I'd have to answer.

A Small Prayer

I have never seen her,
have only heard her voice
close to my ear.
Yet I know she is beautiful
because we all are
when we help
some other poor traveller
as she did last night
when I went searching
for an old friend
and could not find the way.

Please, God,
make good things
happen to her
all day, and to any other
telephone operators
who are kind to drunkards.

On the Burning of Witches

He was one of those famous local characters.
Like The Fox, so called because his hair is red
and he wears it in a pony-tail, or Quack-Quack,
    who quacks like a duck.
He was The Old Guy Who Talks to People and
    Has to be Watched in the Stores.
I hated him. Not for what he said to me
every time we came face to face in the market:
"Well, here's old Santa Claus" or "How's the
    weather up there?"
I hated him for how he said it. He looked and
    sounded
like every bully I've ever encountered,
    starting with
Pig-Faced Avard in First Grade: his voice
    a steam-organ
in a nightmare, with a boil leaking on his neck,
over-ripe lips, and razor-blade eyes set in
    a lump of white pork.

When a boar-pig attacks a man, it goes for
    his testicles.
Thomas Hobbes believed that witches ought
    to be hanged,
although he didn't believe in witchcraft.
They deserved to die, he thought, because
    they believed
their spells could cause suffering, even
    death,
and yet they persisted in them. He contended
that such malice was sufficient to justify
their execution. The Old Guy Who Talks to People
was like those witches. You could feel it.
Now he's dead. The firemen couldn't get to him,
although they could hear him screaming.
His real name was published in this morning's
    newspaper.

That's all. Except I wish I hadn't hated him.
I tell myself that a man so powerless
could not have been evil. The shopkeepers may have had
a right to hate him. He stole things, they said.
But he never harmed me.
                          Speaking of witches,
my way of dealing with him was this:
          I'd stare him out of existence.
I suppose that means that I too practise
          the Black Arts.

A Drive in the Country

If we had come to this turn in the road
ten seconds sooner, that would be our blood
there on the pavement.
                          The police wave us on.

A half-ton truck passes us
on the wrong side.
                    I veer
and almost collide with a stationwagon.
The driver yells at me.
                          Traffic is light
today.
          In the past twenty miles
we've had only two close brushes with death:
an experience so commonplace
on any highway that we talk instead
about the lobster rolls we bought
at a roadside stand and how they compare
with other lobster rolls we've eaten.

Subway Psalm

It's the first storm of the winter
and the worst since 1888,
the girl on television said.

I keep slipping in my leather-soled shoes.
Twice I've turned into a windmill
in my efforts to keep from falling.

At the top of the stairs leading down
to the subway, Johnnie watches me,
not just with his eyes but with his arms and legs.
He'll do his best to save the old man.

That's how I must have looked at him
when he was five or six years old.
Now he's twenty-six, and it seems
we've traded places.
                    Why are you laughing?
he asks me.
              The honest answer is:
Because you look so funny, standing there
like that, my beautiful son,
and because I've loved you
for such a long time and because this
is the finest storm I've ever seen
and everything is exactly as it should be.

The Weekend God

There ought to be a name for the Weekend God
of the working-class. Call it an angel
or a saint, if you prefer. Still, it ought to
      have a name.
A face would follow in no time,
since this is a real god which men and women worship.

I've worshipped him myself, climbed the days of
      the week
like a ladder, with every rung bringing me closer;
and if when I got there it was never
quite as good as I had hoped,
afterwards it always seemed to have been better.

Yes, there ought to be a name for the Weekend God.
There ought to be shrines raised to him
in places like Sudbury, in cities where at dusk
the sun dissolves in acid, creating a sky
of purple, scarlet and brass,
like the garments of the Whore of Babylon,
like a blind man's last remembered
thunderous moment of sight.

A Jansenist with a Snow Shovel

I shovel snow out of the mouth
of my driveway where the city plow
pushed it, and into the street.
I'm only putting it back where
God left it, Constable. I say this
to each approaching set of headlights.
But nobody stops. Nobody reminds me
I'm breaking the law. Nobody has to.
I can never look a cop in the eye
without thinking he's about to charge me

with something. Maybe I've neglected
to zipper my pants, and he'll say
it's indecent exposure.
I don't dare check
because he'll arrest me for sure
if I reach for my groin.
A man with my attitude
oughtn't to throw snow
into a public thoroughfare.
He might die of a heart attack.

He Reflects upon His Own Stupidity
for Michael Pacey

For the first twenty-five years of my life
I never met anyone who was stupid
in quite the same way as I am.

Oh, I knew many, many people
who would have been judged subnormal
by a professional psychologist
—for whatever that is worth:
not much, I imagine, since almost all
the professional psychologists I've run into
have been lunatics or fools.

But I never met anyone who was an idiot
about doors, as I am. I turn my hotel key
this way and that, that way and this,
can seldom get out of a car without help.

If we were measured by our success with locks,
I would be assessed as possibly trainable,
but certainly not educable.

I'm equally stupid about many other things.
And, dear God, it used to be lonely.

But now almost everyone I know is stupid
in much the same way as I am.
Not merely my friends but casual acquaintances,
yes, and enemies too, keep locking themselves out,
and getting lost,
and have trouble changing a tire.

My stupidity matches theirs.
I have found my tribe and am more at home in the world.

Helen's Scar

Helen, my cousin, says she still has the scar
from the time I pushed her out of the plum tree.

I don't even remember the plum tree.

"It must have been an accident," I say to her.
"It was no accident," she says. "You were mad at me."
She laughs. "It bled like the devil. I was scared
        to death."

How old were we then? Ten or eleven,
which means that she's seen that scar every day
for close to forty years
and will continue to see it
for the rest of her life.
It's not bad. But it's always there.

I did it;
and I don't even remember the plum tree.

On Uniforms and Decorations

While sitting opposite an American soldier
in an airport departure lounge, it occurred to me
that it would be helpful sometimes if we all wore
ribbons and badges and stripes to show where we came from
and where we had been and what had happened to us there.

"But we'd have to wear uniforms then," objects a friend,
a professor of English in corduroy pants
and an old tweed jacket with leather elbows.

He Attempts to Love His Neighbours

My neighbours do not wish to be loved.
They have made it clear that they prefer to
        go peacefully
about their business and want me to do the same.
This ought not to surprise me as it does;
I ought to know by now that most people have a
        hundred things
they would rather do than have me love them.

There is television, for instance; the truth
        is that almost everybody,
given the choice between being loved and
        watching TV,
would choose the latter. Love interrupts
        dinner,
interferes with mowing the lawn, washing
        the car,
or walking the dog. Love is a telephone
        ringing or a doorbell
waking you moments after you've finally
        succeeded in getting to sleep.

So we must be careful, those of us who were
        born with
the wrong number of fingers or the gift
of loving; we must do our best to behave
like normal members of society and not make
        nuisances
of ourselves; otherwise it could go hard
        with us.
It is better to bite back your tears,
        swallow your laughter,
and learn to fake the mildly self-deprecating
        titter
favoured by the bourgeoisie
than to be left entirely alone, as you will be,
if your disconformity embarrasses
your neighbours; I wish I didn't keep forgetting
        that.

Great Things Have Happened

We were talking about the great things
that have happened in our lifetimes;
and I said, "Oh, I suppose the moon landing
was the greatest thing that has happened
in my time." But, of course, we were all lying.
The truth is the moon landing didn't mean
one-tenth as much to me as one night in 1963
when we lived in a three-room flat in what once
        had been
the mansion of some Victorian merchant prince
(our kitchen had been a clothes closet, I'm sure),
on a street where by now nobody lived
who could afford to live anywhere else.
That night, the three of us, Claudine, Johnnie and me,
woke up at half-past four in the morning
and ate cinnamon toast together.

"Is that all?" I hear somebody ask.

Oh, but we were silly with sleepiness
and, under our windows, the street-cleaners
were working their machines and conversing in
        Italian, and
everything was strange without being threatening,
even the tea-kettle whistled differently
than in the daytime: it was like the feeling
you get sometimes in a country you've never visited
before, when the bread doesn't taste quite the same,
the butter is a small adventure, and they put
paprika on the table instead of pepper,
except that there was nobody in this country
except the three of us, half-tipsy with the wonder
of being alive, and wholly enveloped in love.

The Perfectibility of Man

The perfectibility of man—he kept coming back to it,
although it was far from being the only subject that
        obsessed him.
He would talk for hours about an imaginary village,
        the inhabitants
of which had no need for money, since they grew their
        own food
and made everything else—clothes, furniture,
        musical instruments—
with their own hands. They would treat their ailments
        with herbs.
"We must go back to the soil," he said.
A God-seeker all his life, he read from the
        Bhagavad-Gita
every night before he switched off his bed-lamp. He
        believed
that children ought to be taught to love animals,
        not to hunt them.

But, as has been said, he kept coming back to
the perfectibility of man. "It's a matter of
        cleanliness," he said.
"We must begin by delousing the race, though God knows
        it's not a pleasant task."
Once, at Posen in 1943, he added this, "I am not a
        heartless beast.
I know, as you do, that it is hellish work we are doing.
I wish to God that I had been spared this task—the horror
        of it
burns in my bowels; I am in constant pain. Let us pray that
        our descendants
are never required to perform such duties," and in the
        presence of the officers
of the Death's Head Division of the SS, Reichsführer
        Himmler wept.

Psalm

adapted from the Romanian of Tudor Arghezi

Running with the wind behind me, on horseback
        like Prince Charming,
I have travelled all over the country and
        its forests;
but when I came to the mountains, scarred by ravines,
I found I was unable to conquer their peaks.

In the bright night, when the huge, blind stars
summon me to the heights, the chasms call me too.
I have chosen the longest road across the great plains,
but I cannot overtake you on any path.

I have pursued you through verses, words and
        syllables,
or dragging myself along on my hands and knees,
thinking that such servile and humble efforts
would make you accept me, at least out of pity.

All my life I have tried to snatch an hour's
       talk with you,
but you would always hide as soon as I appeared.
When I grope at your door, whispering sad prayers,
I always find chains, bolts and bars.

Outraged by such obstacles, I feel an urge to
       destroy them,
but realize that I would first have to destroy you.

Working Late

"Honey, would you stop at Dominion
on the way home and pick up a tin
of Italian-style tomatoes?
I have to work late," the nurse says,
talking to her husband on the telephone
in the reception booth on the surgical floor,
while I wait for the elevator nearby,
lying in bed, dressed all in white, wearing
a costume that might be mediaeval,
hose instead of trousers, loins and breech bare
under a smock that ties in the back,
a big, floppy hat, half-bonnet and half-beret,
on my head, a name-tag on my wrist, a clipboard
containing my chart at my feet,
my drugged brain a fog-ridden swamp of fear.

Such an ordinary message for her to send.
Such an extraordinary thing for me to hear.

It is not hard for me to believe
that great matters are being discussed today;
I know the world will go on,
whatever happens to me.

So if she had told him she was leaving him,
and had cried because of this
or for any other reason,
I would not have been surprised.
That would have fitted in.

But tinned tomatoes!
I'm reminded of how infinitesimal a part
I play in the universe,
of how minute is my share of reality.

Guest Spot

Being a guest on a television talk show
must be a little like being Lord
of the Harvest in ancient times.

Young women wait on me, for instance;
one lights my cigarette, another
fetches an ashtray, yet another brings
real coffee with real cream.
They anoint me with oil,
dust my face with powder, comb my hair,
and lead me to the studio where the host
gives me his complete attention in front of
three million people. I've never talked with
anyone who seemed so interested
in what I had to say. It's as if we'd been friends
all our lives. Then

they switch off the cameras
and if I don't get out of here
fast enough, if I try to continue with
the story I started just before
we ran out of time,
my host will start to dance

a little jig, exactly as if
his bladder were full to bursting.

As for the young women, my priestesses,
they won't even see me
if I meet them in the corridor
or pass them on the stairs
on my way out. The Lord of the Harvest
has it worse, of course —
they used to cut his throat.

After you're through being
a guest on a television show,
they don't kill you;
they simply pronounce you dead.

A Poem for Aida Flemming

May God have mercy
on the porcupine
broken free
but with the snare
still around his neck,
the end of it trailing
behind him
and bound to catch
on something,

on the skunk also
with her head
hopelessly stuck
in a tomato tin,

and the bird who won't
let me pick her up
before the cat comes,

and all the other creatures
trapped
and too frightened
to allow anyone to help.

The Cough

Listen to that
cough. You can tell
he won't be around
much longer. Because
the cough is part of
a play we're watching.
It would be the same
if it were a film
or a book. It is only
in real life
that a cough can
simply happen
and bear no relation
at all to the rest
of the action.
Even little children
recognize the
difference at once
when they see reality on
television, and are usually
bored by it — the timing
is off, the transitions
take far too long,
the point of
view is blurred
or ragged, there are
characters who
contribute nothing
to the final effect
or even distract

from it, players
step in and out of
character without so much as
changing their hats to
alert the onlookers.
It's no wonder
the critics feel
that, as a form,
life is inferior
to art. People cough
for no reason
and at weirdly
inappropriate
moments, farce
intermingles
with tragedy,
the hero farts.

Treasures on Earth

Put on pajamas, go outdoors
and join the joggers. Do not eat
butter or eggs. Beware of drink.
Avoid extremes of cold or heat.
Abjure tobacco. Watch for lumps.
Get enough rest. Control your fears.
And, barring accidents, you ought
to live for years and years and years.

That is what the doctors told her.
The lady did as she was told.
In return for her exertions,
she knows the joys of being old.
Installed in Sunset Manor House,
she now partakes of such delights
as crosswords, paint-by-number kits
and semi-monthly bingo nights.

How Beautiful Art Thy Feet with Shoes

I suppose it's because so many
poets and artists have never had enough
love from women—as boys they were hideous
in their own eyes, as I was, who thought myself
half-brother to Quasimodo
and looked upon every girl as Esmeralda—
I suppose it's because of this
that they've devoted so much time
to portraying the wonders
of her nakedness, to celebrating
her thighs and breasts
so that some love poems sound more like
commercials for fried chicken,
and hardly ever mention
moments like this when I look up and see you,
through the window, getting out of a cab
with your arms full of Christmas parcels
(they always seem to be
Christmas parcels, even in July and even if
they're only books from the public library)
there must have been times, many times,
over the years, when you came home from somewhere
without your arms filled with parcels,
but I don't remember any of them now,
nor do I recall a time when you didn't come in
either bursting to show me something
or trying to hide something from me:
I've never known anybody so fond of arranging
surprises or so inept at keeping secrets;
and I know how long it takes you to complete
the smallest transaction, how much you like to
look at things and touch them, and how you're always
getting involved in long conversations with
old men in waiting rooms, little kids on tricycles,
the high school students who work part-time in supermarkets,
how you even say, "Hello, dog," if you meet one—

all this, and so much more, goes through my head
as I catch a glimpse of you, getting out of a cab
with your arms full of parcels, as they always are,
and am reminded, suddenly, of how much I love you.

Just Now I Heard My Father Singing

Just now I heard my father singing
an old, old song he used to sing
when his hands were busy
with something, as mine were until
I heard that voice: he has been dead
for eight years!

Just now I heard my father's laughter.
That, too, came from my mouth.

The Thief

Having myself been scared silly when I was young
of any girl made of flesh and, God help us, blood,
I am in sympathy with the boy, said to be slow but
        not retarded,
who has been taken into custody for stealing panties
from the laundry rooms in our apartment building.
They say he had a trunkful of them. It reminds me
of those other thieves, treated as praiseworthy,
in the old folk tales; Jack of Jack and the Beanstalk
climbing in through a window of a castle to snitch a harp;
it was no crime to rob a giant in those days.
If the King heard about it, he gave the thief his daughter
in marriage; and, as everybody knows that carried
        with it a guarantee
of living happily ever after. Mind you, that was

well before
the invention of panties; for that matter, drawers
      of any kind
are believed to have been unknown before the 16th century
and, naturally, are first mentioned in a sermon
by the Cardinal-Archbishop of Milan in which he said
      that God Almighty
intended woman to keep her bottom bare, in
      remembrance
of Mother Eve's weakness. All that was long, long ago,
and once upon a time; but I can tell you this from experience:
that to a boy like that—who would even today trade
      his cow, if he had one,
for a handful of beans, not so much because he was
      a fool
as because he was too bashful to argue, and afterwards
hate himself with an almost murderous hated for being
      such a bumpkin—
to a boy like that, every female, without exception,
is a giantess, ready and able to grind his bones to
      bake her bread.

I Have a Friend

I have a friend who loves me so much
that he apologizes on my behalf
to people I've only just met
for acts of mine they've never seen me commit.
He wants to make sure they won't be offended
by anything I do when they get to know me better.

He loves me that much.

The same friend makes certain I find out
what others say about me.
If they're unkind, then he makes excuses

for them, as he does for me
and asks me to forgive them.

He loves me that much.

The Best Man and the Maid of Honour

For the third time in my life I am best man
    at a wedding;
and, once again, the maid of honour is a young
    woman I've never met before.
It seems very odd for us to be dressed
    like the bride and groom,
to be treated much like them, to walk
    arm-in-arm as they do;
odder still, to accompany them into the vestry
where we all four sign our names, as though
    in secret,
with everyone else shut out, except the priest;
oddest of all, to discover once again that
    the two of us,
playing parts that are of no importance
    to anyone else,
are truly set apart from all the others
—perhaps it is because we share so little
    but with such intensity
that for this short while, this space of an
    hour of so,
we are not merely a man and a woman brought
    together
by chance, but partners in a strange, brief
    marriage of our own.

Funny Face

Ah, funny face,
it's so good to have you back,
after all these years,
lying close to me again,
all naked and warm.

Do you know how long —.

Damn!
She's gone.
Just like that.

And here I am,
half-drunk and alone
in a strange town.

But, God,
it was real,
while it lasted.

I wonder if somewhere,
maybe in another
hotel room
very much like this,

there's a woman I knew
a long, long time ago
and she just now awoke
from the same dream as I did.

Mother and Son

She goes on with her story,
this woman whose twelve-year-old son
has drifted into the party;
her mind is still with her guests.
But her flesh has claimed possession of his.

She pushes his hair back from his eyes,
curls a lock of it around her finger,
while continuing to entertain us
with her wit. The touch of her hand
embarrasses him, but only a little;
he shrugs slightly, that is all.
Now she smiles at him
as if conscious of his presence
for the first time.
It's a loving smile, of course,
but not altogether a friendly one:
there's pride in that smile
and a sense of power,
even a hint of cruelty. She's a normal parent.

She pinches his earlobe now, plays with the buttons
on his shirt, talking with us all the while.
He wriggles for an instant, and then
surrenders, half-gratefully,
half-resentfully, to her caresses.

They both know she's the stronger,
that she'll be the stronger for a while yet,
that he couldn't break away from her
even if he could make up his mind
that it's what he wants.

Bobby Sands
for Robert Weaver

I did not cry for Bobby Sands, but I almost did,
thinking of my grandmother whom I loved, and who
     loved me,
and of how her voice would break when she told me again
how her grandmother died in a field in County Wexford
with green stains on her lips, her hands filled with grass,
and of how in that same year the English wagons
escorted by English troops carried Irish grain
down to English vessels for shipment to England.
     Yes,
yes, that was a long, long time ago; but somebody should
remember Mary Foley, somebody should weep for her,
even if it is only a drunken listener
to lying ballads. Being human, we
each of us can bear no more than a particle
of pain that is not our own; the rest is rhetoric.
Better to shed a tear for Mary Foley
than to rant or babble about suffering
that is beyond our capacity to comprehend.
And what of Bobby Sands? We talk too much,
all of us. In common decency, don't speak
of him unless you have gone at least a day
without food, and be sure you understand
that he loved being alive, the same as you.
Then say what you like. Call him a fool.
Call him a criminal. You'll get no argument
from me. I'll agree with everything
you say in dispraise of gunmen. Oh, but Mary Foley's
ghost was left in my keeping.
I know in my heart that if he had come to me
for a place to hide I could never have shut him out.

A Necktie and a Pair of Socks

He was the only person I've ever met
who was like me in not feeling any need
to switch on the lights.
We'd sit in the living-room
of the boarding-house where we both stayed,
letting it get dark around us,
and I'd listen to him talk
about how he'd been a drunk and how he'd joined
Alcoholics Anonymous and how, during the war,
he'd got to know Charles Laughton
and Prince Felix of Luxembourg.

He bet me ten dollars against a funeral wreath
that he'd be dead before Remembrance Day,
lost the bet, paid up, and three days later
died of a heart attack; when I heard him moaning
at about four-thirty in the morning, I thought
he must have fallen off the wagon;
that's what everybody thought, I suppose;
he was sitting in his shorts, doubled over
in agony, and there were nitroglycerine
tablets scattered everywhere.
He was the first person I'd ever seen die.

But the reason I'm telling you this
is that the undertaker asked me
to pick out some clothes for him
and naturally
I grabbed the first necktie I saw
and the first pair of socks,
without thinking—if I'd thought about it,
I'd have figured what difference does it make
what a dead man wears?

And Mrs. Dawes snatched them away from me.
"He hated that necktie," she said,
"and, look, there's a hole in the toe

of this sock." Our landlady, a fat old woman
who had spent her entire life,
not only the years of her life,
but her entire being
in that one little town.

We stood there, pitying
one another's stupidity.
I know now that she had the right.

Until That Night

"You don't love me!" he said.
And, oh, what a weapon that was
to use against her.
                              Until that night
(actually it was between
four and five o'clock in the morning
and he was three-quarters drunk,
half-sick, and nobody anywhere in the
world was answering the telephone),
when, all of a sudden, he thought to himself:
"Merciful Jesus, maybe it's true."

He Sits Down on the Floor of a School for the Retarded

I sit down on the floor of a school for the retarded,
a writer of magazine articles accompanying a band
that was met at the door by a child in a man's body
who asked them, "Are you the surprise they promised us?"

It's Ryan's Fancy, Dermot on guitar,
Fergus on banjo, Denis on penny-whistle.
In the eyes of this audience, they're everybody
who has ever appeared on TV. I've been telling lies

to a boy who cried because his favourite detective
hadn't come with us; I said he had sent his love
and, no, I didn't think he'd mind if I signed his name
to a scrap of paper: when the boy took it, he said,
"Nobody will ever get this away from me,"
in the voice, more hopeless than defiant,
of one accustomed to finding that his hiding places
have been discovered, used to having objects snatched
out of his hands. Weeks from now I'll send him
another autograph, this one genuine
in the sense of having been signed by somebody
on the same payroll as the star.
Then I'll feel less ashamed. Now everyone is singing,
"Old MacDonald had a farm," and I don't know what to do

about the young woman (I call her a woman
because she's twenty-five at least, but think of her
as a little girl, she plays that part so well,
having known no other), about the young woman who
sits down beside me and, as if it were the most natural
thing in the world, rests her head on my shoulder.

It's nine o'clock in the morning, not an hour for music.
And, at the best of times, I'm uncomfortable
in situations where I'm ignorant
of the accepted etiquette: it's one thing
to jump a fence, quite another thing to blunder
into one in the dark. I look around me
for a teacher to whom to smile out my distress.
They're all busy elsewhere. "Hold me," she whispers. "Hold me."

I put my arm around her. "Hold me tighter."
I do, and she snuggles closer. I half-expect
someone in authority to grab her
or me; I can imagine this being remembered
for ever as the time the sex-crazed writer
publicly fondled the poor retarded girl.
"Hold me," she says again. What does it matter
what anybody thinks? I put my other arm around her,

rest my chin in her hair, thinking of children,
real children, and of how they say it, "Hold me,"
and of a patient in a geriatric ward
I once heard crying out to his mother, dead
for a half a century, "I'm frightened! Hold me!"
and of a boy-soldier screaming it on the beach
at Dieppe, of Nelson in Hardy's arms,
of Frieda gripping Lawrence's ankle
until he sailed off in his Ship of Death.

It's what we all want, in the end,
to be held, merely to be held,
to be kissed (not necessarily with the lips,
for every touching is a kind of kiss).

Yes, it's what we all want, in the end,
not to be worshipped, not to be admired,
not to be famous, not to be feared,
not even to be loved, but simply to be held.

She hugs me now, this retarded woman, and I hug her.
We are brother and sister, father and daughter,
mother and son, husband and wife.
We are lovers. We are two human beings
huddled together for a little while by the fire
in the Ice Age, two hundred thousand years ago.

from An Exchange of Gifts: Poems New and Selected

A Song to Be Whispered

Your body consists of so many provinces
that I, a man of salt, must break off my fingers
one by one —
            like so!

See how they fly,
become birds in an orchard.

Oh, my love, it was
God Himself who wove
the skin that clothes you.

Yet the eunuch who escorts
Bathsheba to the King's House
mutters, as always,
"No good can come of it."

You Can't Get There from Here

There is almost always a lilac bush — lilac was the smell
of my childhood, a fine free smell that sets colts galloping
along cool rivers in my mind — and there are almost always
red rose bushes and, sometimes, an apple tree
or even an orchard, where the deer feed on windfalls; and in
        the tall grass
you may come upon a pair of sheep shears, like monstrous
        scissors but made in one piece
as tweezers are, and a grub-hoe, like a two-bitted axe
except that one bit is a hammer; and if you dare to go inside
what remains of the house, there could be a schooner
on the floor at the head of the stairs to the cellar,
its three-foot-long hull on its side, its masts broken, its rigging
rotted; and we'll be there watching
from the dark by the vegetable bins — there was never any

light to switch on, and you'll not have brought with you
a lantern to find us,
but we will see you; oh, we will see you.

For Hans Christian Andersen

Any child can see
the Emperor wears no clothes.

But there are other versions
of that old story.
                In this one
His Majesty knows very well
that he is naked; he can feel
the goose-bumps on his buttocks,
his scrotum shrivels in the cold,
and the soles of his feet
are blistered from walking
such a long way on cobble-stone.

Furthermore, the onlookers
are neither knaves nor fools; well, at least
no more knavish and foolish than we are.
They see as clearly as the child does;
more clearly in a way,
perceiving as they do
that they too have goose-bumps
and not a stitch on their backs
that was not put there
by the mind.
                What is an Emperor,
after all, except another word
for form—call it order,
if you like—it is that
which opposes Chaos, which is another word
for nakedness: call it nothingness,

if you like.
            My child,
why keep crying out
what everybody around you already knows?

Two Visitors from Utah
for Nancy Bauer

The doorbell rings.
            I come face to face with myself.
Myself of 1955, when I was more than a quarter of a century
younger. Two boys with the kind of haircuts
that seem designed to instill humility.
                        Their suits and ties
make them move as young soldiers do
when on leave, almost demurely.
            Of course they're Mormons
who go as missionaries somewhat
as young English aristocrats used to go
on the Grand Tour,
                        except that their purpose
is not to learn but to teach.
            Shall I tell them I love
their Prophet and that, like him,
            I was a farmboy
who opened the Bible like a door
and saw no difference
between the hill where he went for the cows
            and the hill where the King-to-be,
                        young David, tended his sheep?
Oh, we knew,
            Joseph Smith and I,
                        that it had all happened
a long, long time ago like the stories our grandparents
told us about their grandparents.
                        But we had touched the stone
            on which Abraham would have sacrificed

his son, if God had been less merciful;
and if word had come—
a neighbour shouting it—
that there were Philistines encamped
by the river in which we swam,
and a giant leading them,
we would not have been surprised.
We would have fetched our sling-shots.
Shall I tell them
that I too went barefoot
all summer (the worst of it was running
on fresh-cut hayfields, the stubble like toothpicks;
Joe Smith would have known that);
and, still barefoot, talked with an angel of the Lord
who spoke in Jacobean English?
Shall I tell them
that I know their Prophet better than they ever could?
I love him because he wrestled
with the farmboys who followed him
out of Egypt—
try to picture Moses,
Confucius, Buddha, Zoroaster, Mohammad or Jesus
wrestling,
rolling over and over on the ground
not in holy frenzy,
but for the sheer fun of it.
He said that being
a Prophet was a part-time thing
(just as a poet is a poet only
while writing a poem.)
He also danced—
not with the Holy Spirit, but with women,
whom he desired so much that he could never
have called down the wrath of the Lord upon Bathsheba
as Nathan did.
He taught that even God
had a body like ours,
and that we could become
gods—which would suggest

that our God was once every bit as human
as we are,
         that before he created our universe
he too danced and wrestled and made love,
even cursed and swore as the Prophet Joseph did
                  when he was not being a Prophet.
         But, of course, I don't
mention any of this to the two innocent
         little gray parrots on my doorstep.
         I simply tell them
that I'm very busy and, besides,
         they'd only be wasting their time
                  by talking to me.

1914-1918

Thinking again of all those young men who were given
         the same first name,
Canada, once they had reached the place which we in our
         innocence then
called *Overseas*, doubtless with the same intonation
as Frankish peasants had used eight centuries earlier
in speaking of the sons who had followed their steely Lords
         to *Outre Mar*;
thinking of how a German officer remembered this for half
         a century as the strangest thing
he saw in four years of war — the Canadians walking,
simply walking, in no apparent order, but like any group
         of men going anywhere,
into a hailstorm of machine-gun fire that flattened
         them like wheat,
"They did not even look like soldiers, yet fought like
         Prussian Guards,"
I wish, as they would have done, who were much like me,
though they were so much younger, that God's bad brother,
having killed them, had said *Enough!* and had not
         proceeded

to prove their deaths were pointless; if they had to
        die
(and all of us do; oh, all of us do), then I wish
that we could say that we are who we are because they
        were who they were.
That much, at least, has been given others. I think of names:
Salamanca, Antietam, Leningrad. I think of Polish miners
singing of Polish horsemen, a Cuban schoolchild placing flowers
at a wall filled with old photographs.
                        All of it lies,
perhaps, or romantic rubbish, though those young men
        would not have thought it was.

My country has no history, only a past.

Between the Lines

Although it is nowhere mentioned in the Gospels
(St. John With His Head in the Clouds would not have noticed;
St. Matthew, who at heart never ceased to be a bureaucrat,
would have been unable to make it fit
his preconceptions; St. Luke, who was both
artist and physician, would have rejected it
        as tangential
or ascribed it to something physical: indigestion,
        perhaps, or exhaustion;
and St. Mark would not have been there when it
        happened, he is said to
have got his information from St. Paul, who
        was not there either
and would not have approved if he had been) —
Jesus laughed.

The Writer-in-Residence's Poem

He was one of those kids who say they want to be poets.
"This one is pompous and not overly bright," I thought
as I thumbed through the typewritten lists he had handed me
of words like "lonely" and "love" and "Apocalypse,"
and listened to him say he knew he had talent and only
      wanted to be told
whether he was heading in the right direction.

The worst of it was he didn't know when to go — and
      knowing when to go is far more important
than being talented or wearing clean underwear.
He sat in my living room for one hour, two hours, three —
with me aching to say, "Go away, please, you're making me
      so lonely
that if you don't leave soon I may burst into tears."

Still he stayed.
             He had an irritating manner
of putting his hand in front of his mouth and half-turning
      away when he spoke
as if afraid of what might come out,
and when I spoke to him, which was less and less often
as the evening wore on, he scowled as if concentrating
so hard it was painful.

"Thank God, that's over," I thought when he left.
It wouldn't have been so bad if it hadn't been
for those disgusting mannerisms. Then I realized why
his gestures had seemed so familiar — that hand
in front of the mouth, those shifty eyes, that scowl;
and I almost ran after and embraced the poor bugger.
For he had been labouring to be me —
me in the flesh, I mean, out of his longing
for what he innocently imagined me to possess
and believed that he wanted to be.

He Gives Himself Good Advice and Does Not Take It

Never treat the young as your equals.
Be more patient with them
than their closest friends would ever be.
Much the same rule applies to almost everybody
who recognizes you from your picture
in the newspapers.
                      Learn to be
subtly condescending.

Such is the advice I give myself,
who am middle-aged and a very minor
public figure.
                  And sound advice it is,
grounded in long experience.

The problem is, I can never follow it,
being held back, not so much by modesty
as by a constitutional incapacity
to feel superior to anyone —
                         which is not a virtue
since it means I argue
with students,
               treat readers
who approach me as they treat me

when I ought simply to smile
knowingly —
                they would accept that
                        gratefully.
As it is, I often hurt or anger
or even disgust them because they give
so much more weight to my words than I do,
take me so much more seriously
than I could ever take myself,
and, saddest of all, seem unable
to conceive that nobody,

however old or famous
is very different,
                    seen from the inside,
than they are.

Driving a Hard Bargain

What would cause a man to haggle over the price
of the rifle which, later that same day,
he used to kill himself?
                         As a young reporter,
I thought, "Capitalism!"
                        The poor bastard knew what it was
to ask the landlord if he'd wait another week, and then
thank him for answering, "I don't seem to have much choice
in the matter, do I?" in the tone of voice
and with the facial expression of a gentleman
on horseback tapping his boot with a whip,
knew what it was like to make his wife cry every payday
as men on low wages almost always do (it begins with an
        argument
over some small luxury—perhaps a gift one has bought for
        the other, a bottle of wine
to celebrate her birthday, a colour TV she has secretly rented
for him to watch the Grey Cup game—and the realization
that because of it something else will now have to be
endured or postponed or done without or given up).
"No," the sales clerk said. "This guy was loaded."
"Drunk?" "Nah, loaded with dough. And guess how much
he made me knock off the price. Are you ready for this?
Two measly bucks."
                   Could it have been habit then?
I once knew the owner of a substantial business
who, after his secretary had gone home, searched through
        the wastebaskets
for envelopes that bore uncancelled postage stamps.
The same man had gone in at night or on a weekend

and, with a screwdriver, adjusted the soft-drink machines,
so that they'd not disgorge the bottle-caps,
some of which were worth two dollars in a contest.
He might have dickered in the face of death.
I don't know. I do know that for twenty years
I've wondered about that man who killed himself.
Perhaps, when in the store, he was not yet aware
of how he would use the rifle. Perhaps he expected
to go on a hunting trip with friends. Enough can happen
in an hour to make a man decide he'd rather
be dead.
               Or, for whatever reason, would he still be
alive if the clerk had refused to sell for any less?

Field Day

At first there is some doubt as to whether the
          battle will be between paper soldiers
or summer employees of the Department of Tourism:
          High School students in polyester
imitations of 18th-century uniforms — at this point
          the Principal
makes a startling announcement: real soldiers
          are present
with real guns. King George's Redcoats — burly fellows
          with flushed faces,
lobsterbacks, "the scum of the earth," Wellington
          called them,
and he ought to have known. There is a volley
          of musketry
and we carry in an officer, one of King Louis' men,
          who mutters something
about not belonging here; he wears the white uniform
          of the Old Regime,
the breast of his tunic blood-red, and that redness
          spreading...

The Country I Was Born in Was Ruled by Kings

The country I was born in was ruled by Kings.
They stood in back, in front and on either side of me,
as I bent over my schoolbooks; one was fat and wore a beard,
another was thin and wore a beard, yet another was thin and beardless.
All three wore red coats with blue sashes and a Milky Way of medals—
I saw the faces of the same men on the coins with which I
    bought Cracker Jack.

This was long ago, you must remember, before pictures lost
    their magic,
before television, before I had ever seen a movie,
in a time and place where comic books were so rare
that they seemed like a continuation of the Bible,
which also contained pictures; I thought of Captain Marvel
in the same breath with David and Goliath.
    Every picture was a vision
sent by God; my mother's Kodak, with its black snout,
was a thing of mystery: once I unwound a film,
in search of the pictures inside it, and found nothing.
It was not merely the pictures; every morning
we sang "God Save the King," and another hymn,
such as "Jesus Loves Me." Nobody ever said
we belonged to God and the King; there was no need to say it;
they were there, as our grandparents were there: nobody had to say,
this is your grandmother, this is your grandfather; we had
    always known it.
To put it another way, we no more believed in Kings
than we believed in Uncles; there was a blood relationship
involved, and like any other blood relationship,
it was nothing to make a fuss about, yet something
that nothing could alter. My King is long since dead.
Still, as a child of the 1940s,
I think I know exactly what my ancestors
meant when they inscribed upon those monuments,
the words, "For King and Country."

Black Jack

"You've won my railroad in Brazil," said the boy.
"And your steamship line," said the man. "And your ranch
    in Kansas."
"And my private army in Mexico."
"I won that hours ago."
"And Spain and Africa."
"And Australia and Asia."
"And all of America."
"Even Antarctica." The man
    shuffled the cards.
"I guess you must own the whole world by now."
"I guess I must," agreed the man.
"But you haven't got heaven," the boy cried. "And you
    haven't got hell!"

"No, you still own heaven and hell."
"I'll stake heaven and hell against the earth then."
"Agreed," laughed the man. "Who's turn to deal?"
"Yours."
"And the dealer takes all ties."
"That's what you said."
The man dealt the cards.
"I'll pay 21," he grinned.
"An ace and a king," yelled the boy. "I own earth, heaven
    and hell!"

The man gathered up the cards.
"We'll play again tomorrow night," he said.

Home from the Wars
for Walter Learning

His hand in his mother's, her
scented with dried rose petals
and spearmint, the whole city
turned upside down, spilling out a torrent
of people, the flood rushing down
to the harbour where even the cloth flags
joined in the clapping and the ships' horns
wallowed in it—

"There's your father!" she said.
But there were so many,
all the same greenish-brown
scum and mud colour,
so many of them on the decks
of the troopship, looking down
as if from a cloud in a nightmare,
every last one of them
judging him,
it seemed, and his mother
had let go.

　　　　　But he didn't cry
until he hung suspended
in the air while the stranger's
coarse wool sandpapered his face;
and he's not sure if it was then
or in memory years afterwards that he saw
a gull die in each of the man's eyes
as they do when small boys with fishing lines
hook them
　　　　　and he cried again.

Boswell's *Life of Johnson*

Eight hundred pages.
Two hundred thousand words.
The biography of a great man.

Once, penniless, he
walked the streets all night.

One sentence.
Two lines of type.

Hunger. Cold. Despair.
Thoughts of suicide.

He Enters His 50th Year

Nine-tenths blind without my glasses
and growing deafer every year
(they tell me it's hereditary),

threatened with diabetes, forced out of bed
by my bladder two or three times a night
(they tell me this is the surcharge
on all those forty-ouncers of gin),

bursitis in my elbow, receding gums, a loose tooth
(my doctor and dentist advise me to put up with it
as long as I can and then they'll try something
which, they warn, will quite possibly make it worse),

I feel myself dissolving like a snowman,
coming to pieces like an old book.
But I'm not complaining.
It is not as bad as it sounds.
There are compensations.

For one thing, I've accumulated such a company
of past selves, enough of them to fill the stage
in a sizeable theatre, that it is easier to believe
the person I am is only one among many, to look at him
in almost the same way I would look at anyone else.

For another thing, I can now laugh out loud
at incidents such as my first time with a girl
I knew would let me do it. Having read Havelock Ellis,
I knew about foreplay. Oh! My hands and mouth did
ingenious things to her 15-year-old body.
I remember especially a game with her thighs,
        the prescription
called for the fingers to tip-toe ever so slowly
towards the root of her womanhood, touch it so deftly
and retreat so swiftly she could not be sure
whether what she felt was real or imagined,
then to begin again, insect-like, at her knees.
That worked perfectly. She lay moist and squirming,
eyes screwed shut, mouth open — and then
I couldn't get it up. I couldn't get it up.
Havelock Ellis hadn't warned me
this might happen. I wanted to die.
How I wanted to die. And afterwards, alone in bed
I thought for a long time about various ways
of killing myself. Good God, what if she told
somebody?
        I address the rest of this:
to the boy I was: I could never laugh at you unkindly.

The Fox

For weeks I've heard him barking in the woods
that half encircle the oatfield, each bark
set in a space of silence, like a word
printed on paper. Dogs are drivellers

or blusterers, no doubt because they speak
mostly to humans. This could be the cry
chosen to signal other warriors.

A fox, I've seen him twice, but only when,
preoccupied with something, I've looked up
for no particular reason and seen
a flash of flame just as it has been snuffed out.

Why He Became a Collector of Trivia

When he was a small boy, messages such as this
arrived almost daily. *There is a place called India.*
There was a man called Socrates. There lives a beast
known as a unicorn. There exists another
known as a rhinoceros.
Once he watched the moon bleed. Once a fire-eater
came to his village and ate fire.
He was told his country was at war.
He learned to look at a clock and know what time it was.

As a child, he saw continents
rise out of the sea. Now, in middle age,
he can only re-visit them
as a tourist, and come back with trinkets.
St. Augustine thought it remarkable that St. Ambrose
read without moving his lips. Richard the Lionheart
is the first Englishman known to have used a handkerchief.

The Sculpin

"Like an orgasm," I thought, watching the weir fishermen
empty their nets of herring, an onrush of life
spouting into the hold of a boat, and the boat rocking.

And, later, "If only human beings died as it seems to us that
      herring do,
swept away by their dance, their bodies mirrors for the sun."
But that was later; though the fish were dying, thousands of them,
swimming frantically in the air that to them is nothingness,
while I watched the weirmen at work I no more thought of death
than of the children who might have been born of the sperm
      I wasted.

Yet, I had cursed myself and the two American women
fishing with rods from the wharf's edge. They were harmless creatures,
tourists like me, and had hooked a sculpin,
a fish to which they bore a macabre resemblance,
being bloated and with strange protrusions and colorations.
Their jokes about its ugliness ought to have been funny,
and might have been, except that it lay writhing
at their feet, while they laughed their horrible
Pink Lady and Bingo Night laughs, and kept poking it:
God, how I hated their fingernail-polished toenails, and
      myself for not
rescuing their victim; I had wanted to
elbow them aside, somehow remove the hook,
put the fish back, gently, in its own element.

"The difference is in attitudes," a part of me says.
The weirmen are so sparing of everything, even words and
      movements;
nothing is wasted. They would understand
those old breech-clouted hunters said to have asked
forgiveness of their kill. I suppose the truth
is that when I saw the herring, I saw herring,
and when I saw the sculpin, I saw myself.

My Father's Body Was Found by Children

My father's body was
found by children.
Boys from the neighbourhood
who thought he was asleep
in his chair until
they came back next day
and saw he hadn't moved.
Children often visited him,
I'm told. He'd wrestle
with them if he was drunk,
converse with them soberly
at other times. His shack
was the sort of dwelling
a twelve-year-old would
build for himself,
in his last years he lived
the way a small boy would
if allowed to live alone.
Huck Finn at seventy.

To think he might have been
a child all his life
if less had been asked
of him and more been given.

To think I'm afraid
of him, even now,
half-expecting to look out
some night and see him
standing there:
I fear that most.

Who's Going to Understand?

Oh shit
what's the use
who's going to understand
love is my waking up
and there's a pack of cigarettes
beside the bed because
there weren't any
last night and Claudine
doesn't smoke but she walked
three blocks and back
or more
with this same package
of cigarettes
in her hand...

This Is What I Wanted to Sign Off With

You know what I'm
like when I'm sick: I'd sooner
curse than cry. And people don't often
know what they're saying in the end.
Or I could die in my sleep.

So I'll say it now. Here it is.
Don't pay any attention
if I don't get it right
when it's for real. Blame that
on terror and pain
or the stuff they're shooting
into my veins. This is what I wanted to
sign off with. Bend
closer, listen, I love you.

Acknowledgements

Collected Poems has benefitted from the help, generosity, and professionalism of many people. Thanks to icehouse poetry editor Ross Leckie, who phoned one day and gave me the chance of a lifetime to edit a book like this one. *Collected Poems* would also not exist without the labour and enthusiasm of Goose Lane people Susanne Alexander, Julie Scriver, Martin Ainsley, and Kathleen Peacock. Special thanks to Jill Ainsley, for editing the introduction with a keen eye and fine-tuning other aspects of the book; Elizabeth Eve, for her careful review of the manuscript; Allison Wagner and Erin Vance of Special Collections and Archives, the University of Calgary Library; artist Stephen Scott, for letting us use as a frontispiece his vivid sketch of Alden; Robert Gibbs, for years of dedication to the poet's work; Claudine and Johnnie Nowlan, for believing in this collection; and, above all, to Alden Nowlan, for giving us so many magnificent poems.

ooooo

The following poems were previously published in *Alden Nowlan: Selected Poems*, edited by Patrick Lane and Lorna Crozier (House of Anansi Press, 1996, reissued in 2013) and are reprinted here by kind permission of House of Anansi Press:

"I, Icarus," 151; "Long, Long Ago," 152; "And He Wept Aloud, So That the Egyptians Heard It," 153-54; "Daughter of Zion," 156-57; "Britain Street," 159-60; "For Jean Vincent D'Abbadie, Baron St.-Castin," 162; "July 15," 175; "A Mug's Game," 176-77; "The Word," 183-84; "Day's End," 184; "The Last Waltz," 187; "The Wickedness of Peter Shannon," 188; "In the Operating Room," 189-90; "Morning of the Third Operation," 191-92; "The Mysterious Naked Man," 195; "Hymn to Dionysus," 197; "Country Full of Christmas," 200; "Snapshot," 203; "The Mosherville Road," 204-5; "A Poem about Miracles," 219-20; "Ypres: 1915," 223-26; "A Black Plastic Button and a Yellow Yo-yo," 245; "The First Stirring of the Beasts," 251; "An Exchange of Gifts," 257; "Chance Encounter," 263-64; "The Palomino Stallion," 273; "Why He Wanted to Abolish Capital Punishment," 313-14; "Mistaken Identity," 314-15; "Fair Warning," 316; "The Iconotrophic Instant," 322-23; "Canadian January Night," 333; "The Married Man's Poem," 336; "He Raids the Refrigerator and Reflects on Parenthood," 344-45; "Cornflowers," 346-47; "Johnnie's Poem," 346; "Written While Waiting for Another Chest X-ray," 361-62; "For Yukio Mishima," 372-73; "Old Town Revisited," 397-98; "They Go Off to Seek Their Fortunes," 398-99; "For My Grandchildren, As Yet Unborn," 400-401; "He Takes His Leave," 407-8; "At a Distance He Observes an Unknown Girl Picking Flowers," 412-13; "The Social Worker's Poem," 423-24; "The Old

Editor's Notes

Collected Poems includes all of Alden Nowlan's poetry published in his chapbooks and collections, his two new and selected volumes, the compilation *Five New Brunswick Poets*, and the book of his one long poem for voices. Poems that appeared only in periodicals or exist only in manuscript are not included here. Elements of typography such as dashes, ellipses, quotation format, and placement of poem dedications — varied in the poems' original publications — have been made consistent throughout *Collected Poems*.

The Rose and the Puritan
This sixteen-poem chapbook was derived from an initial gathering of seventy poems.

"A Night Hawk Fell with a Sound Like a Shudder": reprinted in *Under the Ice*, with the indentations removed.

"A Poem to My Mother": reprinted as the second poem in *Playing the Jesus Game* under the title "The White Goddess," with the final stanza removed, and in line 12 "my mother" changed to "O mother." See 267.

"A Letter to My Sister": reprinted in *Playing the Jesus Game* under the title "The Time of the Fire," with several revisions. See 267.

"Hens": reprinted as the first poem in *Playing the Jesus Game*, with dashes rather than commas in the final line and "picked" corrected to "pecked." Later version used here.

"Two Strangers": reprinted in an extensively revised version in *Under the Ice*. See 91-92.

A Darkness in the Earth
"Flossie at School": reprinted in *Playing the Jesus Game* as "Flossie."

In *Early Poems*, two poems from *A Darkness* — "About Death They Were Wrong," "The Gunfighters" — appear to have been inadvertently left out. They are restored here in *Collected Poems*.

Wind in a Rocky Country
"Our Brother Exalted": reprinted in *Smoked Glass* as "Our Exalted Brother" in a version two lines longer, with many revisions. See 521-22.

"Summer": reprinted in *Under the Ice* as "Poem," then in *Playing the Jesus Game* as "Atlantic Coast: Summer."

"I Knew the Seasons ere I Knew the Hours:" reprinted in *Playing the Jesus Game*, with "damned" in line 6 revised to "damn." Later version used here.

"For Nicholas of All the Russias": originally printed with lines left-justified and no dropped line, this poem was reprinted in *Playing the Jesus Game*, with "Stranger, knocking" as a dropped line. Later version used here.

Under the Ice

"Poem for Elizabeth": reprinted in *Playing the Jesus Game* under that title, but in *Under the Ice* originally entitled "You Said."

The Things Which Are

The title and epigraph for this collection are from Revelation 1:19 (King James Version), though Nowlan excludes the conclusion of the verse: "…and the things which shall be hereafter." The title also echoes 2 Corinthians 4:18: "While we look not at the things which are seen, but at the things which are not seen: for the things which are seen are temporal, but the things which are not seen are eternal."

Five New Brunswick Poets

The selection of Nowlan poems in this multi-poet compilation included the ones included under that title in *Collected Poems*, as well as seven poems reprinted from *Under the Ice*.

Playing the Jesus Game: Selected Poems

While this book is subtitled *Selected Poems*, it was in fact a "new and selected," including twenty-four poems that had not previously appeared in earlier books of Nowlan's.

"Stars" and "The Palomino Stallion": these poems were reprinted in *I'm a Stranger Here Myself* but only appear in the *Playing* section in *Collected Poems*.

In one of the more curious facts about Nowlan's publications, his poem "Playing the Jesus Game" supplied the title for his first American selected volume, but it never appeared in one of his books or chapbooks. It was published in the special Nowlan issue of the *Fiddlehead* (no. 81, 1969) and later in Patrick Toner's biography of Nowlan. The poem reads:

Playing the Jesus game
I don't smile at strangers
because that might frighten them
into summoning the police.

Playing the Jesus game
I open the trapdoor in the top of my head

and let out the angel
that everyone believes
is an optical illusion.

I see an angel, they think.
I must be going blind or crazy.

So my angel can touch them,
once, gently, with the flat of his sword.
He can play his guitar for them.

But if anyone asks me what I'm doing here
I'll tell them I'm waiting for a bus
because that is a lie that almost anyone would believe.

The Gardens of the Wind

This poem for voices was commissioned by Robert Weaver for CBC Radio's
popular literary program *Anthology* as one of six poems broadcast in February
and March, 1970. That July CBC published the six poems in the book *Poems for
Voices*. The other poets in the series were Margaret Atwood, Phyllis Gottlieb, Tom
Marshall, John Newlove, and Al Purdy. A dozen years later, in 1982, Thistledown
Press in Saskatoon published Nowlan's poem as a separate book, in a limited
edition of 150 signed copies, with a new introduction by the poet. Nowlan's
background commentary included the following:

> As a writer who works in many genres, in part from choice and in
> part from economic necessity, since I'm a writer by trade as well as
> a writer by vocation, I have many times been commissioned to write
> in prose—everything from scripts for television variety shows and
> situation comedies through newspaper and magazine articles to a
> history of Campobello Island.
>
> This was the first and only time that I have been commissioned to
> write a poem. Frankly, it was a discomforting experience. In the first
> place, I am a sprinter whose longest poems seldom run to more than
> one typewritten page in length—and this time I was running the
> marathon. For another thing, it was an entirely new and disquieting
> experience for me to undertake writing a poem not simply as an
> adventure but as a job of work.
>
> The subject I chose was the RCAF Flying Training School—
> we called it simply "the Airport"—that was perhaps the central
> external fact of my childhood world and which has pervaded the

borderlands of my imagination ever since. Ours was rural settlement, with a population of at most thirty families living along eight or ten miles of dirt road.... Although I was born in 1933, I never once talked on a telephone (or tasted a hamburger) until I was nineteen.

Then—and it must have been in 1940—they began to build the Airport, and soon the sky was filled with little yellow Biplanes called Fleets, and everywhere we looked there were airmen, hundreds of them, in wedge caps and blue uniforms. In the depths of my imagination, the hangar at the Airport is still the largest building in the world....

You have to understand that the Airport was not so much an addition to our community as a partially open doorway into a parallel universe. The reality of the Airport and the reality of the Settlement frequently touched, but never merged. I suppose it was a little—perhaps only a very little—like the relationship between any aboriginal people and the first expedition from the Outside.

The pivotal image in *The Gardens of the Mind* is an old man who refuses to sell his land to the Airport. There was such an old man in our settlement—although not, let me stress, the same old man as in the poem. Everyone in the settlement thought he was crazy. I supposed that he was, considering the land there never yielded anything except thistles, rocks and despair. But I've always liked crazy people, being half-crazy myself. I felt good, years later, on one of my very rare visits to Katpesa Creek, when I saw that in truth the grass and daisies were consuming the cement runways of the now abandoned Airport, or would have done so except for the efforts of an amateur flying club from Halifax who drove down on the weekends to play around with gliders and what-not.

Between Tears and Laughter

For this Nowlan collection and the subsequent three, the publisher, Clarke Irwin, made a design decision to lower-case most words in the titles of both the collections and the individual poems. For instance, *I Might Not Tell Everybody This* became *I might not tell everybody this*, and "The Dream of Two Voices" became "The dream of two voices." Those design decisions later led to confusion, with some editors and anthologists transcribing the titles with most capitals removed. Nowlan's typescripts in the University of Calgary Special Collections archives confirm that his own use of capitalization in titles was conventional, with most words after the first one—except for articles, prepositions, and conjunctions—capitalized. In *Collected Poems*, Nowlan's punctuation has been restored to the titles.

I'm a Stranger Here Myself

This title was originally given to a song in a 1943 Broadway musical, *One Touch of Venus*, with lyrics by Ogden Nash and music by Kurt Weill.

Smoked Glass

A late typescript of this collection bears the title *Between the Lines*.

I Might Not Tell Everybody This

The title derives from section 19 of Walt Whitman's "Song of Myself": "Does the daylight astonish? does the early redstart twittering through the woods? / Do I astonish more than they? // This hour I tell things in confidence, / I might not tell everybody, but I will tell you."

In Nowlan's later collections, especially the final one, a few poems with longer lines pose complicated questions for editors. In some cases it appears that line-breaks — in particular, ones involving one or two words indented after an usually long line — were determined by a designer's choice of page width rather than by the poet's aesthetics. (In some cases, however, even on typescripts such isolated words appear where the page is too narrow for what appears to be essentially a single line.) For subsequent reprints of such poems in selected volumes of Nowlan's poetry, different decisions about adjusting line-breaks were adopted by different editors and/or designers. *Collected Poems* continues in that tradition, with careful thought given to present extra-long lines in ways that remain faithful to the poems' rhythms, pacing, and appearances.

An Exchange of Gifts: Poems New & Selected

The section "New Poems" in this collection published two years after Nowlan's death included "Ghost Stories" and "He Attempts to Love His Neighbours," but these poems had already appeared three years earlier in *I Might Not Tell Everybody This*.

Dedications

Note: The Patrick Toner and Gregory M. Cook biographies of Nowlan can be consulted for details about the recipients of dedications in the poetry collections.

A Darkness in the Earth – To C.M. [Claudine Meehan]

Under the Ice – To Claudine For One Reason and To Fred Cogswell For Another

The Things Which Are – To Raymond Souster with admiration / To Harold Plummer with affection / and to Johnnie with love

Bread, Wine and Salt – To Claudine and Johnnie with Love

The Mysterious Naked Man – To Claudine and Johnnie with love and to St. Jude Thaddeus, because I promised

Playing the Jesus Game: Selected Poems – To Claudine and Johnnie with love

Between Tears and Laughter – For Claudine and Johnnie with love
I'm a Stranger Here Myself – For Claudine and Johnnie and Jim Stewart with love
Smoked Glass – For Claudine and Johnnie and to Burt Burgoyne
I Might Not Tell Everybody This – For Claudine and Johnnie and Walter Learning
    with love

Bibliography

Poetry

The Rose and the Puritan. Fredericton: Fiddlehead Poetry Books, 1958. [as Alden A. Nowlan]

A Darkness in the Earth. Eureka, California: Hearse Press, 1959. [as Alden A. Nowlan]

Wind in a Rocky Country. Toronto: Emblem Books, 1960. [as Alden A. Nowlan]

Under the Ice. Toronto: Ryerson Press, 1961. [as Alden A. Nowlan]

The Things Which Are. Toronto: Contact Press, 1962.

Five New Brunswick Poets [with Elizabeth Brewster, Fred Cogswell, Robert Gibbs, Kay Smith]. Fredericton: Fiddlehead Poetry Books, 1962.

Bread, Wine and Salt. Toronto: Clarke, Irwin, 1967.

A Black Plastic Button and a Yellow Yoyo. With illustrations by Charles Pachter. Toronto: Massey College Press, 1968. [limited-edition, 28-page folio of which only 20 copies were printed]

The Mysterious Naked Man. Toronto: Clarke, Irwin, 1969.

Playing the Jesus Game: Selected Poems. Foreword by Robert Bly. Trumansburg, NY, New Books, 1970.

The Gardens of the Wind. In *Poems for Voices,* ed. Robert Weaver [with Margaret Atwood, Phyllis Gotlieb, Tom Marshall, John Newlove, Al Purdy]. Toronto: CBC, 1970. Reprinted as a separate book by Thistledown Press, Regina, 1982.

Between Tears and Laughter. Toronto: Clarke, Irwin, 1971.

I'm A Stranger Here Myself. Toronto: Clarke, Irwin, 1974.

Shaped by This Land. Paintings by Tom Forrestall, poems by Alden Nowlan. Foreword by Barry Lord. Fredericton: Brunswick Press, 1974.

Smoked Glass. Toronto: Clarke Irwin. 1977.

I Might Not Tell Everybody This. Toronto: Clarke, Irwin, 1982.

Early Poems. Fredericton: Fiddlehead Poetry Books, 1983.

An Exchange of Gifts: Poems New & Selected. Ed. Robert Gibbs. Toronto: Irwin Publishing, 1985.

What Happened When He Went to the Store for Bread: Poems by Alden Nowlan. Ed. Thomas R. Smith. Foreword by Robert Bly. St. Paul, Minneapolis: Nineties Press, 1993. 2nd edition by The Thousands Press, Minneapolis, 2000.

The Best of Alden Nowlan. Ed. Allison Mitcham. Hantsport, NS: Lancelot, 1993. [includes prose]

Selected Poems. Ed. Patrick Lane and Lorna Crozier. Don Mills, ON: House of Anansi Press, 1996.

Alden Nowlan & Illness. Ed. Shane Neilson. Victoria, BC: Frog Hollow Press, 2004.

Between Tears and Laughter: Selected Poems. Foreword by Patrick Lane. Introduction by Patrick Lane and Lorna Crozier. Afterword by Gregory M. Cook. Highgreen, Northumberland, UK: Bloodaxe Books, 2004.

Fiction

Miracle at Indian River. Toronto: Clarke, Irwin, 1968.
Various Persons Named Kevin O'Brien: A Fictional Memoir. Toronto: Clarke, Irwin, 1973.
Nine Micmac Legends. Hantsport: Lancelot, 1983.
Will Ye Let the Mummers In? Preface by Robert Weaver. Toronto: Irwin Publishing, 1984.
The Wanton Troopers. Fredericton: Goose Lane Editions, 1988.
The Wanton Troopers. Reader's guide edition. Afterword by David Adams Richards. Fredericton: Goose Lane Editions, 2009.

Drama

Frankenstein. With Walter Learning. Toronto: Clarke Irwin, 1973.
The Incredible Murder of Cardinal Tosca. With Walter Learning. Toronto: Clarke Irwin, 1978.
The Dollar Woman. With Walter Learning. New Canadian Drama 2. Ed. Patrick B. O'Neill. Ottawa: Borealis Press, 1983.

Non-fiction

Campobello: The Outer Island. Toronto: Clarke, Irwin, 1975.
Double Exposure. Fredericton: Brunswick, 1978.
White Madness. Ed. Robert Gibbs. Ottawa: Oberon, 1996.
Road Dancers. Ed. Robert Gibbs. Ottawa: Oberon, 1999.

Index of Titles

Index of First Lines

I've seen Christ born, a stranger in the
wind, 82
I've seen my great-grandfather only
once. 404
Ice storm: the hill 333
If, three-quarters of a century from
here, 447
If I am sentimental 68
If I came in 104
If I could be certain, God, that 554
If I go mad or, rather, say to hell 555
If I had been born blind 454
If I live to be a very old man 549
If I think hard enough 412
If only we adults were as wise 413
If the intern were out to persuade me
457
If the relationship between 354
If we had come to this turn in the road
604
If we were able to 349
If you had not said you loved
her— 441
If you like, 178
If you want to ask 427
Immersed in night, my senses sharpen,
hear 122
In cities the embittered ones are
cunning; 96
In Esdraelon, twenty miles from
here— 86
In my boy's cave of dreaming before
sleep, 129
In my grandfather's house 153
In my youth, no one spoke of love 492
In summer-coloured dresses, six young
girls 70
In the days of the people who are
gone—that was the way 220
In the euthanasia division 364
In the last hours of the Cuban missile
crisis 371
In the next house they're punishing a
child. 71
In those old wars 164
Infant (Anglo-Catholic name 271
Ireland was not 399
Is this what it's like to be old? 201

It has been so long, Barbara, since I last
wrote a poem for you 336
It is always the same 429
It is dusk now, and the secretive
fishermen 590
"It is not death that frightens me," she
said, 136
It is not elephants. I would not laugh at
them 489
It is nowhere so dark 204
It is ordained that the mad should not
dance with the mad 254
It seems I always saw the Indian
woman 152
It takes even more than this to make
you cry 203
It was as if I'd opened 407
It was not the weight 335
It's five o'clock in the morning and the
new-dropt calf 274
It's good sometimes 314
It's not hard to begin 462
It's not the same here, the chairman
536
It's snowing hard enough that the taxis
aren't running. 462
"It's so good to talk with somebody
586
It's summer yet but still the cold 52
It's the first storm of the winter 605

Jacintha's Red Indian has skin as white
as the dream 351
Jack Stringer kissed his mother twice a
year, 74
Jessie, my cousin, remembers there
were gypsies 64
Johnnie comes into the room 355
Just now I heard my father singing
619

"Kill me," begs my wife or my grown
son 465
Kneeling with fastened wrists before
the skull 71
Knock so I'll know 361
Know that I am Napoleon, the great,
the magnificent tiger. 319

This book, typeset in Calendas Plus and Adobe Caslon Pro, was printed and bound in Canada by Friesens in Altona, Manitoba, on 55 lb. Rolland Enviro FSC Natural Antique.